Fairies

In my opinion this is the best book on Fairy and quite possibly the only one you will ever need. Morgan Daimler is my guru on all things fairy and this book is now my new go-to guide. Leaving behind all the gossamer wings and flowery petal skirts (thankfully) this book covers all you need to know and more from traditional fairy to the modern world and everything in between. If you want to step away from the glitter and into the REAL world of fairy then this book is a must have. Highly recommended.

Rachel Patterson, author of *Kitchen Witchcraft, The Cailleach* and *Moon Magic*

Impeccably researched and delightfully well written, *Fairies – A Guide to the Celtic Fair Folk* is a book that every pagan who is interested in following the fairy path should read. Morgan Daimler is a leading expert on traditional Celtic fairylore and this is her finest work on the subject to date.

Lucya Starza, author of *Pagan Portals – Candle Magic* and *A Bad Witch's Blog*

Living in the Irish countryside where fairy raths, paths and strange goings on are part of everyday life, I was captivated by *Fairies: A Guide to the Celtic Fair Folk*. As with all of Daimler's books I was impressed by her thorough research, her clarity of writing and the inclusion of a chapter giving basic guidelines for dealing with fairies. There is so much to commend in this book that I believe it is the most thorough guide to the Good People I have read.

Jane Brideson, Artist and blogger at *The Ever-Living Ones – Irish Goddesses & Gods in Landscape, Myth & Custom*

Other Books by Morgan Daimler

Fairycraft
Following the Path of Fairy Witchcraft

Fairy Witchcraft
A Neopagan's Guide to the Celtic Fairy Faith

Irish Paganism
Reconstructing Irish Polytheism

Gods and Goddesses of Ireland
A Guide to Irish Deities

The Morrigan
Meeting the Great Queens

Brigid
Meeting the Celtic Goddess of Poetry, Forge, and Healing Well

Where the Hawthorn Grows
An American Druid's reflections

Fairies

A Guide to the Celtic Fair Folk

Fairies

A Guide to the Celtic Fair Folk

Morgan Daimler

Winchester, UK
Washington, USA

First published by Moon Books, 2017
Moon Books is an imprint of John Hunt Publishing Ltd., Laurel House, Station Approach,
Alresford, Hants, SO24 9JH, UK
office1@jhpbooks.net
www.johnhuntpublishing.com
www.moon-books.net

For distributor details and how to order please visit the 'Ordering' section on our website.

Text copyright: Morgan Daimler 2016

ISBN: 978 1 78279 650 3
978 1 78279 696 1 (ebook)
Library of Congress Control Number: 2017932673

A CIP catalogue record for this book is available from the British Library.

Design: Stuart Davies

Printed and bound by CPI Group (UK) Ltd, Croydon, CR0 4YY, UK

We operate a distinctive and ethical publishing philosophy in all
areas of our business, from our global network of authors to
production and worldwide distribution.

CONTENTS

For those who seek the truth in the legends.
This book is dedicated to those who give me reasons to
believe. With great thanks to Aileen Paul, for your support
and encouragement.
And thanks to Gemma McGowan for being the amazing
priestess you are, and for everything at Tlachtga, the dark
moon, Samhain, 2016.

Imram – A Poem

Like a shadow, shifting, seeking
what I've found yet still must find,
wrapped in motion, wrapped in time,
bound yet still compelled to bind
echoes like ripples of each action
as here and there merge in my mind
spirit balanced in the eager edges

Wandering the Otherworld is chancy
though the fairy road is always near
tempting and teasing and tangling
touching this to that, and there to here
a bare breath away, a whole world apart
pulled and pushed by hope and fear
I am compelled to turn and return again

I am on wings, flying, swiftly silent
eyes keen in the darkness of night
seeking what is waiting for me
someone found in shade and light;
I am a white hind in trackless woods
running, racing, sharp and bright;
illusions hold the truth of form here

The paths I walk are distant memories
the place I rest a long forgotten tale
my companion, fierce and fearsome,
so that, compared, I seem faint and frail,
there is music, sourceless, around us
and the moon, a lantern, clear and pale,
so painfully idyllic I look for thorns

Dark and dangerous this dreaming
like ground ivy, twining, creeping
intoxicating as sweet rowan mead
into my heart and mind softly seeping
leaving no corner or crevice empty
planting, tending, nourishing, reaping,
changing from the core to make anew

I feel it digging deep and deeper
wearing me away like water on stone
working relentlessly towards its goal
weaving through flesh, blood, and bone
strong its power, stronger its purpose
for in the most primal intent it was sown
and every wish comes with its cost

Days, or Years, or Decades, or Hours
time has no anchor here, it drifts
I am carried with its restless motion
turning and twisting as it all shifts
but I knew before I bargained that
they are clever when they give gifts
and I valued gingerbread over gold
M. Daimler, copyright 2016

Introduction

Go not to the elves for counsel for they will say both no and yes.
J.R.R. Tolkien

Fairies have long fascinated and frightened people and a complex set of traditions has risen around them that reflects this. In a Celtic context these beliefs and practices are often called the 'Fairy Faith' and represent the sum total of what humans have learned about fairies over countless generations. Despite its name the Fairy Faith is not actually a specific religion itself, although it is most strongly associated with Christianity, and anyone of any belief system can follow the Fairy Faith.

This book is not a text on the modern idea of what fairies are, and really there's little need for such a book. There are already quite a few on the market that are aimed at a pagan audience and written from that perspective. What this book is meant to be is a text for pagans focusing on the older understanding of fairies while still seeing them as a part of our very modern world. It focuses largely on the Celtic fairies and to some degree closely related cultures with similar fairy beliefs, but fairies can be found around the world and in every culture as far as I know. It would be impossible, though, to discuss every fairy from every culture in any depth in a single book, so instead this book will aim at offering a deeper view with a specific focus.

As we begin it is probably best to be clear that if you are expecting friendly little flower fairies or ephemeral nature spirits this book is not going to give you what you are looking for. The American cultural view of fairies since the Victorian era seems to be very strongly influenced by a subconscious reflection of idealized human culture. Prior to that time we see a widespread, real belief in the Good People as a force to be respected and feared, propitiated and protected against. But starting around the

Victorian period we see an increasing cultural diminishment of the fey into cute winged children and nature sprites, essentially harmless and entirely pleasant. They become the province of children and a thoroughly domesticated garden. This, I think, can rightly be viewed as a reflection of the wider culture of the time, which was one of the middle class, of repression and sanitization, one that in many ways sought to rewrite unpleasant stories into pleasant ones to create an illusion of a better world.

And today's pop culture fairies also reflect aspects of our culture, shifting into spritely little eco-warriors who show up to impotently bemoan the modern human destruction of the environment, as if we haven't been merrily clear-cutting entire countries and driving species to extinction for millennia. The modern crisis may be a more extreme threat to our own survival, but humans have had an enormous impact on the world around us for as long as we've existed in significant numbers. We may well be courting our own destruction and unlike the Gentry we don't have an Otherworld to return to if we ruin this one, but arguably They have never cared about the things we do to the world around us as long as we leave Their places alone. While there would seem to be no reason for Themselves to suddenly and inexplicably turn to warning us about saving our environment, it nicely reflects our own contemporary socio-environmental concerns. There is a certain logic as well in the Victorian garden sprite/nature spirit being assumed to be somehow concerned with the state of our environment in toto as more people seem to forget that the fey are ultimately beings only partially of this world. And also, more people forget that we and our survival are actually inconsequential to most things that aren't us.

What this book *will* give you is an understanding of fairies from the perspective of traditional culture and folklore, and fairies as they are to the people in the cultures that still believe in them. The idea here is to remove the filters layered over modern understanding because of these views and provide instead the perspective of the cultures that the beliefs come from. So to begin I want to look at a couple of basic things including the use of euphemisms, how to identify fairy activity around you, and how to properly respect fairy places in our world.

Euphemisms

I realize at this point I've already used the word 'fairy' numerous times, but it's actually considered unwise to say that word aloud, lest it attract their attention in a negative way. Many people feel that they don't like being called fairies and if you do so it could anger them. To provide some perspective there was even a running joke on a recent sacred sites tour of Ireland I did that no one should say 'the other 'f' word' and I know people who avoid the word entirely. Instead of saying fairy there is a longstanding tradition of using euphemisms, with the idea that calling them a name that is by its nature positive will remind them of their own potential goodness. Or, in other words, you call them something nice hoping they will act nice to you if they happen to hear you saying it. There are many of these names, but all are designed to avoid offending them. A selection from Irish and Welsh folklore include:

- Daoine Maithe (Good People)
- Daoine Sith (People of Peace)
- Daoine Uaisle (Noble People)
- Aos Sidhe/Aos Sí or Daoine Sidhe/Daoine Sí (People of the Fairy Hills)
- Telwyth Teg (Fair Family)
- Mother's Blessing
- Gentry
- Fair Folk
- Other Crowd
- Good Neighbors

- Themselves

This is not a new concept, in fact we have evidence of the use of euphemisms in folklore dating back several hundred years. There is a 16th century description of Welsh fairy belief that tells us that the Telwyth Teg were greatly revered and that people who believed in them would not *'name them without honor'* (Wilby, 2005, p.23). The Lowland Scots use of the term *'Seely wicht'* (blessed creature) goes back at least 400 years. You can see looking at the list of suggestions that most are descriptive and most intrinsically include the idea of the fairies as good. This wasn't necessarily because people believed they were inherently good or kind, but to remind them of their potential to be so.

The word fairy itself has a long and convoluted history and an uncertain etymology. Ultimately the word fae first appears around the 12th century in French and Latin texts referring to a supernatural woman, an enchantress; two centuries later we see the use of the word fairie in Middle English denoting both the land such beings come from and as an adjective to describe things and beings whose nature is supernatural (Williams, 1991). It's uncertain at what point the word came to be used for individual beings. In older periods other words were used in the general sense that we use fairy today, to indicate a non-specific Otherworldy being, and these included elf and goblin, with elf having a more benign application and goblin a more malevolent one. There is some supposition that the word fairy may be a shortened form of Fair Folk (Wedin, 1998). In the older belief it was thought to be bad luck to call the Daoine Sí by that name (or any name using 'sí', previously spelled sídhe), but interestingly this prohibition seems to be shifting to the term fairies, which of course was originally used as a way to avoid offending them. In modern practice some people will use terms including the word sí while many other people have a strong prohibition against referring to them by any form of sí or using the word fairy, sticking instead entirely to euphemisms (O hOgain, 2006).

Is it Fairies?

One of the first things to look at when you have unusual or inexplicable activity around you is whether it might be fairies. They are of course only one option of several, including ghosts, but fairies tend to have some specific signs unique to them that you can look for. Keep in mind that some signs of supernatural presence are similar between different types of spirits, for example a feeling of being watched or certain types of smells with no obvious sources. Others, though, are more specific to fairy activity and when these are present can be an indicator that it is indeed fairies, which is helpful in deciding how to move forward and deal with the situation. You don't necessarily need to be sensitive or able to directly see these beings; for people who cannot see spirits or otherwise sense them there are practical 'real world' things to look for.

As always the first thing you want to do is look for the most obvious and likely explanation to rule out the mundane causes. Applying Occam's Razor is the best way to start; to paraphrase: *'The simplest explanation is usually the right one.'* If you hear laughter or music, is there a possible real world source nearby? If electronics are glitching, is there something objectively wrong with them? Start with those obvious sorts of explanations. However, to go from there to an Arthur Conan Doyle quote (apropos enough since he was quite the believer in fairies himself): *'When you've eliminated the impossible whatever remains, however improbable, must be the truth.'*

So, what follows is my personal suggestions for what to look for when checking for fairy presence.

Unexplained, laughter, voices, or music – one indication that the fey are around is hearing laughter or voices that seem to have no discernible source. If you hear music with no source it will be music unlike anything heard on Earth. You can sometimes hear voices speaking when ghosts are present, but with the fey it's usually the sound of conversations, often in an indecipherable language. In some cases this may also include the sounds of hounds or horses passing by.

Objects disappearing – the fey are fond of stealing items; unlike ghosts who just move them, the fey outright take them, sometimes for a short amount of time, sometimes for months or years. Car keys are the most common item taken, but jewelry is close second. The object will usually disappear from plain view then reappear at some point in a different place.

Movement in your peripheral vision – to people who don't have second sight or spirit sight, fairies may appear as a flash of movement in your peripheral vision. Of course the fey can also choose to show themselves if they want to, even to someone who normally couldn't see them.

Elf-locks – waking up with matted hair, with no logical reason for it to be this way; this can also happen to animals. This is more common if you've annoyed or offended them, but nonetheless is a sign of their presence unique to them. You do want to be certain there isn't a logical reason for it because hair does mat on its own. However, if you don't usually have a problem with this or you know there's no logical reason for it, but you wake up with a significant tangle or mat of hair, then it could be fairies.

The presence of a 'fairy ring' – a ring of mushrooms or darker green grass – has long been believed to indicate the presence of fairies. I'd note that entering an active fairy ring is considered dangerous, as it can radically alter our sense of time and a night dancing with the fey can translate to anywhere between seven and a hundred years passing in our world. Usually though when we see a fairy ring growing in our yard or the woods, it only means They have been there, not that they are actually there dancing at that moment.

Chores being done or things being put away – an old sign of fairy presence was household chores being done while the family slept, or items being put away. The fey are generally known to prefer neatness, and some of them, especially house spirits, like to keep our homes and yards in order. Any helpful Otherworldly spirit can indicate its presence by aiding with anything around the home from minor things to more major ones that will keep things running more smoothly.

Your cat acting oddly – cats in my experience seem to be very sensitive to fairies. This can mean either that the cat seems to enjoy their presence or that the cat is flat out terrified of them. Either way, cats acting unusually freaked out can be an indicator of the Other Crowd being around. We are talking about cats here though so use your judgment as to what qualifies as a cat being unusually freaked out. Often it seems to mean the cat seeing and chasing something that you can't see, particularly at a time when a flying bug wouldn't be an option. On a related note horses also seem sensitive to fairies, should you have one.

Respecting Their Places

Many people lump nature spirits in with fairies and that is both true and untrue. Fairies are a broad category of beings and they can and do include both beings of this world and beings from the Otherworld that choose to come here. In the next chapter we will take an in-depth look at the Otherworld, but I want to discuss here the importance of showing proper respect to the locations in our own world that are associated with or claimed by the fairies, whether that means true nature spirits or not.

A land spirit or the spirit of a natural feature such as a tree or plant is strongly connected to the place it calls home. This is only logical really, as that physical place or object is for them like our body is for our soul – it acts like an anchor for the spirit in this world. If you think of it this way then it's easier to understand why we should be careful and respectful of places that belong to these spirits. This doesn't necessarily mean that all natural spaces should be inviolate, life after all is a cycle of growth and death and it can involve destruction, but just as we should show respect to the animals and plants we use for food, we owe respect to the natural places and the spirits that inhabit them. It's also always good to keep in mind that nature spirits have the ability to influence the mood and atmosphere of a place, so happy nature spirits are always better than angry ones. Generally angry land spirits will express their feelings by making the area they influence unpleasant, causing the atmosphere of the area to be uneasy or unhappy, or cause bad dreams in people living nearby.

Respecting nature spirits is a straightforward proposition: don't be needlessly destructive, don't take down trees, move large rocks, or make any big changes to an area without giving the land spirits a bit of notice (I recommend a couple days, when possible), and don't muck up natural places in your yard or local woods with human junk or refuse. If there is a particular nature spirit, such as that of a tree, that you want to connect to you can make offerings to it and talk to it. Offerings are also a good idea if you do have to do major landscaping or tree removal; honey works well, as does planting new growth or working to clean up any human messes.

Besides land spirits that exist as an intrinsic part of the world around us, there are also places that belong to the fairies that are spirits of the Otherworld. These are not land spirits and are not tied to the land in these places, but they have laid claim to them and feel a strong sense of ownership about them. Folklore and modern anecdotes show that interfering with or damaging places that belong to the fairies is a profoundly bad idea, and that they tend to respond in a fairly direct fashion. In Iceland both road construction and drilling that upsets the Hidden Folk tends to result in machinery breaking, ill luck, and strange happenings until the construction stops or the damage – usually to a boulder that is associated with them – is repaired. In Ireland folklore says that to interfere with a fairy tree or fairy hill can result in bad luck, illness, or even death. They are also not averse to destroying the offending human construction that is on their territory; one recent event in 2007 that made the news in Ireland was a series of telephone poles too close to a fairy hill, which kept mysteriously falling down.

Traditionally places that belong to the fairies are best left alone; it is unwise to interfere with them or build on them. There are many stories, not only in Ireland but also in Iceland, of people who damaged or dug into fairy places only to suffer great ill luck, illness, or even death. In some cases even going into a place that belonged to the fairies posed a risk; in one story from Ireland a young man interfered with a well that was known to belong to the Fair Folk and in response they cursed it; when the man next went to drink from it he fell in and drowned (Ballard, 1991). If you choose to visit them it is best to do so during the day and to be careful not to leave behind a mess. It's also advised not to relieve yourself on the ground in the area, as that is known to offend them as well. Add to that a general suggestion not to say anything provocative in those areas, especially anything that belittles or questions their power or influence because they do respond to verbal insults. As long as you are careful not to break things, not to leave behind trash, and not to verbally provoke them, you should be alright.

Chapter 1

Fairyland

And do you not see that bonny road,
That winds about the ferny hillside?
That is the road to fair Elfland,
Where you and I this night must go.
The Ballad of Thomas the Rhymer

In my experience when we seek Fairy we always start by seeing the parts of it that most reflect ourselves and what we want to see. Perhaps that's a greater truth of life in general, that we always see ourselves reflected first in the things around us, before we see those things as they truly are. And so when we hear people talking about Fairy and their experiences with it we will find a wide array of descriptions, from the frightening to the fantastic, the terrifying to the enticing. None of them are wrong, and none of them are exactly right either, and that's your first lesson about Fairy: it is in all ways and always a contradiction.

There's a wide array of teachings about Fairy in different spiritual contexts and most of them tend to treat the Otherworld as one homogenous place; this is understandable and difficult to avoid. I think there's a huge need for caution though in not over-generalizing an individual's perceptions and experiences into universal truths about Fairy. Because it isn't like a single city that can be summarized neatly – rather it's more an entire world with places of civilization and places of dangerous wilds; confusing one for the other won't end well. Perhaps one person always goes to one place and has one type of interaction, and that's fine, and passing along teachings based on that is fine, but that one place is not the sum total of what Fairy is, any more than Boston is what Earth is. The same holds true for the beings within it –

becoming an expert in mice doesn't give you any experience with wolves, if you understand what I'm saying, and vice versa. As we look at what and where Fairy is, keep this in mind and understand that when people talk about 'Fairy' they are either making broad generalizations, like we do when we say 'Earth' or the 'mortal realm', or else are meaning it in a specific sense, but using the general term.

Defining Fairyland

So, what then is Fairy? That is a complicated question, as there are many worlds besides our own, and the world of Fairy is only one of them, if indeed it is one single world. It goes by many names: Fairy, Fairyland, Elfland, Elfhame, Elphame, Elvenland, an Saol Eile (the Otherworld), and in other cultures there are places that may be analogous to the Celtic Fairy, such as Ljossalfheim. These places aren't the same place, but they are similar in context as being the home of beings that are a type of fairy, in that case the Alfar.

The term Fairy is an old one for the land in which Otherworldly beings dwell, and indeed we see authors such as Chaucer using the generic term 'elf' for the inhabitants and the term Fairy for the place almost exclusively (Williams, 1991). Although my own preference is to refer to the place as Fairy, capital 'F', and the inhabitants as fairies, lower case 'f', it is common in folklore – particularly Scottish – to see it referred to as Elfame or Elfhame. There are a variety of spellings given, but for convenience I am using the more modern version here. An older example can be found in this quote from the 16th century witchcraft trial of Bessie Dunlop: '*The guid wichts who winnit in the court o' Elffehame*' (the good creatures who dwelt in the court of Elfhame) (McNeil, 1956). In the Irish, the realm in which the Good People live is sometimes called An Saol Eile, which is usually translated as 'The Otherworld'. However, 'Saol Eile' literally means the 'Other Life' and this is important to remember as we contemplate what exactly the Otherworld is.

The simplest definition of what Fairy is would be the place that fairies live, but that can easily become circular logic depending on how we are defining fairies. It may be easier to say that Fairy is a place that is a separate world associated with beings that would normally be considered fairies, where time runs differently, and where the presence of magic is considerably stronger than here. Folklore tells us that fairies may live in lakes, or hills, or mountains, but it was always less that they literally existed in the water or physical ground of those places and more that those places acted as doorways to the Otherworld. The nature of the Otherworld itself is not widely agreed on either in folklore or by scholars. In the oldest mythology, Fairy was a world full of fantastical things such as animals that could be killed and eaten one day and rise alive and whole the next morning. During the medieval period Fairy was often equated to a near Heavenly paradise, sometimes described with the exact same phrases found in ecclesiastical texts discussing Heaven, but gradually came to be associated more strongly with the land of the dead (Firth-Green, 2016). There was also an association of Fairy with Purgatory, reinforced by medieval stories that explicitly connected the two, although it was never clear that they were in fact the same place (Firth-Green, 2016). In the same way in the Irish material we see this idea hinted at with references to all souls of the dead having to go to Tech Duinn, the house of Donn, Donn being both a God and King of Fairy and his house being in the Otherworld. The only consistent thread to be found was a belief that, however similar Fairy may seem to our own world, it was a place foreign to living humans and inhabited by strange and uncanny beings.

I do want to clarify one point of confusion here that I often run across. The Otherworld, what I call Fairy, is not the only other realm of existence, and there are several other well-known ones that are often confused with or conflated with Fairy. The astral plane, for example, is not the same as Fairy, but rather is a different and unique place. The astral seems to be more closely connected to our world and more strongly influenced by it, while Fairy is connected to our world, but not as a mirror image or a place we can influence from within our world. The axiom that applies to the astral plane, '*As above so below*', would not apply to Fairy, which exists independently from our reality in that sense. This is where it becomes important to remember that there are many other worlds besides our own, but they are not all the Otherworld of Fairy.

Time

One distinctive feature of Fairy is the flow of time; in most cases time in Fairy seems to move at a different pace than on Earth. We may see a single night go by in Fairy while years pass on Earth, or in one anecdote years passed for a man in Fairy while only minutes passed here (Briggs, 1976). We see a variety of stories where a person joins a fairy dance for what they believe is only a single night only to find at dawn that years, decades, or even a century has passed while they danced. In the tale of King Herla a single night of feasting in Fairy occurs while 200 years pass on mortal Earth (Briggs, 1976). There is no clear predictable pattern to this, however, and the fairies themselves seem exempt from the disjointed temporal effect, as they often and regularly cross between the two worlds, even maintaining friendships with mortals over the length of the person's lifetime, without difficulty. The same is obviously not true for mortals, or at least not without fairy aid[1], as we see many mortals doomed by their time in Fairy because they return to a world that is utterly changed from the one they left by nothing more esoteric than the passage of time.

Describing Fairy

Fairy has been described in many ways in folklore, from a world

15

that is much like our own in its appearance to one that is quite fantastic in nature. One description says that Fairy has no sun, moon, or stars, and that all its springs contain blood, which flows there from the mortal world (Acland, 1997). The blood in the water could be a metaphor for the connection between fairies and the mortal dead, which we shall discuss in more depth later, or it could be meant to be interpreted literally. Blood has a lot of important symbolism, but it also very literally carries vital substances including salt, minerals and metals, and healing compounds. Fairy can be a wilderness or a massive city, wild or civilized. In one story from Pembrokeshire, a shepherd who travels to Fairy describes a shining palace with a variety of gorgeous gardens (Briggs, 1976). A Welsh description from an anecdote describes a great city with large houses where all the people never seemed to lack anything (Gwyndaf, 1991). It is often described as exceedingly fair, green, and pleasant, although also usually said to be in a perpetual twilight; the great halls are said to be rich and full of treasure and jewels (Acland, 1997). In the Irish myth of the *Echtrai Nera* it would seem that when it is summer in Fairy it is winter in our world, as Nera goes into a fairy hill on Samhain (Halloween) and is given a flowering branch from a fruit tree to prove his story when he leaves. In contrast, however, the *Gesta Regnum Britannie* describes Fairy as a land of perpetual spring, abundant in flowers and fruit, and without any illness or unhappiness (Firth-Green, 2016).

Finding Fairy

In the Irish sources it seems to be both a cohesive place that is not our world, and also a collection of related or contiguous places that are not here. Sometimes these are described as islands, or beyond the ninth wave, but most often the Otherworld is anchored in or reached through the sí, the fairy mounds, or other Earthly objects. It – or they – can be reached by sailing to the west (in Irish folklore), by finding doorways often in mountainsides, or by finding doors opened into fairy hills. Entrances to Fairy exist in marshes, caves, rocks, lakes, riverbanks, underground tunnels, and even in heavy mist (Gwyndaf, 1991). In some stories getting to Fairy is as simple as stepping through a doorway, while in others it can only be reached through an arduous and difficult journey.

Reaching Fairy in the stories can be easy or quite difficult. In some tales a person has only to step through an opening in a fairy hill or into a fairy ring to find themselves in the Otherworld, while in other stories a long and complex journey is involved. In the ballad of *Thomas the Rhymer*, Thomas describes traveling with the Fairy Queen on her white horse through a desert, wading through rivers, going where there is neither sun nor moon, and wading through blood up to the knee to get to Fairy (Acland, 1997). In one Welsh story a midwife is taken to tend a fairy birth by riding a white horse[2] with the father-to-be along many paths, between a cleft in a split boulder, into a cave, and a great distance through darkness (Gwyndaf, 1991). We see the passage through darkness repeated in the story *'Reinbrun'*, where the eponymous protagonist must pass through gates in a hillside, ride through darkness, then cross a river to reach the fairy castle that is his destination.

Joining a fairy dance can lead to a person's death, or may make years seem like a single night, but in many stories it is also a way that we see people being taken into Fairy (Briggs, 1976). One might note that this is a riskier method, and by no means a certain way to reach Fairy, and as well those taken in dancing do not always want to go. In the ballad of *Childe Rowland* the protagonist's sister is taken unwillingly to Fairy after going counterclockwise around a church, and the protagonist himself obtains entry to an elfin hall by walking three times counter-clockwise around it chanting: *'Open door! Open door! And let me come in!'* (Acland, 1997) This example from the ballad along with the stories about fairy rings may show us that moving counterclockwise – what's called 'withershins' in the source material – has a purpose and a power of its own that helps open the way to Fairy.

In contrast, in medieval belief the Otherworld could be reached in a person's dreams, and interactions there were as real as those in the waking world (Bitel, 1991). Indeed, it is not an uncommon belief even into the modern period that Fairy can be reached in dreams and trances and that a person can be 'away with the fairies' as the saying goes even though they are still physically present in our world. One person in Ireland about a hundred years ago said it was possible for a person to go into a trance and be with the fairies for several hours or several days, or less commonly for years (Evans-Wentz, 1911). In such cases the person afterwards might have no memory of the events they experienced, or equally likely would claim no memory because they were under a prohibition not to speak of anything they had seen while among the Other Crowd. The idea that a person can be physically in our world, but also in Fairy, possibly in spirit or perhaps in some other sense, is an old well-established one. People who were believed to be taken by the Gentry would fall into trances, sometimes able to speak and relay information, but sometimes completely lost to mortal Earth for a time (Evans-Wentz, 1911). This process of entering Fairy in trances and dreams is no less valid or real than entering the Otherworldphysically. In the past it was taken just as seriously by people. It is very important to keep this in mind if you feel you might be having dreams about Fairy, going to Fairy in your sleep, or entering Fairy in trances as you must behave as if you are really there, with all the required caution and etiquette, in order to emerge safely again.

Some people wander Fairy unwittingly while some go there intentionally. Others are taken by a member of Fairy either permanently as a spouse or servant, or else for a set temporary period, often as a servant. In the second case the person is usually returned to mortal Earth after either a year or seven years, although occasionally other periods of time are noted (Briggs, 1976). There are usually specific prohibitions relating to Fairy if one wants to return to mortal Earth again. The most common one is that you cannot eat or drink any food while there or you will be bound to stay forever. In the ballad of *Thomas the Rhymer* we see a different version, where Thomas must remain completely silent, or else he will be trapped forever in Fairy. In a story from Ireland of an abducted child, the fairies were not able to keep him because he had a blackberry thorn under one fingernail (Ballard, 1991). They had a prohibition on them that they must remove all Earthly things from him within three days or return him (Ballard, 1991). They took his clothes and, as the story goes, washed him thoroughly, but they were unaware of the small thorn's presence, and so when the three days were up had no choice but to bring him back. Ballard suggests that this was a symbolic removal of the boy's humanity, which the fairies had three days to complete, and because they could not remove everything – could not effectively remove all traces of mortal Earth and make the boy one of themselves – they had no choice but to return him. Excluding *Thomas the Rhymer*, where it seems Thomas was an exception based on the terms under which he was taken into Fairy by the Queen, the overall pattern involves changing the person or binding them to Fairy. This can be done by removing all external traces of mortal Earth – and one might assume, after three days, all internal traces as well through the normal natural processes – or by having the person internalize Fairy itself by eating or drinking a substance from it, which we may suppose contains its essence[3].

Rescue from Fairy

There is a long tradition of people being rescued from Fairyland by those still on mortal Earth. Yeats relates a story of a policeman who rescued a girl who'd been taken, by burning all the ragwort in a field associated with the fairies. The Rev. Robert Kirk, author of *The Secret Commonwealth of Elves, Fauns, and Fairies*, was said to have been taken by the fairies and later to have appeared to a friend and said he would be seen in church on a certain day and, if his friend acted, he could be freed (Bennett, 1991). His friend failed to take the proper action at the appointed time, and Kirk was never seen again. In the ballad of *Tam Lin* Janet rescues Tam Lin by pulling him off a fairy horse as the Fairy Rade passes by and holding him without faltering when the Fairy Queen transforms him into a variety of fearsome things. In the ballad *The Faerie Oak of Corriewater* a sister tries to save her brother in a similar manner, but when he is turned in her arms to fire she panics and is killed by the flames. There were also means of freeing people from the Slua Sidhe by tossing items in the air including gloves or a knife and yelling: '*This is yours that is mine.*' When we study the stories we find three main patterns emerging: gaining the return of people by threatening something the fairies value, rescue by passing trials to free them, or exchanging something else for the person. Each of these three methods has its own risks, and none comes with guarantees. Usually threatening something the fairies value means being willing to destroy those things normally held sacred by the fairies, including their trees and hills. The trials one must undergo vary, but may mean holding onto a person while they seem to change into frightening things, or sometimes finding a specific weapon and using it to kill or destroy someone or something. In the ballad *Childe Rowland*, for example, the protagonist must take a sword and travel to the castle where his sister is being held, beheading anyone who speaks to him; when he reaches the castle his sister greets him and he sadly kills her, only to find out that it was just a test and she is still alive. His older brothers had failed to save her and had fallen into an enchanted sleep because they could not bring themselves to kill her when she spoke.

To Stay or Go

Even those who go willingly to Fairy must adhere to specific
prohibitions to stay there. In a tale from Pembrokeshire, a young
man taken into Fairy after joining a fairy dance lived there
happily for years, under the single prohibition that he not drink
from a fountain in the center of a garden. When he finally did so
he was immediately returned to mortal Earth, where he realized
only a few minutes had passed (Briggs, 1976). In another story,
this one from Cornwall, a girl who was brought to Fairy to act as
a governess for a little boy broke a prohibition put on her not to
touch her eyes with the ointment she put on the child's eyes, and
when she is found out she was cast out for it (Briggs, 1976). The
Fey Folk seem swift to punish even those who they have adopted
as their own, when those people break rules set upon them.

Those who succeed in returning from Fairy rarely come back
unchanged. Thomas served the Fairy Queen for seven years and
was rewarded with the gift of prophecy, but also an inability to
speak anything but the truth; both a blessing and a curse. In one
tale of a girl who joined the fairies in a night of dancing, she was
able to escape by refusing a drink, and being given a bit of
enchanted ground ivy as a charm, but was warned that when she
heard the fairy music again and danced she would be taken into
Fairy forever (Briggs, 1976). The threat to take her back when she
heard the music a second time is unusual, as in most cases once a
person is freed from Fairy, willingly or not, they are not taken
back again. Some people who were saved from Fairy or otherwise
returned from it died shortly afterwards, pining away for the
Otherworld, as in the story of a man rescued from a fairy ring
who could not reconcile his night dancing with the year that had
passed for everyone in his town (Briggs, 1978). Others were
haunted by their experiences and were described by one source
as pale, thin, and with unsteady eyes (Firth-Green, 2016). More
often though those who returned after too much time had passed
would simply crumble to dust as the years they had missed on

mortal Earth seemed to overcome them on their return.

The Scottish witches who owed loyalty to the Fairy Queen claimed during their trials that they would be taken to Fairy to see the Queen or otherwise do business with the fairies, and their repeated travel between worlds did not seem to harm them. This may perhaps be because they had a guide bringing them and returning them. In Irish tradition there were and are those who regularly visit Fairyland and they are also thought to be slightly odd or unlike other people. I have heard it called being 'touched by the fairies', 'off with the fairies' or 'away with the fairies', which are also euphemisms for being eccentric or slightly mad. Fairy leaves its mark on a person and going to the place changes something deep inside them, whether the visit is temporary or permanent.

End Notes

1. Some mortals, such as the witches who claimed to have gone to Fairy and met the Fairy Queen or otherwise mingled with the fairy folk there regularly traversed back and forth. However, they also had the help of either a particular fairy guiding them, or were there at the Queen's bequest and one assumes under her power. There are some other exceptions to the distortion of time, and people who are able to travel safely back and forth. Overall, it should be understood that a distortion of time is a serious concern and should not be dismissed lightly.

2. It is certainly interesting that we see the white horse as a repeating motif in these journeys; Thomas the Rhymer is also brought to Fairy on a white horse, and we see white horses elsewhere appearing as significant.

3. This theory seems quite solid, as it also works in reverse in stories. Not, as it happens, on fairy brides who come to Earth under strict conditions and usually bound by having a literal piece of themselves – such as the Selkie's seal skin – held

captive. No we see it in stories like that of the Green Children (see Katherine Briggs entry under that heading in her 1976 *Dictionary of Fairies*) where beings of Fairy have all that makes them fey stripped away, are fed mortal food and clothed in mortal clothes, are baptized, and eventually lose their Otherworldly essence and become mortal entirely. From this we may deduce that it is the process of eliminating the essence of one world and inculcating the substance of the other into a being that in effect makes that being either fairy or mortal.

Chapter 2

Basic Facts about Fairies

There are more things in heaven and earth, Horatio,
Than are dreamt of in your philosophy.
Shakespeare, *Hamlet*

We use the term fairies very loosely to describe all inhabitants of the Otherworld as well as some spirits tied more closely to our world, but there are some general things that can be said about them. We will be looking at common questions asked relating to fairies and looking to the general patterns we see in folklore for answers; as always there will likely be exceptions to any rule when it comes to the members of Fairy. However, this chapter will give a person a good idea of the basics before the book gets into the more detailed aspects of fairies and looks at some specific types and common interactions.

Do Fairies Have Physical Forms?

Among some people in modern belief, fairies are often assumed to be entirely insubstantial; that is they are described in the same terms as ghosts or other incorporeal spirits and are said to have no physical forms that can be touched or interacted with. This view has become so widespread in some groups that the idea of fairies having any physicality is considered ludicrous, and yet a brief look at folklore shows that in Celtic cultures historically, as well as other cultures such as the Norse, these spirits were always assumed to have a physical form that could be interacted with. A quick survey of a variety of stories in folklore provides evidence of fairies acting in very physical manners, but also being compared to formless things like the wind – so which is it?

Now I'll start by saying there are some understandable

reasons why people tend to go with the insubstantial view. Firstly fairies are usually invisible to humans (unless they choose otherwise or the humans have some special ability or talisman) and this invisibility naturally lends itself to an assumption of a lack of substance. Yeats recounts a tale of a group of the Other Crowd who wanted to play a game of hurling, but were unable to touch the ball until they found a human to play the game with them; many people tend to interpret this as necessary to give them solid form in our world (Yeats, 1893). It's also true that one of the better known historic texts on Elves and fairies, the Rev. Robert Kirk's *The Secret Commonwealth of Elves, Fauns, and Faires* refers to the Good People as having bodies that were like a *'condensed cloud'*, *'congealed air'*, and compares them to astral forms (Kirk, 1691). They were generally believed to be able to either become invisible to mortal eyes or to become insubstantial entirely and pass through solid matter (Firth-Green, 2016). This certainly paints a picture of a being without physical form. Many types of fairies, including the Slua Sí and the Wild Hunt are also described as traveling through the air, a feat that is easier to reconcile if they are assumed to be intangible.

However, that being said, even Kirk goes on to discuss a variety of things that are done by the Good People of a very physical nature. He mentions them using solid weapons, for example, and that they steal nursing mothers to wet-nurse fairy babies, these women being physically removed and sometimes returned unharmed years later. People who are taken and returned relate stories of living among the fairies, which involve activities much like those found among humans including spinning, sewing, cleaning, and cooking. Similarly we see many Welsh tales of the Fair Family in which they are physically inter-acting with people, often by kidnapping women, children, or babies (Sikes, 1881). In one notable tale a boy who was taken by the fairies steals a golden ball from them and finds his way back out of Fairyland to make a gift of the ball to his mother (Sikes,

1881). It is quite clear in that story that the boy is acting in a physical way with the fairies – such as playing with the King's son – and that the golden ball is tangible and exists as something that humans can touch and take. Ballads like *Tam Lin* and *Thomas the Rhymer* also offer examples of people interacting in very physical ways with the Good Folk, as do the myriad tales of Selkie wives. W. B. Yeats related a story of a woman whose mother had a friend among the Good People who similarly could be substantial and gave the woman one day an herb for protection; this was passed to her from the fairy woman's own hand (Yeats, 1893). In the ballad of *Lady Isabel and the Elf-Knight* the eponymous protagonist Lady Isabel lulls the Elven knight who means to murder her to sleep and then ties his hands and kills him with his own dagger, proving both his physicality and mortality[1].

Perhaps the best answer to this question can be gained by looking at the Norse and Germanic evidence. Here we see that Elves are considered both insubstantial and also able to take physical form. Grimm relates a story of an Elf-maid who entered a house like smoke through a knothole, then married the son of the family, bore him four children, only to eventually leave the same way she had entered (Grimm, 1883). He also states that Elves are strongly connected to butterflies because both are *'the product of repeated changes of form'* (Grimm, 1883, p 462). In this way then it is not a matter of Elves and fairies either being insubstantial or having form, but rather a matter of them being both, or at least able to be one or the other. This can be a difficult concept to grasp, but another valuable lesson if you want to deal with fairies is to work to let go of an either/or mindset and instead embrace the idea of multiple possibilities even when those possibilities seem to be contradictory.

In Celtic lore fairies are known to both shape-shift as well as use a type of magic called glamour to deceive the eyes of those looking at them. Glamour is used not only to obscure the fairy's own appearance, but also to make other objects look different than they actually are, so that a handful of leaves may look like gold or a dank cave may seem like a palace. In the ballad of *Tam Lin* the Fairy Queen uses her magic to make Tam Lin appear as several frightening things in the arms of his lover Janet, including a burning brand (Acland, 1997). Beyond magical manipulation of the viewer, fairies are also often said to be able to change their shapes in truth, so that the Púca, for example can fly through the air as an eagle, or run across the land as a horse or goat, or appear as a small wizened man.

Ultimately folklore shows us stories of fairies that are shadowy and can pass through the physical substance of our world as well as stories where they are as solid and able to affect our world as we are. In some cases the choice between forms seems to be theirs, in others, such as Yeats' hurling tale, there appears to be a more formal set of rules in play. In the end it would seem that it is true that fairies are both insubstantial and tangible, and that we should not assume they are limited to either.

What do Fairies Eat?

Like everything else to do with Themselves there's actually no one simple answer and it depends a lot on what sort of fairy we're talking about. There's also been a lot of speculation, even going back to the 17th century and the writings of the Rev. Kirk, that fairies may not eat our solid food at all, but rather absorb the essence of the food, what Kirk called the 'foyson', Campbell called the 'toradh[2]', or Evans-Wentz called the quintessence. It was for this reason that food offered to the fairies, or which it was believed they had consumed the essence of, was not considered fit for human consumption nor even for animals to eat (Evans-Wentz, 1911). Again, though, this may be something that is true of some types, while others do literally consume the item itself. Without getting into what may be traditionally offered to fairies, but only looking at what folklore tells us they are known to consume, here are some general things we can say to give people an idea of what different fairies eat:

- Some fairies eat 'corn' (a general term for grains), bread, and drink liquor and milk (Kirk, 1691).
- Fairies will steal, and presumably eat, any and all human food and produce if the owner of it speaks badly about it, by taking the 'toradh' out of it so that it gives no value to the humans (Campbell, 1900).
- Fairies are known to take the 'substance' from such crops as turnips and grain, and will take butter if they can (Evans-Wentz, 1911). They will also steal quality food from the hearth that is cooking, such as meat or vegetables, leaving behind something wasted or unpleasant in its place (Wilde, 1920).
- The Corrigans and Lutins are fond of meat, especially beef, and will steal and butcher cows to prepare their own feasts (Evans-Wentz, 1911).
- Some fairies are said to use glamour to make their food appear as delicious fare like to what humans would eat when really it is leaves, weeds, roots, and 'stalks of heather' (Briggs, 1976).
- Several types of fairies, including Hags, Kelpies and Water Horses, are known to eat human flesh. Briggs mentions one such reference to a fairy court's feast, which consisted of the prepared and cooked body of an old woman (Briggs, 1976, p 145). Similarly tales of the Hag Black Annis mention her penchant for eating children; Kelpies can trick people into riding them, tear them apart and eat them (Briggs, 1976). On a related note the Baobhan Sí drinks blood, and the welsh form of the Leanann Sí, the Lhiannan Shee, is also said by some to have a vampiric nature (Briggs, 1976).

- It is said that some Irish fairies eat fruits, vegetables, honey, and drink milk, but do not eat meat (Lysaght, 1991).
- The Good Neighbors of Orkney and Shetland eat oatmeal, fish, and drink milk (Bruford, 1991).
- In Wales the fairies eat eggs, butter, and drink milk (Gwyndaf, 1991).
- Yeats recounts a tale of one of the Gentry who passed a Halloween with a family and ate with them a meal of duck and apples, although she had only a single bite from each portion (Yeats, 1892).
- It is said that some fairies eat rowan berries. Indeed, rowan berries were also said to have been the food of the Tuatha De Danann by some accounts (McNeill, 1956).
- Several types of fairies appear to either be fond of barley or to grow it as their own crop, and to eat it. Milk is also widely reported to be consumed by fairies, not only cow's milk, but also goat's milk and the milk of deer (Briggs, 1976). This widespread love of grain and milk is particularly interesting in folk belief as it echoes much older myth from the *De Gabail in t-Sida* where the Tuatha De Danann retreat into the sí (fairy hills) and cause all the crops to fail and cows to go dry until an agreement is reached whereby they will be given a portion of each harvest, specifically 'ith' (grain) and 'blicht' (milk).

To summarize, milk was often mentioned, as were grains, which would seem to be prepared in ways similar to humans; most sources including Briggs and Campbell refer to the fairies' use of grains ground into meal, for example. Baking is mentioned, as is cooking more generally, and when fairy feasts are mentioned, barring the more macabre ones, they seem to be filled with the same dishes humans would eat. Besides an emphasis, perhaps, on dairy and baked goods, generally fairies seem to eat much the same foods humans do, although certain types of fairies are more specific in their diets and some of course eat things we would not. While they are often noted to take the essence from foods they are also equally often said to eat the food itself, so both seem equally possible.

Colors and Clothing

There are several colors that have come to be associated with the Good Neighbors over time. Generally they are related to us through descriptions of clothing and of animals, although by far the most detail can be gleaned by looking at clothing descriptions. The clothing itself, when described in stories, is usually similar to that of the people living in the area, although sometimes a bit out of date in style (Briggs, 1976; Yeats, 1893; Kirk, 1891). The colors may be interpreted as symbolic or simply as representing widespread preferences by the Fair Folk.

Green

Green is probably the most well known of fairy colors. Several euphemisms for the fairies in different areas are based on the color green including Greenies and Greencoaties (Briggs, 1976). In some places, like parts of Scotland, it is so strongly associated with the fairies that it is considered unlucky for women in particular to wear green (Briggs, 1976). In the ballad of *Alice Brand* the couple in the story anger the Fairy King by wearing green, which he calls '*the fairies' fatal green*' (Acland, 1997). The Cu Síth of Scotland are said to have green fur. In many traditional descriptions fairies are described as wearing green; often they are said to wear green clothes and red hats, especially the Trooping fairies (Lysaght, 1991; Gwyndaf, 1991; Briggs, 1976). In other sources they are simply said to wear red and green (Bruford, 1991; Ballard, 1991; Evans-Wentz, 1911). In many cases green is said to be the primary color worn along with a touch of red, for example a fairy lady might wear a green dress with red slippers or a fairy man might wear a green outfit with a red feather in his hat (Briggs, 1976). In other descriptions given of fairies in folklore and anecdotes they are seen wearing green only (Evans-Wentz, 1911). In many descriptions of the Queen of Fairy, such as we see for example in *Thomas the Rhymer*, she is described as dressed richly and in green. Briggs relates green to the color of death in Celtic folklore (Briggs, 1976, p109). In contrast, however, Evans-Wentz suggests green is associated with renewal, rebirth, and immortality (Evans-Wents, 1911). The truth may be somewhere between the two, with the color having layered symbolism of death, life, and immortality.

Red

Red has long been associated with the Otherworld and with Otherworldly beings in Irish mythology and in fairylore. In Irish mythology when a figure appears who is described as 'red' or wearing all red they are almost invariably Otherworldly in nature, something we see in *Togail Bruidne Dá Derga* as well as the *Táin Bó Regamna*. Red in Irish mythology is a color associated with blood and more generally with death by violence; in the *Tain Bo Cuiligne* we can see an example of this in the prophecy given by Fedelm to Medb where the words forderg (very red) and ruad (red) are used figuratively to indicate blood and bloodstains. Red hats are associated with fairies, not only the eponymously named Red Caps who dye their caps in blood, but many others as well. In folklore fairies are sometimes described as wearing green clothing and red hats (Lysaght, 1991). They may also appear dressed entirely in red, although this could be considered a bad omen, relating to an anecdotal tale of a red clad fairy who would appear at births to foretell the baby's death (Ballard, 1991). As well, a woman who saw the fairies in Newfoundland and was hit by elfshot from them, saw them dressed all in red (Rieti, 1991). Although this may indicate that red clad fairies are generally more dangerous, as with most things fairy related, it is not a firm indication. Leprechauns, Cluricauns, and the Fir Darig were traditionally known to wear red clothes, and they could be either harmful or lucky depending on circumstances and how the person interacted with them (Briggs, 1976).

White

In one Shetland account the fairies appeared as two opposing forces, one wearing white the other black (Bruford, 1991). A variety of fairies were known to wear white in particular and these included the Silkies (a type of English Brownie), the White Ladies, and the Tylwyth Teg (Briggs, 1976). Yeats related a tale of two boys who saw a white-clad figure circling a bush (Yeats, 1892). Isobel Gowdie described the Queen of Elfhame as wearing white as well. Many fairy animals are described as being white with red ears, and this includes cows, deer, and dogs. In Old Irish white was a color that among other things was associated with corpses of the battle dead, which were described as bloodless. It was also said in some folklore that fairies had white blood, which was sometimes found on the ground after they had fought.

Grey

The Trows of Orkney are noted to wear grey (Bruford, 1991). So strong is this association that one of the euphemisms used for the Trows is 'the Grey Neighbors' (Briggs, 1976). In addition a variety of stories, including one recounted by Yeats in Celtic Twilight, describe a fairy appearing clad in a grey cloak (Yeats, 1892; Briggs, 1976). One famous fairy horse in Irish mythology was the Liath Macha or 'Macha's Grey' who appeared out of a sí and returned there after being mortally wounded. Grey is another color whose ultimate symbolism may relate back to death.

Black

Black is generally speaking an ill-omened color. To see a fairy wearing black was an omen of death, although not necessarily for the person seeing it (Ballard, 1991). A variety of fairy dogs and hounds are described as black in color, and these are usually, although not always, death omens. Black Dogs are large and shaggy with flaming eyes, and in stories might be helpful or could be dangerous (Briggs, 1976). The Cat Sidhe are said to be black with a white spot on the chest.

Blue

Manx fairies are described wearing blue, usually with red (Briggs, 1976). There was also a sighting of a fairy market at Blackdown where the fairies seen were noted to be wearing both the usual red and green as well as blue (Briggs, 1976). There is a type of Hobgoblin in Somerset, called 'Blue Burches' who was known to wear blue pants from which he got his name and similarly a fairy called 'Blue Bonnet' who was known to wear a blue hat and worked in mines (Briggs, 1976).

Multicolors

There are also several sources that mention fairies wearing many colors, in the sense of a crowd of the Other Folk all arrayed in different colors, as well as wearing plaids or tartans. One Welsh account of two brothers describes them seeing an assortment of smaller fairies dancing wearing many different colors (Gwyndaf, 1991). Scottish accounts going back to the 17th century describe some Highland fairies wearing plaids and this seems to be true into the modern period as well (Kirk, 1891; Briggs, 1976). We should not, therefore, assume that because certain colors are prevalent that they are necessarily restricted to these.

It's also worth considering that while these colors are likely still powerful and significant to the Good People, were one to see them today they would most likely be dressed in fairly modern attire. Although they are occasionally seen in archaic dress they are more usually seen in clothes that are either slightly out of date or contemporary and, as the Rev. Kirk, Yeats, and Briggs all noted, usually in the styles of the same region they are appearing in.

Fairy Morality

The ethics of Fairy are often sharply at odds from human ones and this is a key thing to grasp when trying to learn about fairies and understand their actions. We cannot measure their actions by our own expectations, or we will consistently be baffled and often appalled by what they do. We will also put ourselves in danger if we act based on our own morals or human etiquette without realizing that fairy expectations are so foreign from ours.

The Good Neighbors are private beings and this is seen in a variety of ways, but one sure method of angering them is to violate that privacy or to speak too openly about experiences you have with them. There are some who say that the Rev. Robert Kirk, who wrote about the Good People of Scotland in the 17th century, was ultimately taken by them for his writing. In the widespread stories found in most Celtic countries where a midwife is borrowed by a man of the fairies to help his wife in childbirth, when she is able to see and identify him later – because she accidently touches one of her eyes with a special ointment which grants sight of the unseen – he either puts out the eye she sees him with or blinds her entirely. In some cases a person who was taken into Fairy for a relatively short amount of time, usually a year, who speaks too much is punished by being barred from ever returning there (Briggs, 1976). It was generally understood that even if you heard fairy music or the noise of Themselves passing by you should not look around to try to see them or you'd be punished for it (Ballard, 1991). Katherine Briggs outlines three basic tenets of fairy privacy, that is that they dislike being watched, don't want people trespassing on their land, and don't want people they show favor to bragging about or even in most cases talking about the good things they receive from the fairies (Briggs, 1976).

Those who steal from the Other Crowd do so at great peril, although the reverse does not hold true as the Fey Folk are well known for taking from mortals, especially milk, food, and people. Herein lies another valuable lesson in dealing with Themselves: do not think that imitating their own behavior will gain you anything, but understand that there are different rules for fairies and mortals. Those who have the ability to see the fey often catch them in the act of taking milk from cows or stealing in human markets, and if they know they are being seen they tend to retaliate against the viewer (Briggs, 1976). Fairy theft is not limited to the Unseelie Court either, or the fairies that more clearly mean us harm, but is a pastime of all the fey including the ones who are usually considered magnanimous towards us. One theory holds that fairies can only take something if the rightful owner has spoken ill of it, been stingy, or if the item is ill-gotten (Campbell, 1900). This may be true in some cases, but certainly not in others; in fact the reverse is true of some stories of changelings in which it is believed that complimenting a baby's good nature or beauty opens them to abduction by drawing the fairies' attention to the child.

In another example of fairy morality being different between fairies and mortals, while fairies have no compunctions about stealing from mortals they are extremely quick to punish those among their own number who steal from other fairies. As Katherine Briggs describes it, even the good fairies adhere to a motto of: *'All that's yours is mine, all that's mine is my own,'* when it comes to mortals, but apply a much stricter sense of fair play among themselves (Briggs, 1976, p. 154). For example, there is at least one story of a young Trow boy who was banished from Fairy for stealing from other Trows, a banishment that appeared to be permanent.

Oddly although fairies willingly steal from humans they also sometimes borrow from people with proper manners, asking permission first and promising repayment, although the repayment is not always in kind and can be for a greater value than what was borrowed (Briggs, 1976). It is also possible to borrow safely from the Fey Folk, if a person is polite in the asking and scrupulous in the repayment. In one anecdotal story, a farmer who had suffered several reversals of fortune went out one day to a place where it was known that a man who had been taken by the fairies frequently appeared and asked him for a loan from the fairies of what to plant; the loan was given with the agreement that the exact same amount would be given back on the same day a year later (MacNeill, 1962). Such debts are safe enough to undertake as long as they are repaid on time.

The Good Neighbors are always strictly honest with their words and they expect the same from the humans they deal with. No fairy will say anything that is not strictly true nor will they break a promise (Briggs, 1967). Lying to any member of Fairy is rarely a good idea, as is breaking your word with them. Even the worst of what we would call the Unseelie will not lie, although they can easily twist the truth around so far that their words are taken to mean something else entirely. Semantics is an art form among the fairies. In this way talking to the Fey Folk requires a very different mindset than talking to a human being, because while we may assume a human is lying and look for the dishonesty in their words we will be caught in the trap that the fairies weave with the truth of their words.

Fairies also have a very different view of indulgence than many human cultures do, and this view applies to a variety of areas. It would be fair to say that fairies embrace a much more hedonistic attitude than most human societies and religions, which can also confuse people who find it difficult to reconcile the fairies' embracing sexual and personal freedoms with policies of strict honesty and adherence to oaths. To understand this aspect of Fairy we must understand that fairies are ultimately beings who embrace orderliness and generosity above all things, but they are also, as Yeats puts it, beings of *'unmixed emotions'*.

They love completely and hate completely, without any reservation. They expect their own laws to be followed even if a person is ignorant of them, yet they disregard human law as inconsequential and are as likely to favor a person who is seen as respectable in human society as one who has a reputation for law-breaking. For example there is one story of a man who made whiskey for a living and was favored by the fairies; they taught him an herbal cure for eczema and acted to save him when he set out on an ill-fated meeting with the Devil one night (Briggs, 1967). They are also known to favor illicit lovers and to have no compunction against engaging in such affairs with mortals themselves. As with all dealings with fairies, however, one must be cautious to keep any oaths made to them and to keep their secrets, or risk losing their favor. Their reputation for sexual lasciviousness was so well known that hundreds of years ago a human woman who was sexually loose in defiance of social norms was called a fairy, an idea that later shifted to homosexuals (Briggs, 1976).

There are also some general characteristics that fairies prefer in both people and, it seems, themselves. These include generosity, politeness, cleanliness, and cheerfulness (Briggs, 1976). Although fairies can be jealous of what they have and of their places they are also known to be generous to those they favor. Good manners are often the key to fairy amity and rudeness a quick route to punishment. A good illustration of this is seen in the story of Lusmore, where the protagonist is polite and helpful to the fairies he encounters and is healed of a deformity, while another seeking to repeat his feat acts rudely and brashly and is deformed even more in punishment (Yeats, 1888). Cleanliness is another factor that fairies often look for and appreciate, and with a few select exceptions embody themselves. Fairies also prefer people who have happy hearts and merry dispositions, generally speaking, although some do feed on our negative emotions.

The Good People are quick to both reward those who please them and punish those who offend them. There are stories of rewards given by the Good People such as gold that turns into leaves or gingerbread at dawn, but in many other tales the rewards they give are tangible and remain. These can include actual wealth as well as health and good luck, and in some cases knowledge or even a magical object or charm. Punishments, however, are usually harsh and can include years of illness, painful physical maladies, madness, ill luck, and death.

Fairies and the Dead

The relationship and connection between the fairies and the dead is a complex one, and likely always has been. The human dead aren't fairies, except when they are. Fairies aren't the human dead, except when they might be. The places of the dead belong to the dead, except when those places are fairy mounds, like the Neolithic tumuli. Even the Slua Sí, whose name means 'Fairy Host' is sometimes said to consist of the spirits of human dead, as in some cases does the Wild Hunt, making it hard to draw any clear lines between the groups. In a very general sense we can say that human ghosts are not the same as fairies, but fairies can include people who were once human. The key difference may be, as we shall see, is how exactly the human came to join the fey.

There is an old Celtic belief, recorded by the Greeks and Romans, which hints at the idea of rebirth or reincarnation, that a person born in our world was dying in the Other World and a person who died in this world was born in the Other World. This idea, perhaps, explains the reason that fairies who wed mortal men were known to cry at births and laugh at funerals. It may also explain in some way why the Irish name for the Other World, an Saol Eile, literally means 'the Other Life'. It is not just another world in the sense of being a place, but it is also another life, another type of existence.

There is some suggestion that the initial depiction around the

16th century of fairies as small beings was actually related to the connection between fairies and the dead and the belief that human souls were small in appearance when separated from the physical body (Briggs, 1976). In turn this idea may reflects a related idea, that the soul was separate from the body and could leave it at times, either temporarily or permanently. We see this in the folktales were a person is taken by the fairies, but their dead body is left behind and in anecdotes where a person goes into a trancelike state while their spirit is off with the fairies. The idea that the soul can be separated from the body and once separate has a reality and substance that can even be injured is an old one seen in multiple sources (Walsh, 2002). It may be difficult for us to grasp the idea of a soul as a tangible, physical thing when our modern culture tends to prefer the idea of souls as insubstantial and ephemeral, but it's clear that the older belief gave the soul substance.

Another level of entanglement is more straightforward, that is sometimes fairies are known to take people to join them and often these people were thought to have died. In a wide array of folklore from Ireland and Wales we see stories in which a young woman is thought to die and is buried, only to be seen later among the fairies in one context or another. In at least one story it was a young man who died and was buried, only to have a fairy doctor tell his family that he was among the Other Crowd; when they attempted to retrieve him he appeared and begged to be allowed to stay with the people of the sí (Briggs, 1976). The Scottish witch Alison Pearson claimed a dead relative was among the fairies and that it was he who acted as her familiar spirit with them (Wilby, 2005). In the ballad of *Alice Brand* we find a story of a man who is mortally wounded in a fight and while everyone assumes he has died he has actually been taken into Fairy as a servant to the Elfin King (Acland, 1997). Getting back to the earlier point about the soul as a tangible presence, we must understand that these are people with presence and physicality who were interacted with and who are clearly counted among the ranks of the fairy people.

Several particular types of dead were more likely to be counted among the fairies. Babies and children, especially if they had been pleasant natured or beautiful in life, as well as brides and handsome youths, were often known to be taken by the fairies and should anyone in that demographic die it was suspicious. Additionally there was a long history of saying that both those killed by violence, the 'sword-killed', as well as great heroes, had been taken into Fairy, and we see this being applied to everyone from King Arthur to Thomas Beckett (Firth-Green, 2016).

In the book *The Fairy Faith in Celtic Countries*, several anecdotes are related that connect the Good People directly to the dead, in both the sense of describing some fairies as being humans who have died as well as saying some of them are people who were taken and thought to have died. One person related a story about a woman who died and shortly after, before the body had been buried, her husband was visited by one of the Good People who told him she wasn't dead, but taken by the fairies; the husband then waited by the body with the door open and his wife came in to see her infant, at which time he grabbed her (Evans-Wentz, 1911). After being restrained and struck with a charm he had prepared the wife returned to her body, as the story was related, which revived and she went on to live a long mortal life (Evans-Wentz, 1911). In another tale with a less pleasant ending a bride died at her wedding, only to appear to her new husband later and tell him that she was actually among the fairies and that if he went to a certain place he would see her passing by and could save her (Evans-Wentz, 1911). The husband went as she'd told him to but when he saw his bride among the fairies passing by he found himself paralyzed and unable to move to grab her; he never saw her again after that, but refused to re-marry (Evans-Wentz, 1911). The people interviewed in that section of the book, who were relating the beliefs of different areas of Ireland around the turn of the 20th century, also made it clear that there were fairies who were never human and had never been human, assigning them origins among the Fir Bolg and Tuatha De Danann, as well as saying they were fallen angels. There were also those among the human dead who could and did return as ghosts or other types of undead spirits that were not considered fairies. Most who died did not become fairies, but passed to another afterlife in common belief, showing that there was no assumption that becoming a fairy was the norm.

The subject of the fairies and the dead is not a simple one, but it is clear that the two groups are intertwined. There are those beings who were never human spirits and those human spirits who are not and will not be fairies. But there are also those who were once human and are now fairies because the fairies themselves added the human to their ranks. The different layers of belief make it apparent that while there was crossover between fairies and the dead there was also distinction and separation of the two groups in other ways. If one could imagine it as a Venn diagram we would see fairies as one circle, the human dead as another, and the area where the two circles overlapped would represent those who fall into both groups – how small or large that is no one can say for certain.

Fairies, Demons, and Angels

Another complicated topic is whether fairies are demons or angels. Generally speaking, fairies seem to fall into a category of their own that is distinct from a Judeo-Christian worldview and shows clear signs of pagan origins. However, fairies have been understood within a Christian context for long enough that aspects of the beliefs around them have adapted or become synchronized. Because of this we see fairies in both folk belief and the writing of the pre-modern literati being described as or equated to both demons and angels.

41

A variety of fairy beings are referred to as Goblins in Old Irish including the Each Uisce, Púca, Fíthal, and Gruagach (eDIL, n.d.). Goblin[3] itself is a term that was often understood as or used as a cognate with the word imp. In the Anglo-Saxon we see the word Aelf similarly grouped with Goblins, demons, and specters, and also being used as an equivalent to Incubus (Hall, 2007). We see a pattern in the Scottish witch trials of the accused witch claiming they dealt with fairies only to have their accuser refer to those fairies as demons (Wilby, 2005). This reflected a common pattern wherein the literati saw fairies as demonic and placed them within the realm of such spirits while the lower classes of society referred to those same spirits as fairies or even as angels (Wilby, 2005). It may perhaps be argued that calling fairies demons was a matter of perspective and represented a continued process of demonizing the older pagan folk beliefs. It can also be argued that it was often the lower levels of society, the common people, who would call them fairies while the educated class were quick to label them as demons, seeking to fit them into a carefully regulated and divided worldview. What the peasant woman or blacksmith might call a fairy – or more likely by the slightly more specific name of Elf, Goblin, Púca, or Gruagach – the priest or scholar would label a demon, Incubus, or imp (Williams, 1991; Wilby, 2005; Hall, 2007).

Even those who saw fairies as demons, however, tended to class them separately from the demons who served Lucifer in Hell. In this view there were two distinct classes of demons: a lesser group who might punish men and cause mischief, but rarely did great evil, and a greater group who were truly malevolent and destructive (Firth-Green, 2016). There was an implicit acknowledgement that these fairies labeled as demons had not fallen all the way to Hell, but remained on Earth in a sort of middle state between true demons and something more benevolent. In some tales we even see a character described in different versions as either a demon or fairy who acts to help and guide the protagonist (Firth-Green, 2016).

Interestingly in the story *Esclarmonde* the fairies seem to be credited with having power over demons, in that they use their magic to save someone from demons trying to drown him (Firth-Green, 2016). This is in direct contrast with other sources, discussed later in this book under the section about the teind to Hell, wherein it is implied the fairies are tenants to or under the authority of Satan, which would reinforce the idea of fairies as lesser demons. This may be a complicated subject that cannot be given a simple answer; ultimately it may be that what constitutes a fairy or a demon is a matter of perspective and a person's worldview.

There was also a similar point of view that saw fairies as angels or as related to angels. In his trial for witchcraft, Andro Man claimed he was visited by a spirit that he alternately described as a fairy and an angel (Wilby, 2005). Looking outside of the Celtic culture for a moment we see evidence that the Icelandic Alfar, at least textually in Snorri Sturulson's writings, were described in ways meant to evoke comparison to angels (Hall, 2007). One of the most common stories within folklore explaining the origin of fairies claims that they are fallen angels, neither demonic nor heavenly, who are seeking redemption and a return to Heaven. Common questions fairies are known to ask mortals during encounters are whether fairies have souls and whether they will one day be redeemed within the Christian faith (Evans-Wentz, 1911; Yeats, 1888). While some folklore did deny souls to the fairies, and thus any hope of Christian redemption, there was also a line of belief going back to the 13th century in England that claimed they might be pardoned at Judgment Day. In this view fairies were fallen angels who were being punished by the Christian God, but who still followed his will and so would return to Heaven at Doomsday (Firth-Green, 2016).

A common angelic narrative attached to fairies says that they were angels who were neutral during the war in Heaven, and because they refused to choose a side God cast them out, but they did not join Satan and his demons in Hell. Another frequently seen version of this story states that when Satan rebelled God was so angry that he threw open the doors of Heaven and all of the angels were being pulled out and into Hell, until he was convinced to show mercy and close the doors. When the doors of Heaven closed, those angels who had fallen into Hell became demons, but those who were trapped in the limbo between Heaven and Hell became fairies. Both of these stories are clearly framed in a Christian worldview and can be seen as attempts to explain the existence of fairies in a way that makes sense in monotheism. This attempt met with only partial success and while it gained some ground among the common people scholars never fully accepted fairies as either redeemable demons or ambiguous angels; texts often differentiated between fairies and any kind of angel, and the Church rejected the idea of demons who could do good (Firth-Green, 2016).

Fairies and the Gods

It's an often repeated belief that the fairies are the Gods, diminished. In Ireland the terms Aos Sí and Daoine Sí, which both mean 'people of the fairy mounds' are used for the fairies, but also by association with the Tuatha De Danann (McKillop, 1998). The Tuatha De Danann are a group of divine beings who invaded and settled Ireland after driving out a previous group of chthonic beings, the Fir Bolg. Most people see the Tuatha De Danann as the Gods of Ireland, and a wide selection of myths exist about their exploits. When the first humans came to Ireland, in the myths, they fought against the Gods and drove them into the fairy hills. However, no crops would grow and no cows would give milk until an agreement was reached with the leader of the defeated Gods. Humans had to offer a portion of their harvest, some of their milk and grain, and in return the Gods would allow the land to flourish. This belief is directly related to the modern belief that the fairies can also influence the health or failure of crops and are due a portion of what is grown and gathered (Evans-Wentz, 1911).

Many people believe that when the Gods went into the fairy hills they lost their divine status and became the fairies (Briggs, 1976). Lady Wilde referred to them as *'cave fairies'* and said they were spared by the Gaels and allowed to go into the fairy mounds because of their skill as poets, musicians, and artisans (Wilde, 1888). This idea was widely adopted in folklore, which depicted the Tuatha De Danann and the fairies themselves as physically small[4], possibly using this as a metaphor for their loss of power and divine status.

The early period of anthropology and folklore in academia saw a great many interesting theories about fairies appearing, many of which linked the Gods to the fairies. This idea also took hold in folk belief creating a great deal of confusion between the Irish Gods and the fairies, and leaving us with a multitude of stories featuring beings listed elsewhere as deities being depicted as fairies instead. For example a variety of the Fairy Queens and Kings of Ireland were once found in mythology as deities or divine supernatural beings. Also because of the story of *The Taking of the Sidhe* as well as local folk belief and attributions from other myths we see many specific well known fairy hills being called the homes of members of the Tuatha De Danann. Sí na Broga (Newgrange) has belonged to several Gods, most notably the Dagda and Oengus mac ind Og, and the Sí of Cruachan is associated with the Morrigan, for example.

The subject is not necessarily so straightforward as the Gods simply being turned into fairies though, as we see references in Irish mythology to *'the riders of the sí'* before the Irish Gods have gone into the sí (fairy mounds). This would seem to imply that the sí and the beings within existed even before the Gods were exiled into the mounds. Mythology also tells us that the Gods themselves may have come from the Otherworld originally, appearing in clouds or mists, and we may perhaps say that when humans pushed them out of our world they simply returned at least partially to the one they came from. After going into the sí we often see different fairy beings, usually referred to generically as Goblins and specters, accompanying the war Goddesses Badb, the Morrigan, and Nemain when they appear in the *Táin Bó Cuailgne*. In that same myth when the epic hero Cu Chulainn is badly wounded the God Lugh appears out of a sí and takes Cu Chulainn into it and when the hero returns to mortal Earth he is accompanied by a man of the sí who relates what has occurred during the three days he was gone. The Goddess Morrigan is said in multiple stories, including the *Táin Bó Cuailgne, Táin Bó Regamna*, and *Dindshenchas* tale of Odras to emerge from and return to the sí of Cruachan. This would seem to establish a strong early connection between the Gods and the fairies, with these myths dating back usually to the 9th or 10th century CE. Later 19th century poets and authors would conflate the two groups, making the Tuatha De Danann themselves into fairies; yet even in these written attempts to reduce the Gods they retain obvious and sometimes explicit divine powers and abilities that transcend what are credited to other fairies (Williams, 2016). As F. Marian McNeill tells us in her book *The Silver Bough*: '*...the Tuatha appear in medieval tales as the Side, or fairy hosts. They are not, however, regarded as ordinary fairies, but rather as 'the gentry of the fairy world.'* (McNeill, 1956, p. 28) From this we may perhaps conclude that while the Irish Gods, the Tuatha De Danann, find a place within the sí they are not truly fairies as we generally understand the term, but rather occupy an upper echelon within Fairy.

End Notes

1. It may be worth noting, however, that he was bound with his own belt and killed with his own blade, suggesting, perhaps, that his own possessions or items from his own world had

greater power over him. Given the lack of detail in the ballad, this is only supposition, and it is possible that rather than any deep metaphysical significance it was simply pragmatism on Lady Isabel's part.

2. Literally 'fruit', but probably in this context meaning produce, profit, or substance.

3. We will discuss Goblins in more depth in a later chapter

4. This idea of the Gods literally shrinking in stature is particularly interesting when juxtaposed with their original stature, which was often described as large or mighty, in some cases even gigantic.

Chapter 3

The Courts and Divisions in Fairy

The guid wichts who winnit in the court o' Elffehame
(The good spirits who dwelt in the court of Elfhame)
Bessie Dunlop describing a group of fairies she had met,
McNeill, 1956

People have tried for a long time to categorize and divide Fairy and its inhabitants to better understand them. It seems to be human nature that we have an easier time comprehending things we can label and put into a box, but that concept doesn't work well with Fairy. There is no simple, clear-cut way to group the beings of Fairy that doesn't either leave a lot of room for fluidity or ignore a variety of them for convenience. However, there are several historic methods of division found in folklore that are still used today and can be helpful for people approaching the subject who need a fairly quick way to immediately understand a few basic things about a particular member of Fairy. The most common of these are the division into Courts, the grouping based on social structure, and division based on locations where they prefer to live.

The Seelie and Unseelie Courts

By many accounts the beings of Fairy are divided into two courts, the Seelie and Unseelie. This is often simplified as the 'good' and 'bad' fairies, or as F. Marian McNeill says the *'gude wichts'*[1] and the *'wicked wichts'* and this concept is still seen in modern fairy beliefs. This was initially a Lowland Scottish belief that later spread (McNeill, 1956). Although in more or less common use now I think we lose the nuances between the two when we try to reduce them into such blunt terms as good and bad (or worse good and evil) and also that many modern people may not fully understand the concepts of seelie and unseelie. So let's look at what exactly seelie and unseelie mean, and how the two courts were traditionally understood, as well as the likely original roots of both as a single entity.

The words seelie and unseelie come to us from the Scots[2] language, itself an amalgam of a variety of languages found in the Lowland areas of Scotland. Although its most often seen today as 'seelie' it also appears in older texts in a variety of forms including sely, seely, seily, sealy, with seely being the most common (DSL, 2016). It is often a term in Scots dictionaries associated with the fairies and given as an adjective to describe both a fairy court and the disposition of individual fairies themselves. Meanings for seelie are given ranging from happy, blessed, lucky, fortunate, and good natured, as well as having connotations of bringing good luck (DSL, 2016; Jamieson, 1808). In contrast, unseelie – also spelled oonseely, onseely, unsealy, or unseely – means dangerous, unlucky, unfavorable, unhappy, unholy, and ungodly (DSL, 2016). The word unseelie, in the form of unsely, can be found as far back as the 16th century meaning unlucky or miserable, but was generally applied to times, places, and animals (DSL, 2016). I have been unable to find any older references to unseelie being applied to fairies.

The Seelie Court is described in relation to the fairies specifically as the 'pleasant or happy court, or court of the pleasant and happy people' and is also given as a general term for all fairies (Jamieson, 1808). In folklore the Seelie Court can act benevolently at times for no reason other than the sake of kindness, as we see in the 1783 ballad of *Allison Gross*, where the eponymous witch of the story punishes a man who refused her sexual advances by bespelling him into the shape of a worm. The unfortunate man is cursed to circle around a tree every day in this form, until one Halloween *'when the Seely Court was riding by'* and the Queen stops, picks up the worm, and uses her magic to restore his original shape to him (Child, 1882). They are also known to be extremely generous to those whom they favor and to be kind to the poor, giving bread and grain as gifts (Briggs, 1976). It was believed that members of the Seelie Court would help those who propitiated them and that this help took various forms including the fairy doing work for the human around their home or farm (McNeill, 1956). They can also act in ways that go against what we would consider goodness, or at least in ways that bring harm to humans, without a clear reason. We see this in the *Ballad of Lady Mary O' Craignethan* where the lord's daughter is quite deviously kidnapped by a man of the sí to be his bride. The lord then curses the fairy folk, wishing that the Devil might take three of them instead of one as his tithe, and swearing to cut down every oak, beech, and ash in the country, to which the priest begs him *'dinnae curse the Seelie Court'* (Sand, Brymer, Murray, & Cochran, 1819). This illustrates that it was in fact the Seelie Court that was believed to be behind the kidnapping, although as we shall see later the term Seelie Court itself may have served as a euphemism for all fairies, rather than a specific term only for the benevolent ones. Despite its reputation as generally kindly, the Seelie Court was known to readily revenge any wrongs or slights against themselves, and even a fairy who would be considered Seelie, such as a Brownie, could be dangerous when offended or harmed. The Seelie Court is not known to harm people without reason though and generally will warn people at least once before retaliating against offenses (Briggs, 1976).

The Unseelie Court is for all intents and purposes the antithesis of the Seelie Court, as implied by the name. The Unseelie Court is described as always unfavorable to humans and is closely linked to the Slua Sí, the malicious Fairy Host who torment people and cause illness and death where they visit (Briggs, 1976). The Slua itself is strongly tied to the dead and is known to kidnap hapless mortals and force them to help with the Host's entertainment, usually harming other humans, before dropping them in a location far from where they were grabbed. The Unseelie Court comprises many solitary fairies of a malicious nature, those who feed on or enjoy hurting mortals for sport, although not all Unseelie fairies are solitary (Briggs, 1976). The Unseelie Court was seen as constantly ready to cause harm or injury to mortals and was avoided as much as possible, and many different protections existed against it (McNeill, 1956; Briggs, 1976).

However, just as the Seelie Court could cause harm if motivated to, and sometimes without having any clear reason at all, so too the Unseelie Court's denizens might occasionally act kindly towards humans without any obvious rhyme or reason. For example Kelpies are usually considered Unseelie by most reckonings, as they trick people into riding them only to kill and eat the person once they have gotten back to their watery homes. However, in several stories a Kelpie will fall in love with a mortal girl and put aside his own bloodthirsty nature for her sake. In one such story the Kelpie even put up with being tricked by the girl, captured himself and forced to work in his horse form on her father's farm for a year, and still loved her enough in the end to choose to marry her (McNeill, 2001). So while it may be convenient and often expedient to divide the Other Crowd up into the two courts based on how they relate to us, we should be very cautious about seeing the division as a hard line or seeing a perceived placement in one court or another as a non-negotiable indicator of behavior.

As mentioned above the term seelie may not have been as specific in the past as it is today and when we look at its usage in older ballads and stories, seelie often appears as a euphemism (DSL, 2016). That means that just like calling Themselves 'Good Neighbors', 'Mother's Blessing', or 'Fair Folk' it isn't done because they are those things, but because we want them to be those things towards us. In other words we are using the term – a nicer term for something generally considered not nice at all –

to try to invoke the nicer aspects of them. To remind them that they can be nice. There is longstanding and deep belief that what we choose to call the fey directly relates to how they will respond to us and interact with us. As this 19th century rhyme illustrates:

Gin ye ca' me imp or elf
I rede ye look weel to yourself;
Gin ye call me fairy
I'll work ye muckle tarrie;
Gind guid neibour ye ca' me
Then guid neibour I will be;
But gin ye ca' me seelie wicht
I'll be your freend baith day and nicht.
(Chambers, 1842)
(If you call me imp or Elf
I counsel you, look well to yourself;
If you call me fairy
I'll work you great misery;
If good neighbor you call me
Then good neighbor I will be;
But if you call me seelie wight
I'll be your friend both day and night)

It should also be noted that the term unseelie referring to fairies is newer than the term seelie and does not appear in the Scots dictionary at all with this connotation, while seelie clearly does. The oldest reference I could find to seelie for fairies is from a 16th century story referenced in a book from 1801; in *The Legend of the Bishop of St Androis* it says:

Ane Carling of the Quene of Phareis
that ewill win gair to elphyne careis;
Through all Braid Albane scho hes bene
On horsbak on Hallow ewin;

and ay in seiking certayne nyghtis
As scho sayis, with sur selie wychtis
(One woman of the Queen of Fairies
that will take goods to Fairyland
through all broad Scotland she has been
on horseback on Halloween
and always in seeking certain nights
as she says, with our Seelie wights)

This reference uses the term Seelie as a generic for fairies with no obvious distinction as to benevolence or malevolence, as do the other ballad references, supporting the idea that at some point there was likely only the concept of the single Seelie Court, used as a euphemism for all fairies. Much like the Welsh calling their fairies Tylwyth Teg (Fair Family) or the Irish use of the term Daoine Maithe (Good People) the Scottish Seelie Court may initially have been a way to speak of the fairies so that should their attention be drawn they would be more likely to be well disposed towards the speaker. This concept, at some later point was divided into seelie and unseelie to better define those beings who either meant humans well, generally, or meant humans harm, generally. While it may seem strange to us now, it is entirely logical that in the past people would have used the euphemistic Seelie Court when referring to the fairies, but not had an inverse negative concept as it would have been seen as impossibly dangerous to even speak of such a group and risk drawing their attention and facing their wrath for it. This could also explain why the idea of the courts as such is unique to Lowland Scots lore and more generally Scottish folklore. It is not found in Welsh or Irish fairylore[3] where euphemisms like 'Fair Family' and 'People of Peace' are still used by preference.

Whether the courts have always existed or not they have certainly been a part of fairylore belief for centuries now and are ingrained in the modern lore. It should also be kept in mind that

while the two courts are a convenient division it is more complicated than that, with a multitude of other possible divisions
going on as well including lesser kings and queens and lords and
ladies. But when most people think of Fairy they think of the
courts, specifically the Seelie Court and Unseelie Court. In
modern parlance these may now be called the Light Court and
the Dark Court or even the Summer Court and the Winter Court,
but though the common names may change the idea remains the
same. The Light Court means us well and the Dark Court
generally does not.

It could be said that the light are the most inclined towards
kindness to humans and who are most likely by nature to have
interests or goals aligned with humans, generally. The magic of
the light tends towards healing, blessing, and increase, which
doesn't mean they can't hurt you if motivated to.

The Dark Court are the most inclined towards seeing people
as a resource – usually food or entertainment – or a nuisance and
are the most inclined to harm humans with little or no provocation simply because they were in the wrong place. The magic of
the dark tends towards decay, ill-luck, and transformation,
although that doesn't mean they can't help a person if they
choose to.

It's not cut and dried at all and there are lots of shades of grey
in between. We should also be cautious to avoid dichotomous
thinking on this subject; it is not simply a matter of good and bad
or good and evil – they are merely what they are and they follow
their own natures the same way anything else does. Perhaps a
key thing to understand in seeking to understand the courts, and
indeed any attempted division of Fairy, is the morality of the Fey
Folk themselves, which is often very foreign to human morality.
While some of the things that fairies find praiseworthy are values
humans share, others baffle us. I mentioned earlier that even
those counted among the Seelie Court can be angered and may
choose to bring harm to a person, and usually this occurs with the

transgression of fairy etiquette.

A Note on the Unseelie Court

Although it's trendy now to see the darker fey as just as kind and helpful as the Seelie Court, merely grumpy and misunderstood, in folklore there was usually a good reason people feared them and that reason was their tendency towards homicidal reactions and eating people. Contrary to what most of the young adult novels and paranormal romance currently on the market like to say, the Unseelie Court aren't the emo bad boys of the fey world who just need a big hug and some understanding. There was a good reason that they were traditionally feared and while it is true that it is not a cut and dried situation, and any member of Fairy can potentially help us or ally with us, we need to be careful not to romanticize the more dangerous fey based on our own desire for them to secretly be kind and gentle.

The Water Horse (an Each Uisce) tricks a person into riding them only to race back to their watery homes, drown, and eat the person. Red Caps dye their hats in human blood. Bogles can bring blight to crops or attack people. So it goes, with those who are usually described as Unseelie being found in that court because they are malicious towards people without provocation. Because, you see, it's not that you have to worry about transgressing and angering them, or being rude and angering them, or anything like that; all you have to do is be at the wrong place at the wrong time and get their attention and they will be inclined to do you harm. Like a tornado or a hungry apex predator, it won't be personal, but it could be deadly.

It is possible for an individual to earn the favor of a member of the Unseelie Court, just as it is possible for someone to anger the normally benevolent Seelie Court, but generally speaking it is dangerous to fall into a mindset of seeing them as safer than traditional folklore paints them, or otherwise romanticizing them. You can choose to interact with more dangerous spirits, but part of the key to doing so safely is the constant awareness that they are dangerous. If you get too comfortable with those beings who we have the most traditional protections against – and with good reason – then eventually something bad will happen. Because all those myths and stories exist because of people who have learned the hard way, just like the reason we're told not to feed wild bears at parks.

Everything in the Otherworld is not safe and not all of the beings who dwell there mean us well. Quite frankly its arrogance on our part to think we know more or better than our ancestors or than the cunning folk and wise people who spent lifetimes practicing their skill. If all these beings were really so safe and easy to deal with, with just the right attitude, then anyone and everyone would have always done so. And we would have no stories of harm, and maiming and death at the hands of these spirits, nor would witches have been seen as dealing with dangerous things. No, the truth is that we cannot simply decide through positive thinking and a belief in the goodness of all spirits that the Other Crowd are harmless; our opinions do not make them a bunch of watered down angels with angst.

I have a lot of respect for grizzly bears and their place in the ecosystem, but that doesn't mean I ever for a moment confuse them with teddy bears and think I can walk up and give a wild one a hug. Or one in captivity for that matter. Because a wild bear, no matter how noble and beautiful to our eyes, is still a wild bear and it's going to do what its nature tells it to do, which may mean ignoring us or may mean ripping chunks out of us. Just so the Unseelie fey may ignore us or they may hurt us, and this is why there are so many folk protections against them.

Trooping Fairies and Solitary Fairies

The second most common way of categorizing fairies, beyond their disposition towards us, is by their sociability towards each other. Within this division we see two options: trooping or solitary fairies. The names are fairly self-explanatory, but it is worth expanding a bit on each group.

Trooping fairies are social by nature and tend to appear in groups although the size of those groups can vary widely. They are often seen wearing green, and have been noted in all sizes from tiny enough to use flowers as drinking vessels to the size of children, to human sized (Briggs, 1976). Trooping fairies can belong to either of the previously discussed courts, and may be either kind to humans or cruel. It is the trooping fairies who are noted to ride across the land in grand processions and hunts, to assemble in courts, and to live in fairy cities and other large communities. They have been noted to enjoy a variety of pastimes including fighting with other groups of fairies, playing games of sport such as hurling, and in the cases of the more maliciously inclined, of gathering together to torment lone humans they run across.

Solitary fairies, as the name implies, are those who prefer to exist in solitude rather than live in groups. These fairies seem to be fond of wearing red, and are more prone to being malicious towards people, or at best neutral. However, there are some solitary fairies who are positively inclined towards humans (Briggs, 1976). Most of the truly frightening or dangerous fairies are solitary, particularly those associated with water of any kind. As with the previous division of seelie and unseelie, some fairies are usually solitary, but may occasionally choose to be social. We see this, for example, in some stories of Brownies, who are generally helpful solitary house fairies, but who may occasionally live or be found in groups.

Location-Based Fairies

The final way that we see fairies categorized in traditional folklore and cultures is based on where they prefer to live. This method is a bit more complicated than those that involve a simple division into two options, but it also allows for more nuances and less generality. There's no real set list of location-based fairies, but the most common would probably be domestic fairies[4], mine fairies, water fairies, wilderness fairies, and mountain fairies. As with the other methods though, this one isn't perfect and not all types of fairies can be easily categorized in this way; the Aos Sí for example may be generally associated with the fairy mounds, but may also be associated with fairy trees or other landmarks.

Domestic fairies include a wide array of beings, mostly benevolent in nature, that choose to live closely with humans. The most familiar may be the Brownie, a helpful fairy who is known to take up residence in a home and do some of the chores after the occupants are sleeping. Fairies who choose to live so closely with humans are, perhaps unsurprisingly, immune from most protections against the Fey Folk, but are also somewhat more dependent on people.

Mine fairies are also closely tied to humans, but in a different manner. Whereas domestic fairies prefer to live where people live, mine fairies happen to coincidentally favor the same places that humans sometimes work in. Mine fairies can be either helpful or harmful, depending on what type of fairy they are. The helpful ones will assist miners by warning of danger and by signaling where to dig to find deposits of ore or minerals; harmful mine fairies in contrast can cause cave-ins and terrify miners with noises and dangerous pranks.

Water fairies include everything from sea-water Mermaids and Nucklevees to fresh-water Kelpies and Lake Maidens. They can be extremely dangerous, such as the Hags who are known to drown children, or helpful like the Merrows who aid sailors in storms. Water fairies as a whole seem to be more mercurial and tend to be more dangerous, perhaps reflecting their connection to the water, which is also changeable and may feel unpredictable. As with everything Fairy though, it's best not to get too locked into one point of view with water fairies as they cannot easily be defined as either wholly good or dangerous. It is also best to remember that just because they are called water fairies for convenience doesn't mean they are restricted to that element; in fact most water fairies are not only capable of leaving the water, but frequently do so. Water fairies are defined as such though because they make their homes in bodies of water or are primarily found in water.

Wilderness fairies are quite simply those among the Other Crowd who prefer to live in the most inaccessible and untamed places. These can be moors, marshes, hills, forests, any place that is far from human settlement and human interference. Those Fey Folk who prefer to live in the wilds are generally either antagonistic towards people or coldly indifferent, although in some rare cases they seem to avoid humans out of shyness or fear. This group can include fairy animals as well, such as the various Cu Sí or Black Dogs, as well as different fairy deer.

The final general grouping that can be made based on locations would be the mountain fairies. As with all the others this group includes both the kindly inclined, like the gentle but shy Ghillie Dhu, and the vicious, like the Gwyllion. Mountain fairies may live on any part of a mountain or in the mountain itself, the key being their preference for being near mountainous terrain.

These three approaches are the most common ones I am aware of in traditional folklore. They represent different specific cultural approaches, although there is a lot of crossover between them as well. The two courts are mainly a Scottish viewpoint, while trooping and solitary is an Irish view, and location-based is often seen in Wales. Each approach has its own merits and can be applied to all fairies, but each also has drawbacks and limitations that should be kept in mind.

End Notes

1. Wicht or wight is a general term in Scots that means both any living being as well as any supernatural being. It is often

used as a generic term to describe a fairy.

2. Scots is also known as Doric and was formed from a blend of Middle and Early Modern English, Gaidhlig, and Norse derived languages.

3. Although I believe in recent decades the idea of the two courts has spread to Ireland, it isn't found in older material to my knowledge and I was unable to find a single reference to the two courts in any of my Irish folklore books. The Irish system is based on a multitude of sí (fairy hills) ruled by different kings and queens, with each being its own kingdom in a way. All the Irish Fair Folk, it seems, are ambivalent in nature and cannot easily be placed into a grouping of 'good' or 'wicked'. When I visited Ireland recently, however, I did hear someone in Armagh retelling the myth of Fionn and Sadb who mentioned the Unseelie Court, so the concept does seem to be spreading.

4. That is, those who prefer to live in human homes or other areas such as mills or farms inhabited by humans.

Chapter 4

The Kings and Queens

But as it fell out on last Halloween
When the seely court was riding by
The queen lighted down on a rowan bank
Not far from the tree where I wont to lie.
The ballad of *Alison Gross*

Whether or not there are two set courts of Fairy, one thing that is clear is that the social structure does seem to operate as a hierarchy ruled ultimately by Kings and Queens. When we look at the bulk of the folklore it is usually a Fairy Queen who holds power, often with an unnamed King at her side or else ruling alone. In only a few Irish examples do we see solitary Fairy Kings. In the later folklore and ballads the Fairy Queens and Kings are often unnamed, going simply by their titles, but in older mythology and some local folklore we do have examples of named Fairy Queens and Kings, often beings who we know were once Gods. It also became fashionable in later poetry and theater to name Fairy monarchy, using names that may or may not be rooted in older fairylore.

The Fairy Queen is usually said to ride a white horse, something we see in both the ballads of *Tam Lin* and *Thomas the Rhymer*. It would seem that in the great Fairy Rades the colors of the horses have some hierarchical significance, with white as the most important[1]. In the ballad of *True Thomas*, the Queen of Elfland is described dressed in green velvet, while Scottish witch Isobel Gowdie described the Fairy Queen as finely dressed in white (Acland, 1997; McNeill, 1956). Accounts of Fairy Queens usually describe them as extremely beautiful, often irresistible to human men they seek to enthrall. These Queens are also described as having powerful magic, able to break spells laid on people and to weave enchantments that are not easily set aside. They can give the gifts of true vision or true speech, but they can also lay powerful curses on those who offend them.

Fairy Kings appear less often in folklore than do Queens. Isobel Gowdie described the Fairy King she met as *'a braw man, weill favoured'* (a splendid man, good looking) (McNeill, 1956). The ballad of *Alice Brand* describes the Fairy King as moody and protective of all that he considers his. When Kings appear alongside Queens it is generally the Queens who seems to have the most authority.

Unlike some other spirits or even Gods, the monarchy of Fairy is well known for interacting with humans, both directly and through intermediaries. Many of the Scottish witches who claimed to have dealt with the Good People said that they met with the Fairy Queen, and sometimes with the King as well (Wilby, 2005). Isobel Gowdie said that the Fairy Queen gave her an abundance of meat to eat, as well as equipping her with elfshot (McNeill, 1956). In several accounts confessed witches claimed to have been given a fairy as a guardian, a type of familiar spirit, usually at the explicit direction of the Fairy Queen[2]. Although the Fairy monarchy was much more directly involved with humans than might be expected, often including sexual dalliances with them, nonetheless the overall relationship was still a formal one. The Fairy Queen or King would summon the person to be brought before them in most cases and would give or withhold gifts as they saw fit. One cunningman described being brought to a great hall where he said the Fairy Queen was seated on a throne holding court, and a 17th century Scottish witch said that when she was brought before the Queen of Fairy she was instructed to kneel (Wilby, 2005). When a Fairy Queen appears in a story or ballad to personally kidnap a human they usually make that person their servant for a period of time, often seven years.

As I mentioned previously though there are a s[Fairy Queens and Kings who are named. Below is a li of the more common ones and their folklore.

Áine

Áine was a Goddess, a member of the Tuatha De Danann in the earliest mythology, but in later folklore she was said to be a Fairy Queen whose sí was Cnoc Áine (Knockainey) in Ireland. Her name means 'bright' and she was seen sometimes sitting in or near Lough Gur combing her blond hair (Evans-Wentz, 1911). In much of her later folklore, Áine is reputed to have love affairs with mortals and several Irish families claim descent from her. The most well known of these human descendants is the third Earl of Desmond, Gearoid Iarla. It is said by some that Gearoid did not die but was taken into Loch Guir and would return one day (Berresford Ellis, 1987). Other tales say that he lives still within the lake and can be seen riding beneath the water on a white fairy horse, while still other stories claim that Áine turned him into a goose on the shore of the lake (Berresford Ellis, 1987). In the story of the *Cath Maige Mucrama* Áine was the daughter of the Fairy King Eogabul and she and her father emerged from their hill one Samhain night only to be ambushed by a mortal king and his servant; her father was killed and she was raped. She cursed the king, a man named Ailill Olum, and swore that she would take away all his possessions and his kingship, which eventually came to pass.

Aine's special holiday was midsummer and people would hold torchlit processions on her hill on that night. In one story a group of girls met Áine on her hill on midsummer and she had them look through a ring; peering through its circle they saw her hill covered in fairies celebrating (Evans-Wentz, 1911).

Aoibhill

Queen of the north Munster fairies, she is associated with Craig

Liath (Evans-Wentz, 1911). There are many variants of her name including Aibell, Aebill, Aoibheall, Eevell, Ibhell, Aibinn, and Eevin; her name means 'radiance, spark, fire' (McKillop, 1998, p 5). Aoibhill is sometimes described as a rival to the Fairy Queen Cliodhona, who once enchanted her into the form of a white cat (McKillop, 1998). Like many Fairy Queens, Aoibhill was known to favor poets; she also had a reputation for predicting deaths, both of her lovers and others (Logan, 1981). Aoibhill appears as a character in Merrimen's poem *Cúirt an Mheán Oiche* as a Fairy Queen advocating for justice and fairness and sitting as a judge over a fairy court.

Bodb

King of the Munster fairies. He is usually given the epithet 'Derg'; his name – Bodb Derg – probably means 'Red Crow'. His father is the Dagda and he is said to have two different homes, one at Sidhe ar Femen and one at Sliabh na mBan (Slievenamon). He has magical pigs who are tended to by a pigkeeper, also a man of the fairies, and the friendship and later enmity between Bodb's pigkeeper and the pigkeeper of the King of the Connacht fairies[3] is featured in the tale of *De Chophur in Da Muccida*. Bodb was renowned for the wisdom of his judgment, and in the myth *Aislinge Oenguso* he helped the Dagda and Aengus find a mysterious woman of the sí that Aengus had been dreaming of (McKillop, 1998).

Cliodhona

Cliodhna is one of the Tuatha Dé Danann in the mythology and also a Fairy Queen in modern folklore associated with Cork in Ireland. Her epithet is Ceannfhionn (fair headed or fair haired) and she is sometimes called 'the shapely one'; her name may be related to the idea of territory or being territorial (O hOgain, 2006; MacKillop, 1998). She is said to be extremely beautiful.

Cliodhna can take the form of a wren, a bird that may be

generally associated with her, and she is also often connected to the Otherworldly Bean Sí (Banshee). By some accounts she herself is considered to be such a spirit, or their Queen, although in other folklore she is more generally the Queen of the fairies of Munster. She has three magical birds that eat Otherworldly apples and have the power to lull people to sleep by singing and then heal them (Smyth, 1988; MacKillop, 1998).

She is strongly associated with the shore and with waves, and the tide at Glandore in Cork was called the 'Wave of Cliodhna'(O hOgain, 2006). In several of her stories she is drowned at that same location after leaving the Otherworld either to try to woo the Tuatha De Danann Aengus mac ind Og or after running away with a warrior named Ciabhán. She has a reputation in many stories for her passionate nature and love of poets in particular, and she is known to abduct handsome young poets or to appear and try to seduce them. In folklore she known for seducing and drowning young men (Smyth, 1988). Several mortal families trace their descent from her including the McCarthys and O'Keefes and she was well known for taking mortal lovers.

The Dagda

The Dagda was one of the premier Gods of the Tuatha De Danann in Ireland, and after the Gods were driven into the fairy mounds it was with him that humans had to reach an agreement to get their crops to grow and cows to give milk. By some accounts it was the Dagda who divided up the sí among the Tuatha De Danann and decided which Gods would live in which fairy mound. In the story *Aislinge Óenguso* the Dagda is called '*the King of the sidhe of Ireland*' establishing his authority over the other fairy hills and by extension their inhabitants.

Diana

Most familiar from Roman and Italian mythology, the Goddess Diana found a place in later fairylore and was said to be both a

Queen of the Fairies and a leader of witches. The name Diana became a common one associated with a leader of the Fey Folk in the post-pagan period (Purkiss, 2000). This may be an example of a form of the *interpretatio Romana* in action, where native Celtic Goddesses were called Diana by outside observers and literati seeking a more familiar name for the Queen of the Fairies. It could also reflect a Christian interpretation that simply homogenized everything under Diana's name in connection to the Good People and the night-roaming dead (Purkiss, 2000). King James I, for example, says this about her in his work *Demonologie*: '*Diana, and her wandering court, and among us was called Pharie [fairy]...or our good neighbors*'. It is possible that Shakespeare's Titania is actually a corrupted version of the name Diana.

Donn

Donn was originally a figure from mythology, one of the Milesians who won Ireland away from the Tuatha De Danann. Donn died before his people reached Ireland, and many people say that he was the first human to die in Ireland and is the first ancestor. His special place is a small island called Tech Duinn (Donn's House) off the Irish coast; besides Tech Duinn (present day Bull Rock, County Cork) Donn is also connected to Cnoc Fírinne in county Limerick and Dumhcha in County Clare.

Donn of Cnoc Firinne had strong aspects of a lord of the Aos Sí, being called Donn Fírinne and was said to kidnap people into his hill who were thought to have died (O hOgain, 2006). It was also said when the potato crop showed any signs of damage or blight that it was because Donn Fírinne and his Fairy Host had fought there the night before, or had a game of hurling, and taken away the best of the crop (MacNeill, 1962). Like many other Irish deities, Donn shifted rather seamlessly from a God – or perhaps primordial ancestor – to a Good Neighbor, albeit a very powerful one. In County Clare, Donn was Donn na Duimhche, Donn of the Dune, and was believed to ride out as a fairy horseman with his army (O hOgain, 2006). Donn Fírinne was viewed with both trepidation and fondness, as he was known to carry off young people and to stir up storms, but he also often helped to guard the crops of the people in his area and seemed inclined to bless those whose paths crossed his rather than to cause mischief (MacNeill, 1962). By some accounts the Maguires trace their ancestry back to Donn (Logan, 1981).

Donn may or may not always have been seen as a deity, but he certainly seems to have been understood as one from at least the 8th century onward, until his shift into an Otherworldly horseman. Some believe that the house of Donn is where the dead go before moving on to the Otherworld (Berresford Ellis, 1987). Folklore tells us that Tech Duinn is a place where the dead go, but not necessarily their final destination. In the 8th to 10th centuries Tech Duinn was seen as an assembly place of the dead, and a place that the dead both went to and left from (O hOgain, 2006). Donn's association with the dead is strong and even his habit of taking people usually assumed the form of young people dying mysteriously, going to his hall one way or another as it were.

By some accounts people used to make offerings to Donn at Cnoc Firinne at Lughnasa, Samhain, and on Bealtaine (Logan, 1981). These offerings could reflect an older view of Donn as a deity or they could be a way for people to show respect to a Fairy King, who like all such Kings, could influence the success of the harvest. These offerings included eggs, flowers, and meat, and on the old date of Samhain (now St. Martin's Day) a rooster would be sacrificed (Logan, 1981).

Ethal Anbual

In Old Irish his name would possibly mean 'Pure Great-Healing'. According to Katherine Briggs he is the King of the fairyfolk of Ulster, although Mackillop calls him the King of the Connacht fairies and says his sí was at Uaman (Briggs, 1976; MacKillop, 1998). In the story of the *Aislinge Oenguso* he is the father of the woman of the sí who Aengus loves and he is captured by the Dagda and forced to reveal her whereabouts.

Finnbheara

King of the Connacht fairies who makes his home in the sí of Cnoc Meadha (Knockma) in Galway with his Queen Una. In one story he was described as appearing on Samhain night in a coach pulled by white horses; he wore all black and was attending a fair filled with the dead, leading Lady Wilde to suggest that he was the King of the Dead (Briggs, 1976). Finnbheara was well known for his love of beautiful mortal women, although his wife was said to be more beautiful than any other woman, mortal or fey. In another tale he appeared as a man on a black horse and invited a mortal back to his home where they shared a meal with all those the man had known who had died during the his life (Briggs, 1976). Although the man ate fairy food and drank the wine offered to him he was allowed to leave and the only harm he came to was a burn around his wrist given to him by one of the dead, a woman he had planned to marry who had died before the wedding (Briggs, 1976). This story, as with the other one on Samhain, again ties Finnbheara strongly to the dead. It is said that when he is present in Connacht the crops flourish, but when he is not there the crops don't do well (MacKillop, 1998). He is known to reward mortals who please him, including smiths willing to shoe his horse, which has only three legs; in one story he healed a woman who was ill and accepted food in payment (MacKillop, 1998).

Gloriana

The name of a Fairy Queen in Spenser's epic poem *The Faerie Queene*.

Grian

Sister of Áine, she lives in the fairy hill of Cnoc Grian. Not much is known about her. In one story she turned five brothers who had attacked her father into badgers and she had a reputation for her magic and skill with Druidism (Logan, 1981).

Gwyn ap Nudd

Once a Welsh God of the underworld he eventually became a King of the Plant Annwn, the underworld fairies (literally 'children of the underworld') and the Welsh fairies more generally. His name means 'White son of Nudd'[4]. He is described as having a blackened face and he rides out hunting with the Cwn Annwn (dogs of the Otherworld), a fierce pack of fairy hounds (MacKillop, 1998).

Gyre-Carling

A Fairy Queen in Fife, Scotland. Gyre is a term for a dangerous type of fairy or giantess, and carling means an old woman (DSL, 2016). So the Gyre-Carling then is a supernatural hag-like figure, said to rule over the fairies in her area. She is strongly associated with spinning and with winter, and it is said that all spinning must be finished before the end of the secular year or the Gyre-Carling will take whatever is left undone (Briggs, 1976).

Mab

Mab was a figure made popular in the 16th and 17th centuries as a Queen of the tiny fairies. It was said that she traveled in a carriage drawn by insects and was the source of dreams (Briggs, 1976). She was said to tangle a person's hair while they slept and it was thought very unlucky to untangle these Elf-knots, which had to be left in untouched. By some accounts Mab is the midwife of the fairies, a handmaiden of the Queen, and a type of pixy who misleads travelers (Brigg, 1976).

Medb

Medb, also spelled Meave, is a pseudo-historic queen in Ireland

and possibly originally a sovereignty Goddess, Meave later came to have some association as a Fairy Queen. There is a great deal of confusion, however, between Meave and the later Mab, who are very distinct figures with unfortunately similar names.

Midir

As with many of those listed here, Midir was one of the Tuatha De Danann who some later believed became a Fairy King. His home was in the sí of Bri Leith, modern day Ardagh Hill in county Longford (MacNeill, 1962). His most well-known myth is the *Tochmarc Etaine*, the story of his marrying his second wife, Etain, who was transformed into a fly by his jealous first wife, Fuamnach. Etain was eventually reborn as a human and married to a human king, and when Midir finally found her again he had to win her away from her new husband. After successfully winning a kiss from her, which restored her memory of her previous life as his wife, he transformed them both into swans and they flew away. In recent folklore he is known as Midas of the mountain and it is said that children who wander on his hill at the beginning of August run the risk of being taken into it (MacNeill, 1962).

Nicnevin

Possibly a name for the Gyre-Carling, but also possibly a Fairy Queen in her own right. A Queen of Elphame and some say of the Unseelie Court, and also said to be Queen of witches and a powerful witch herself (Briggs, 1976). November 11th is the old date of Samhain (before the calendar shift) and is the day most strongly associated with Nicnevin, when it is said she rides out with her court.

In Scots it's said her name means daughter (nic) of the little saint (náomhín). This follows a pattern of witches who have names relating to positions in the Church, including both Nicnevin and her cousin Nikclethin (daughter of the cleric) (DSL,

2016). Other people today claim it means daughter of Nemhain, an Irish Goddess. It may also be related to the Irish word for 'bone' cnáim, hence cnámhín 'little bones', which is the etymology I personally favor, daughter of little bones being so very evocative. Ultimately it is uncertain what the name means. Sir Walter Scott says of her:

> A *gigantic and malignant female, the Hecate of this mythology, who rode on the storm and marshalled the rambling host of wanderers under her grim banner. This hag...was called Nicneven in that later system which blended the faith of the Celts and of the Goths on this subject. The great Scottish poet Dunbar has made a spirited description of this Hecate riding at the head of witches and good neighbours (fairies, namely), sorceresses and elves, indifferently, upon the ghostly eve of All-Hallow Mass.*
> (Scott, 1830)

Oberon

First mentioned as a King of the Fairies in a 15th century French romance, Oberon also appeared in Shakespeare's *A Midsummer Night's Dream* paired with the Fairy Queen Titania (Briggs, 1976). In contrast other sources say his queen was Mab, and while Shakespeare described Oberon as human sized, in the French story he was the size of a toddler (Briggs, 1976). This may reflect the shape-shifting powers of the fairies or the use of glamour to alter perceptions, or perhaps merely indicate the same name being used for two different Fairy Kings between cultures. In *Huon of Bordeaux*, the first place Oberon appears as a Fairy King, he is described as small and deformed, yet extremely handsome, wearing a jeweled gown that glows. This Oberon carries a bow that never misses and a magical horn that cures all illnesses and acts as a cornucopia. A 16th century literary source described Oberon as tiny and said he could not bear sunlight and fled the light of day (Purkiss, 2000). The name Oberon is also strikingly similar to names used for familiar spirits during the Renaissance, including 'Auberon' and 'Oberycom'; in this guise he was invoked as a spirit of luck and to gain power for the person calling him (Briggs, 1976; Purkiss, 2000). This could mean that Oberon was a general term for a powerful male fairy that was later applied as a name for Fairy Kings. In that case, if we also view Diana/Titania as a similar generic name applied to a Fairy Queen there is a logic in pairing the two together.

Titania

Likely a form of the name Diana, this was an uncommon name for the Fairy Queen that was used by Shakespeare (Briggs, 1976). Shakespeare's Titania is proud and willing to contend with her own husband for what she wants, which in the play was the possession of a changeling boy.

Una

Also spelled Oona, she was the Fairy Queen of Connacht and wife of King Finnbheara. Described as a peerless beauty, in one story she appeared with him on Samhain night wearing a silver veil; she is also described as wearing *'silver gossamer'* and with long blond hair that touches the ground (Briggs, 1976). She was said to have 17 sons, and although she is associated with Finnbheara's sí at Cnoc Meadha she also had her own home at Cnoc Sidh Una (Knockshegouna) in Ireland (MacKillop, 1998). There is a story of Cnoc Meadha that tells of a farmer who tried to graze his sheep on the hillside, but all his workers were driven off by the Good People. Finally he hired a piper who knew of the hill's reputation and was willing to take on the work anyway. The piper went out with the sheep and as night fell began playing his pipes, ignoring all the things the fairy folk did to try to frighten him. Finally a great cow appeared, but before she could harm him the piper leaped on her back; the cow in turn leaped off the hill entirely and landed many miles away. The piper clung to her and when she landed he exclaimed at what an amazing jump it had been. At his words the cow turned into Una, the Fairy Queen, and she proclaimed herself impressed by the man's courage and gave him her permission to keep sheep on the fairy's hill.

End Notes

1. The idea of a person of import riding a white horse shows up repeatedly throughout fairylore. We see Fairy Queens on white horses, Tam Lin is described as riding a white horse as a token of his renown, and in an anecdote from Ireland in 1911 we see a man who was taken by the fairies and as the story goes 'made an officer among them' described as riding on a white horse (see MacNeill 'Festival of Lughnasa', p 585).

2. The subject of fairies as familiar spirits for witches will be discussed in greater depth later in this book

3. Interestingly, although Finnbheara is usually given as the name of the Fairy King of Connacht in the story De Chophur in Da Muccida it is said that Connacht's Fairy King is named Ochaill Ochni. This obscure character is not to my knowledge mentioned elsewhere. The name Ochaill may be related to the word for 'hot-tempered'.

4. Nudd may mean mist, as a form of nudden; Nudd is considered a probable cognate of the Irish Nuada.

Chapter 5

Denizens of Fairy

Elves are wonderful. They provoke wonder.
Elves are marvelous. They cause marvels.
Elves are fantastic. They create fantasies.
Elves are glamorous. They project glamour.
Elves are enchanting. They weave enchantment.
Elves are terrific. They beget terror.
The thing about words is that meanings can twist just like a snake,
and if you want to find snakes look for them behind words that have
changed their meaning.
No one ever said elves are nice.'
Terry Pratchett, *Lords and Ladies*

Discussing the beings who exist in Fairy is always a difficult
subject to tackle because, like so many other things fairy-related,
there are very few hard and fast definitions and a lot of names for
beings, which can change their meaning depending on context or
circumstance. On the same hand though it is important to have
some sense of which beings exist within Fairy and generally who
and what they are, and what can be expected from them. It would
be impossible to discuss every kind of fairy in any real depth so
what I would like to do here is look at some of the different
generalized groups of beings within the larger category of fairies
as well as a few specific types that are more well-known, but
perhaps not well understood. For those who are looking for a
more exhaustive listing of every type of fairy, particularly Celtic,
I recommend Katherine Briggs book *A Dictionary of Fairies,* which
is both relatively complete and in-depth in its listing and also
well researched.

Before we begin discussing some of the beings of Fairy it

would also be best for us to remember that the standards we judge by are not universal. What we find beautiful may be ugly to another being, for even the Aos Sí must be ugly to a Goblin who measures beauty by their own kin. We should not fall into the trap of thinking we are the measure of beauty, size, ability, skill, or anything else especially as we seek to understand the beings of Fairy. Although we may sometimes have the idea that all fairies are peerlessly beautiful, it is quite common in folklore to see fairies described as deformed, grotesque, or terrifying in appearance; I suggest leaving behind our human aesthetic and approaching the subject without expectations.

It may also seem as if the majority of the beings listed here are more negative, but that is not because the majority of fairies are themselves more negative. Rather there are two reasons for this. One, this section looks primarily at types of beings that are more general in nature, rather than overly specific, and when looking at generalities it will naturally include both good and bad qualities. Secondly, keep in mind that there is a longstanding prohibition against speaking too much of positive experiences with fairies, lest you offend them and lose their good favor, but there is an equally long-standing practice of passing on tales that act as warnings to others of things that might be dangerous. I believe that the actual reality is more balanced than it might appear, just as each being of Fairy is both helpful and harmful depending on context and the actual numbers of helpful and harmful fairies is probably also relatively balanced.

Aos Si

Aos sí and Daoine Sí both mean 'people of the fairy hills' and are used more or less interchangeably. The terms come from the belief that these beings dwell within the hollow hills, called sí, which are entrances to the Otherworld. As with many of the other groups of fairies we are discussing, the Aos Sí are both a specific group and also a rather general term that applies to a range of different beings. The Aos Sí are most strongly associated with the old Gods and with the nobility of the fairies, and may perhaps be described as the most powerful of the Other Crowd, and generally the monarchy of it, although folklore shows that other types of fairies may have their own Kings and Queens as well. The Aos Sí are the ones in particular that may be called the Gentry or the Daoine Uaisle (Noble People).

Although the name itself emphasizes the fairy hills, the Aos Sí are not limited to the fairy mounds, but can be found as well on mystical islands, usually located in the west, which were sometimes seen in the distance, but could never be reached (McNeill, 1956). Looking at Irish fairylore we see that they are also associated with islands, bogs, lakes, trees, and the air (O hOgain, 2006). Within these fairy hills and other gateways into their realms we find stories of the Aos Sí living in grand palaces and beautiful halls. The lands within the Otherworld are described as beautiful beyond belief, rich in resources of all kinds, and peaceful (Firth-Green, 2016).

Although they are strongly associated with these Otherworldly locations the Aos Sí are not tied to them as true land or nature spirits would be and they are known to travel and move their homes. They enjoy attending mortal fairs and have been known in stories to even attend mortal festivals, such as we see with tales of Áine joining people celebrating on her hill at midsummer, or a group of boys being joined by one of the Aos Sí on Saint John's Eve at their community's bonfire celebration. On the quarter days – Samhain, Imbolc, Bealtaine, and Lughnasa – they move their homes from one hill to another, traveling along established fairy roads (McNeill, 1956). There are also tales of the Fairy Queens traveling alone and of the Fairy Rade[1] riding out at specific times. The Fairy Rade was usually described as a grand procession of fairy knights, led by the Fairy Queen or King, but the name itself can indicates an armed excursion, 'Rade' being Scots for raid as well as ride. Fairy Rades were dangerous to any humans that they came across, but also offered the opportunity to free captives to those brave enough to confront them, such as in the case of Tam Lin who is rescued by his lover Janet during a Fairy Rade.

Physical descriptions of the Aos Sí are fairly consistent, they are generally said to be very similar to humans in height and overall appearance, usually pale, fair-haired, and finely dressed (O hOgain, 2006). Yeats describes a fairy woman in an anecdotal tale as being slightly shorter than average, with brown hair and dressed in human fashions (Yeats, 1892). In stories they are often said to wear green or grey primarily and may have blond or brown hair; they can appear alone or in groups and be male or female. Groups of fairy men sometimes appeared seeking a human to play hurling with them, apparently a requirement for them to play the game, while fairy women might appear with messages or warnings (Yeats, 1892).

The Aos Sí use their magic to either blend in with the humans around them or to become invisible; in some cases they may be seen by a person who has the Second Sight or who has dealt with them before and for some reason retains the ability to see them. Those who can see them are usually wise enough to be subtle with this knowledge, as it well known that the Aos Sí value their privacy and are quick to punish those they feel are spying on them.

There are many roads and paths, called Fairy Roads, that exist between the different fairy hills, invisible to most people. The Good Neighbors travel on these roads, especially at night, and building on or near one always leads to bad luck and often death (O hOgain, 2006). It was also very bad to engage in any activity that disturbed the homes of the Aos Sí, whether that was digging into the fairy hills or cutting down their trees because either action was likely to result in ill-luck or death (O hOgain, 2006). This belief exists to this day and has resulted in protests to divert roads around fairy trees and outrage over the destruction of fairy hills. There was a case in Ireland not too long ago of telephone poles placed too close to a fairy hill, which kept falling down; this inexplicable inability of the company to keep the poles up so close to the hill led many people to say it was the result of offending the Aos Sí.

The Good Neighbors are usually invisible to mortal eyes thanks to their magic that hides them, unless they wish to be seen or the person has the Sight. However, their presence and especially their passage can be perceived in other ways. A person may hear music, talking, or the sound of horses as the Fairy Rade passes, for example. The ability to pass by unseen relies on the use of a type of magic called glamour, one of the fairy folk's most famous powers, which can deceive mortal senses into thinking one thing is something else. This magic is seen in many different fairy stories where a handful of leaves might seem to be a pile of gold coins, for example, or a deserted cave appear as a rich mansion.

The Aos Sí, like most other types of fairies, have been known to marry and have children with humans. There are a multitude of different versions of stories of a bride stolen by the fairies on her wedding day and taken to marry a man of the sí instead and these usually center on the Aos Sí. The Aos Sí also take musicians and midwives, but these are usually only borrowed for a time and later returned to the mortal world. Some, like Thomas the Rhymer, are taken for a specific amount of time, while others – often those who eat or drink anything in Fairy – can never leave and may remain as spouses or servants in Fairy. In some tales a person might join the fairies for a single night of dancing in a fairy ring or enter a fairy hill for what they think is only one night only to emerge and find that anywhere from seven to an hundred years have passed. The Aos Sí were also famous for stealing cattle and horses that they wanted, usually by making the animal appear to sicken and die, but sometimes by taking them out right (O hOgain, 2006).

In Ireland the opposing groups of fairies sometimes battle during the night, often near a fairy tree, leaving behind traces of a white liquid believed to be fairy blood, which people see in the morning (O hOgain, 2006). The Gentry live in a monarchy, but there are also lower class fairies as well as the nobility, and these working class fairies might interact with humans more often than the higher class ones do (O hOgain, 2006). The Fair Folk ride on fine horses and are seen in the company of hounds; generally these animals are either black, white, or grey. The Tuatha De Danann were renowned for their fabulous horses, and these fine animals seem to have either been passed on to or shared with the Aos Sí who also have exceptional mounts (Wilde, 1888).

The Aos Sí are especially active on the quarter days, Samhain, Imbolc, Bealtaine, and Lughnasa. Samhain and Bealtaine in particular are times of very strong fairy influence and so great care should be taken to avoid running afoul of them during these periods (O hOgain, 2006). At Bealtaine it was believed that the Fair Folk might travel abroad, appearing as a stranger at the door asking for milk or a coal from the fire; to give either would mean giving the household's luck away for the year to come (Wilde, 1887). At Samhain the Aos Sí are known to move from one hill to another, from their summer to winter homes, and it is quite dangerous to meet them on a fairy road that night (Estyn Evans, 1957). The Fair Folk are also especially active at twilight and midnight, although as with every other kind of fairy they are not limited in any way to these times.

The Aos Sí can bless or harm people, more strongly perhaps than other fairies, and a main motivation for keeping on their good side is to receive the blessings and avoid the ill luck. Fairies are reputed to give gifts, but these gifts too can be either a blessing or curse, as they might result in prosperity or luck, or they could be illusions that would turn to leaves or grass at dawn. When angered the Aos Sí can cause madness, illnesses, or death, as well as making a person's luck go all bad. Elfshot, a sudden pain, cramp, or stitch caused by an invisible fairy arrow shot into the body, is another well-known fairy illness caused by angered Aos Sí. In many cases it was also believed that elfshot was a power given to witches, which they learned from the fairies – indeed many Irish and Scottish witches were thought to have learned both malediction and healing from the Fair Folk with whom they dealt (Hall, 2005). In contrast though those who were considered friends of the Aos Sí might be taught things like healing and magic, or a musician might be given great skill, or a person may be favored in other ways with special knowledge or gifts (O hOgain, 2006). The Aos Sí might appear as a stranger at the door seeking to borrow something or needing milk or a coal from the fire, alone in a field or wood, or might be encountered on the road; those brave enough to seek them out might choose to sleep on a fairy mound, knowing that the result could either be a blessing or madness.

Baobhan Síth

A Scottish fairy whose name means 'wicked female fairy' in Gaidhlig, the Baobhan Síth is a dangerous spirit that preys on men. They are blood-drinking spirits, but like other fairies are warded off by iron. A story tells of four men out hunting who camped for the night and were joined by four Baobhan Síth; three were enamored of the fairies and fell prey to them, but the fourth fled and hid among the horses until the fairy trying to seize him fled when the sun rose (Briggs, 1976). By some accounts the Baobhan Síth drain all of their victim's blood while another story claimed they also took their hearts.

Bean Sí (Banshee) and Bean Nighe

There are two closely related types of fairy women found in tradition that are often confused with each other in modern lore, the Bean Sí (Fairy Woman) and Bean Nighe (Washer Woman).

The Bean Sí is a female spirit who is known for attaching

herself to a particular family and appearing whenever someone in that family is about to die. In one account a Bean Sí attached to a family near Lough Gur came when a woman of the family was dying and both of the woman's sisters heard sad fairy music playing (Evans-Wentz, 1911). In other stories the Bean Sí may appear on the night of a death wailing or keening in mourning. The Bean Sí has been described as a grey figure or a woman wrapped in a grey cloak, and it is said that only those in the family she is attached to can hear her cry (Ballard, 1991). Others say that the Bean Sí wears white and has long golden hair (Logan, 1981). She brushes her hair with a special comb and it is considered very dangerous even today to pick up a stray comb you find laying on the ground, in case it belongs to the Fairy Woman.

The Bean Nighe appears in bodies of water, most often streams or rivers, washing the clothes or equipment of those about to die. She dresses in green and may have red webbed feet, and will attack anyone who interrupts her at her work (Briggs, 1976). She is a fearsome fairy, an omen of death, but can sometimes be dealt with bravely and if handled properly a person can benefit from seeing her. Those who catch her unawares away from the water and can block her return to the stream earn three wishes, and the truly brave who manage to grab her and nurse from her breast will gain her favor as her foster-child (Briggs, 1976).

Both the Bean Sí and Bean Nighe are sometimes said to be the spirits of mortal women who died in childbirth and remain as fairies until the time they would have died naturally (Briggs, 1976). Other theories trace them back to the war Goddess Badb. It is possible that like so many other kinds of fairies the answer to their origin isn't one or the other, but a combination, with these fairies being made up of some who are mortal dead and others who have always been fairies and may be related to Badb of the Tuatha De Danann.

Bogles

In most cases Bogles are viewed as malicious and dangerous creatures. However, in some areas they have a more benevolent nature. Seen as a particularly evil kind of Goblin generally, in some areas of Lowland Scotland Bogles were thought to only attack murderers, oath breakers, and those who stole from widows (Briggs, 1976). The name Bogle is related to words for both scarecrow and demon (Williams, 1991). In these cases the name relates directly back to the idea that this fairy has a dangerous and frightening nature

Brownies

Brownies can be found in several various forms under different names including Bwcas, Bodachs, or Fendorees, and, in specific cases malicious Boggarts. The name Brownie has no non-English equivalent and may derive from the longer name 'little brown man' (MacKillop, 1998). The Brownie, like so many others discussed here, is as much a type of fairy as a specific fairy being, so that one could say that a Fendoree is a kind of Brownie, and that Boggarts may or may not be considered Brownies depending on the area and the specific folklore. They are one of the few faeries who are specific to human habitations, preferring to live in human homes or sometimes in mills or farms, although they are also often associated with bodies of water, especially ponds (Briggs, 1976). The Brownie will adopt a specific home, coming out unseen in the quiet night hours to clean and organize the home for its human owners.

As the name implies, Brownies are an overall nut brown color, usually appearing as a small, wrinkled brown man dressed in rags (Briggs, 1976). According to Scottish legend Highland Brownies have no fingers or toes, whereas Lowland Brownies have no noses. Since most stories of Brownies involve the noseless ones it would seem that the Lowland are the more commonly seen. In the few cases were females have been seen or appeared in tales they are virtually indistinguishable from the males, but they do seem to be very protective. For example, there is one story of a Brownie who falls in love with a mortal girl and kidnaps her, and in the course of her escape he is grievously injured. His mother wants to hunt the girl down and avenge her son and only the girl's cleverness saves her. In another similar story a girl grinding in a mill at night encountered a Brownie who frightened her and she spilled boiling water on him, killing him and earning the wrath of his wife (Briggs, 1976).

Most tales about Brownies revolve around their place in the human home and what needs to done to keep them happy, as well as what should be avoided. An industrious Brownie expects a bowl of cream and a good cake or loaf of bread to be left out once a week, in appreciation for his hard work (Briggs, 1976). It is important never to thank him aloud or to leave the milk or food out for him as a gift. Rather it must be left out, as Henderson in *Folklore of the Northern Counties* says: '*The housewife will prepare these and lay them out carefully where he may find them by chance.*' (Briggs, 1976, p46). A variety of reasons are offered for this, from the Brownie being bound to serve until he is rewarded with intentional payment to the belief that a Brownie is offended by any implication that he is serving humankind (Briggs, 1976). So should one find a Brownie in one's household it is important to keep it happy by giving it milk and cakes, but be careful not to make an actual offering of them.

The worst thing a person whose house boasts a Brownie can do is leave out a set of new clothes for it. Many a story features a well-meaning homeowner who, on seeing the Brownie's ragged clothes, thought to thank him by making a new, fine shirt and pair of pants, which invariable has one of two results. If they're lucky the Brownie snatches up the clothes, dances merrily singing: '*New clothes, new clothes, now I work no more,*' and disappears never to be seen again. If they're not lucky the Brownie turns Boggart and goes on a rampage, destroying everything in sight before storming out.

Brownies not only do housework, but also help out in mills and farms, helping to bring in the crops and to tend the farm animals. The same rules apply whether the Brownie is in a home or a farm: they expect some food and milk weekly and receiving clothing will either drive them off or offend them so that they become malicious. Additionally farm Brownies are known to become destructive if they are verbally insulted, especially if the quality of their work is questioned (Briggs, 1976).

Although Brownies have an overall good reputation in modern lore as helpful beings who are desirable to have around, in older folklore they were viewed somewhat more ambivalently. While he might be beloved in his chosen home, the Brownie was often feared by those he had no attachment to and his habit of destroying crops and property when angered was reason enough for people to be cautious around him (Briggs, 1976).

Corrigans

A type of fairy found in Brittany that is less of a specific kind of being so much as a general category of beings is the Corrigan. They might be loosely compared to the generic English idea of elves as small, mischievous creatures. Corrigans are social fairies who live in groups and enjoy dancing; where they dance mushroom rings are said to appear (Evans-Wentz, 1911). They wear white exclusively and are the size of young children, but look like an adult in miniature. Corrigans can be very cruel to humans in their power and they are usually less inclined to aid people, but are not always hostile towards them and will sometimes help around homes or farms (Evans-Wentz, 1911). They are nocturnal fairies and only emerge at dusk and during the night-time. In most ways they are exactly like all other Celtic fairies: they are known to steal human children, to punish those who spy on them or repeat their secrets, and to reward those who please them.

Elves

Another term that is found now throughout English-language folklore, but that causes a great deal of confusion, is 'Elf'. This confusion is likely rooted in the fact that Elf, like Goblin and fairy itself, was originally a generic term used for a type of being, rather than a specific being in itself. Looking at the etymology of the word we see that it traces back to Old English and Anglo-Saxon (as alf) and eventually to proto-Germanic 'albiz' and eventually back to Proto-Indo-European 'albho' where it possibly meant white (Harper, 2017). In its Old English and Germanic forms it was translated as 'Sprite, fairy, Goblin, Incubus' demonstrating the range of associations applied to it (Douglas, 2017). Looking at older stories and folklore we find that Elf, Goblin, and fairy may be used interchangeably although Elf and Goblin could have darker connotations, with Goblins being seen as more dangerous than Elves. Also, like the word fairy, the word Elf had a reputation for angering them when used in addressing them (Briggs, 1976).

The word Elf was borrowed into British and eventually Celtic folklore from Germanic and Anglo-Saxon influence, but found a strong place in them once there. The term never entirely lost its generic connotations in English although it came to be applied to several specific beings and the folklore around them remains heavily influenced by their Germanic roots. We see it today applied in modern folklore to beings like Santa's Elves who are envisioned as small, childlike, but industrious, magical, and generally benign.

The English view of Elves as tiny laborers is vastly at odds with the traditional Norse view of the Alfar as tall, beautiful, and powerful beings. If you are familiar with Tolkein's Elves then you have some idea of the older view of the Alfar. This view was shared in Scotland, which had a lot of Norse influence, where the word Elf was used for both the beings and their home, Elfhame, and Elves were seen as much like the Norse Alfar in physical description (Briggs, 1976).

In Anglo-Saxon material Elves are described as invisible or hard to see creatures who could cause wounds or illness and were even able to possess people, linking them in Christian thought with demons (Hall, 2007). They are also clearly ranked as spirits below the Gods, who are referenced as the 'Aesir' in these sources, but Elves still had power over humans. These Elves were believed to live mostly in wild places and their penchant for attacking people and causing illness earned them the label of evil. As with all fairies, however, this view was only one extreme within a spectrum and the body of lore overall was more nuanced, with some Elves in stories acting benevolently.

The Fairy Fool

The Fairy Fool is known by two different names in Irish each of which has a different character. The Amadán na Bruidhne (Fool of the Otherworldy Hall) is a greatly feared fairy, who is most active in June and whose touch brings madness, paralysis, or death to those whose paths he crosses (MacKillop, 1998). It is said by some his touch is the fairy stroke, while others say his power is unique to him. In contrast the Amadán Mór (Great Fool) is a more ambiguous figure who appears sometimes as a King of the fairies or leading the Fairy Host (MacKillop, 1998). Despite his name the Fool is neither foolish nor amusing and should be treated with great caution.

The Fairy Rade

The Fairy Rade is found in ballads, stories, and anecdotes, as the formal riding out in procession of the fairy folk. This is usually described with great pomp and circumstance as a parade of sorts led by the Fairy Queen and featuring minstrels and knights. The word 'rade' in Scots can mean both to ride on horseback or to go out on a raid (DSL, 2016). When referencing the fairies it is found in both contexts, although the more common usage is of the ride.

It presents a sharp contrast to the wild and dangerous riding out of the Slua Sí; the Fairy Rade being more for show perhaps than the purposeful hunting of the Slua. The horses of the Fairy Rade were of various colors, but in the ballads it was said that riding the white horses was a sign of rank. The horses were beautifully caparisoned and described as having bells or even wind chimes woven into their manes (Briggs, 1976).

The Fairy Rade was noted to ride out on days sacred to the fairies, such as the pagan fire festivals. Bealtaine in particular was associated with the Fairy Rade's presence by two Scottish sources, one from 1810 the other from 1825, noting the disturbance caused by the sound of horses' hooves and music as the fairies processed to their celebration (DSL, 2016). A 19th century anecdotal account of the Fairy Rade seen near Bealtaine described it first as the noise of bridles and hooves, then appearing as a glowing troop of green-clad riders on white horses (Briggs, 1976). In both the ballad of *Alison Gross* and the ballad of *Tam Lin* we see the Fairy Rade riding out on Samhain as well.

The Fuath

A general collective term for some fairies in Scotland, the Fuath were fairies that were considered dangerous and potentially ill-inclined towards humans (Briggs, 1976). In Gaidhlig the word Fuath means fairy or specter as well as hatred. According to Campbell in *The Gaelic Otherworld* the Fuath are a type of malevolent specter or apparition that seem to ride the line between ghosts and fairies. Unlike the English term fairies, however, Fuath is slightly more specific in its usage, indicating a certain type of fairy rather than all fairies in general. Generally the beings who made up or were considered part of the Fuath were seen as water fairies, both fresh water and salt water, although Campbell contests this and argues that it is a mistake made by one folklorist who over-specified the Fuath based on a single story of a water fairy (Briggs, 1976; Campbell; 1900).

Glaistig

A complex Scottish fairy, the Glaistig can be both extremely dangerous, particularly to men, and also protective, especially of children and the elderly. John Campbell in *The Gaelic Otherworld* suggest the name Glaistig comes from the word 'glas', which he translates as grey although it actually indicates green, shading anywhere from blue-green to true green to grey-green. Campbell describes her as wearing a green dress with a face that is 'wan and grey' (Campbell, 1900, p 23). A solitary water fairy who may also be called Uaine Maighdean (Green Maiden) she appears as a beautiful young woman, sometimes with the lower half of a goat, which she conceals under her green dress, and seduces mortal men. Once under her power the Glaistig kills them and drinks their blood (MacKillop, 1998). She can also take the form of a goat, showing some shape-shifting abilities, and while she is known to kill she also helped those she favored by watching after the cows, expecting only a bit of milk once a week in thanks (Briggs, 1976). The Glaistig often seems to be tied to a specific location and like the Brownie is known to take on the tasks of a servant, specifically by watching after the herds (Campbell, 1900). As with so many of the fairies being discussed in this section, the Glaistig may be one particular being or may perhaps be a grouping of similar beings, female fairies who live near water and can appear as goats or with a partially goat-like form. The Glaistig was said to have once been a human woman who had been transformed into a fairy after being taken by the Good Neighbors (Briggs, 1976; Campbell, 1900).

Goblins

One of the more well-known types of fey, by name at least, are Goblins, but many people are vague on what exactly Goblins are. So let's take a look at Goblins, what they are, and some folklore surrounding them.

The word Goblin itself dates back to about the 14th century and is believed to possibly come from the Latin Gobelinus, and to be related to the German Kobold; the meaning is given as an ugly fairy or devil (Goblin, 2016). Originally, the word Goblin was not applied to a specific type of fairy being, but rather was used as a generic term, in line with the older uses of fairy and Elf, to indicate a more general type of being. In Scots, for example, we can see more than a half dozen kinds of fairies that are described as Goblins, from Gunnies to Whaups (SLD, 2016). The name Goblin was used in earlier periods as a synonym for other negative types of fairies, such as Thurs and Shuck, both of which had connotations of maliciousness and evil (Williams, 1991). The prefix 'hob' was added in front of the word Goblin, giving us Hobgoblin, to indicate a Goblin-type spirit that was less negative and more benevolent; Hobgoblins were inclined to mischief, but also known to be helpful to people where Goblins were not (Briggs, 1976). MacKillop posits that the word as well as the being was borrowed into Celtic belief from outsiders, likely from Germanic folk belief probably of the Kobold (MacKillop, 1998). The Irish Púca is sometimes described as a Goblin, and Goblins are often seen as equivalent to Bogies. An array of subgroups of fairies are considered Goblins or Hobgoblins including the afore-mentioned Púca (and more general Puck), Bogies, the Fuath – themselves a general term inclusive of specific types – Boggarts[2] and Bogles, who are usually considered the more evil sort of Goblins, the Welsh Coblynau, and Irish Clauricaun and Dullahan (Briggs, 1976; MacKillop, 1998). Even the usually benevolent Brownie is sometimes considered a Goblin, or perhaps more properly a Hobgoblin (SLD, 2016; Briggs, 1976).

When they appear in folklore, Goblins are generally described as wizened or smaller than the average human and unattractive in their features, ranging from grotesque to animalistic. In Rossetti's poem *Goblin Market* the depiction of the Goblins directly relates them to animals describing them with whiskers, tails, and with fur (Rossetti, 1862). Dickens described them as small, with long arms and legs, and rounded bodies (Silver, 1999). These descriptions are typical of those found in older folklore as well where Goblins are usually referred to as grotesque and ugly. Generally Goblins are male and their physical descriptions reflect ideas closer to imps or devils than the usual fairies who appear fair on the outside no matter how dangerous they may be on the inside. This may reflect a belief that Goblins, although a type or kind of fairy, were closer to or on the border of being demonic; this is muddy water at best as there was often a fine line between the fey and demons in the medieval period, particularly among the literati. Briggs suggests that it was particularly the influence of Protestant belief, which edged the Goblins into the category of the demonic as they directly equated them to 'imps from Hell' (Briggs, 1967). In fact imp is often given as a synonym for Goblin, further confusing the issue. Specific types of Goblins, such as the Bogies, were known as shape-shifters as well and could alter their appearance at will in order to more easily deceive people. Because of their fearsome reputation, many people were afraid of Goblins and even the generally more benevolent Hobgoblins (Evans-Wentz, 1911).

Goblins were known to favor specific locations and might set up residence in a home; in one story a Bogey takes over a farmer's field and had to be tricked into leaving (Evans-Wentz, 1911; Briggs, 1976). In Rossetti's poem they have their own market and a well-worn path that is taken to and from it each dawn and dusk. Like many fey, Goblins are usually considered nocturnal and are most likely to be encountered at night (Evans-Wentz, 1911). Goblins of various sorts might also be associated with wilder locations and with the ruins of former human habitations and were known to lead people astray, either as part of a frustrating, but ultimately harmless, joke or to the person's eventual death (Briggs, 1967). By modern reckoning Goblins fall under the dominion of the Unseelie Court and may be either solitary or trooping fairies, depending on what kind of Goblin is being discussed (Briggs, 1976). Hobgoblins, however, are harder to be certain of as they are usually seen as more benign and can be associated with helpful spirits like Brownies.

There is at least one well known piece of more modern literature that refers to Goblins, Rossetti's poem *Goblin Market*, which I will discuss in more depth in a later chapter. In the poem the Goblins appear in a fairly typical form, being deceptive, malicious, and grotesque in appearance. They play the usual role of a group of fairies trying to trick mortals, in this case by getting them to eat dangerous fruit. In the poem when the person the Goblins are seeking to trick resists they become violent, which is also in line with the general temperament normally seen with them. Goblins play a prominent role in the film *Labyrinth* where they are depicted more as Hobgoblins, being somewhat dangerous and set against the story's heroine, but overall more mischievous than actually malicious. Goblins also feature in the Harry Potter novels and movies, and while they physical resemble the Goblins of folklore in those fictitious depictions they are very different in character from the traditional ones, being more similar to common depictions of Dwarves with their focus on money and metalsmithing than folkloric Goblins.

Ultimately Goblins are a difficult group of fairies to define, being both a specific type of being and also a class of being. The word itself is just as ambiguous, the etymology uncertain beyond the 12th century, and the ultimate root unknown. The term Goblin can be used to indicate a specific being that is small, grotesque and malicious or a broader category of beings that were generally described as 'imps' and ran a gamut from devilish to mischievous. When the prefix 'hob' is added it indicates a more benign nature to the creature being discussed; Shakespeare's Puck is referred to as a Hobgoblin in the play *A Midsummer Night's Dream*. However, Protestant influence did add a darker reputation even to the Hobgoblins, who were considered outright demonic in some places. The only way to be certain of the usage of Goblin or Hobgoblin is to look at the context of the reference. However, one can safely say that Goblins were generally viewed as dangerous and to be feared, whatever sort of Goblin was being discussed.

The Gruagach

The Gruagach is a type of fairy similar in nature to a Brownie, but who favors living in barns and helping farmers with cattle. A solitary fairy, the Gruagach is sometimes envisioned as giant or a type of ogre, but usually appears as only human sized (MacKillop, 1998). The male can be either attractive and dressed in green and red or extremely hairy, shunning clothing, and industrious, while the female is said to have long blonde hair and wear a green dress (Briggs, 1976). Donald MacKenzie suggests that some Scottish legends of the Gruagach that depict her as a woman who appears, always wet and dripping, asking to warm herself by a household's fire are actually describing the Glaistig, not the more domestic Gruagach.

The word grúacach in Old Irish means 'hairy, long haired', 'a Goblin' and 'very wise'. It is likely from the meaning of 'hairy' that this particular fairy derived its name. A farm that had a Gruagach present would offer it milk once a week for its labor (Briggs, 1976).

Gwragedd Annwn

The famous Lake Maidens of Wales, their name means 'Otherwordly women'. While many fairies who make their homes in bodies of water are at best mercurial and at worst murderous, the Gwragedd Annwn have a good reputation for kindness and gentle ways. They appear as beautiful young women and are known to make good wives when they marry human men, although like many fairy wives they usually leave if the man violates a taboo relating to them (Briggs, 1976). In many stories of these Lake Maidens this taboo has to do with the husband striking the wife three times. Even if they are forced to leave their family such fairy women stay involved with their children, and one Welsh family renowned for their medical knowledge claimed it had come from a long-distant Gwragedd Annwn ancestor (Briggs, 1976). The Gwragedd Annwn are strongly associated with cattle, both Earthly cows and Otherworldy ones, which may be seen as symbols of abundance and blessing.

Hags

A variety of monstrous female fairies fall into this category all sharing common characteristics and habits. Usually known by specific names such as Black Annis, Jenny Greenteeth, and Peg Powler, these fairies often lurk in rivers and reach out to pull in and drown unwary or misbehaving children (Cox, 1904; Briggs, 1976). Most Hags are specific to a location and are known in that area's folklore. Black Annis lived in the hills of Leicestershire and was said to have a blue face and iron claws, as well as an association with a gigantic cat (Briggs, 1976). Jenny Greenteeth was local to Lancashire and favored stagnant pools, while Peg Powler haunted the river Tees (Briggs, 1976).

The Leannán Sí[3]

Of all the beings in Irish – and more generally Celtic – folklore, one of the most interesting may be the Leannán Sí. The name literally means 'fairy lover'[4] and we see two distinct pictures emerge in mythology and folklore of this type of being, very different in nature although both perhaps equally hazardous in various ways.

The most well-known Leannán Sí is a figure from folklore and is perhaps the more obviously dangerous. The name is often Anglicized to its more phonetic form of 'Leanan Shee'. Yeats

93

described this spirit as one that sought to seduce mortals, and if successful would feed on their life energy while inspiring their creativity; the only escape according to him was to find another to replace yourself in her affections, or else you would be bound to her even beyond death (Yeats, 1888). This Leannán Sí was fond of poets and musicians and other naturally creative people, but her presence meant a short, if intensely productive, life. According to Yeats if a person could resist her allure then she would become bound to their service instead, although one may assume this was the more rare occurrence (Yeats, 1888). The Manx version of this spirit, the Lhiannan-Shee, was more blatantly vampiric in nature; said to haunt springs and wells, invisible to everyone except the man she seduced, she would drain his life until he wasted away (Briggs, 1976). Generally when we hear stories of the Leannán Sí they feature a supernatural female of great beauty who seduces a man and once she has him as her lover she draws his vitality from him causing him to slowly die. In the Irish stories this is done in exchange for extraordinary inspiration, while in the Manx the only thing given is the Lhiannan-Shee's company to the man. However, there are equivalent beings by different names that are more literally vampiric. In Scotland we find the Baobhan Sith, literally 'wicked fairy woman', who seduces a young man into dancing with her and then drains him of blood leaving him dead by morning (Briggs, 1976).

Although usually described as female there is a version of the dangerously seductive Leannán Sí that is male – the Gean-Cánach, or 'Love Talker'. He appears as an attractive young man smoking a pipe, walking in the untamed places, and is quick to seduce women when he can, after which they lose the will to live (Briggs, 1967). There are some clear parallels between these two spirits as both seek to seduce mortals and this seduction results in the person's wasting and eventual death. The biggest difference between the Leannán Sí and the Gean-Cánach is that the Love Talker only lays once with his victim then departs never to be seen again, leaving her to waste away for want of him (or perhaps because he has stolen some vital life energy from her) while the Leannán Sí is a regular visitor to her victim throughout his life and possibly afterwards.

The second, and less discussed, Leannán Sí is a more straight-forward one, a person of the sí of either gender who takes a human lover. Katherine Briggs in her book *Fairies in Tradition and Literature* devotes an entire chapter to this type of Leannán Sí and their place in fairylore. The most famous by far example of this type of Leannán Sí is the story of Niamh and Oisin in the Fenian Cycle. In this tale Fionn's son Oisin is captivated by a fairy woman, Niamh. He chooses to go to Tir na nOg with her, where they live happily together and she bears him a son and daughter. However, as time passes, he begins to miss his friends and wishes to visit Ireland again; Niamh warns him that if he goes he must not dismount his horse because if he touches the ground he will die. Of course while he is there he finds that hundreds of years have passed and all the people he knew have died, and through mischance his saddle slips and he falls, instantly aging when he hits the ground.

With this type of fairy lover they may or may not seek to take the human partner out of the mortal world, and may or may not produce offspring with the human partner in stories. In most cases if a child is produced the family will later trace its lineage back to that spirit, such as the Fitzgeralds tracing their ancestry to the Fairy Queen Áine who was a lover of the Earl of Desmond. Some versions of the story of clan MacLeod's Fairy Flag say that it was a gift from a fairy lover. It is not infrequent in stories for a fairy lover to give a family line they are part of a special item or token as a sign of favor. The Lhiannan-Shee of Ballafletcher was connected to the Fletcher family who had a custom once a year of drinking from a fairy cup, which she had given them (Briggs, 1976).

In some stories the mortal remains in our world, but regularly sees her fairy lover, shunning any human love in turn. In one tale from Scotland a girl had such a fairy lover and made the mistake of trusting her secret to her sister who then spread the tale; in anger the girl's Leannán Sí abandoned her and she went mad from his loss (Briggs, 1967). In a tale from Ireland a young man had a fairy lover who took him into the sí on Bealtaine; a fairy doctor was called for and for nine days and nights sought to get the young man back until finally he appeared and begged to be allowed to remain with his new wife (Briggs, 1967). In many cases like this the human partner is simply taken into Fairy and removed from the human world entirely, often under the guise of having apparently died in our world. In the stories where the human partner stays in our world, but sees her Leannán Sí regularly, she is often required to keep him a secret or lose him. As with all things, however, there are various versions and exceptions to be found[5].

Several folk songs immortalize attempts by mortals to win the heart of a fairy lover, including *Scarborough Fair*, which is based on older folk ballads including *The Fairy Knight*; and the ballad of *Tam Lin*, which also survives as a song today. In the first example the girl wishes for an Elfin knight as a lover or husband and he responds with a list of seemingly impossible tasks she must first accomplish. In the second example a girl takes a fairy lover (Tam Lin who was a mortal taken into Fairy as a child) and only after they have been lovers for a time and she seeks to abort the child she is carrying does he tell her the quite difficult way she must win him free of the Fairy Queen so he can be her husband. Some versions of ballads of fairy lovers are decidedly grim, such as *Lady Isabel and the Elf Knight*, which tells the story of a woman who wishes for an Elf knight on Bealtaine morning only to have him appear and kidnap her to a greenwood where he tells her that he is going to kill her as he has seven other king's daughters before her; she tricks him into falling asleep, binds him with his own sword belt, and kills him with his own dagger then escapes. Similar ballads exist that begin the same way, but where the Elfin knight tries to drown the girl who must outwit him to escape. These represent a clear warning to be careful before wishing for a fairy lover, although most other tales are far less murderous and when they end badly do so because of a failure on the human partner's end to keep their lover a secret resulting in abandonment. We may see echoes of this theme in Keats' poem *La Belle Dame sans Merci*, which tells the story of a knight who loved a fairy maiden who took him *'to her elfin grotto'* and enchanted him only to abandon him. The knight was then left to waste away, pining for what he could not have, although this could also perhaps be an example of the more directly harmful kind of Leannán Sí as well. Looking at these stories and ballads we can see the challenges and difficulties this sort of Leannán Sí presents, as they may not always be as overtly dangerous as the first sort, but they can often lead a person to the same eventual end.

Not all instances of humans with fairy lovers end badly for the human though, as some tales do make it clear that the non-human half of the pairing genuinely cares for the human partner. There is at least one story recorded by Evans Wentz of a man with a fairy lover who immigrated to America and his Otherwordly lover followed him there (Briggs, 1967). A male Leannán Sí who took a human lover was generally concerned for her care and if any children were produced seemed to genuinely care about their welfare (Capmbell; 1900). There are two stories I know about featuring Kelpies who fall in love with mortal women and go against their own nature for the sake of their human partner. In one Irish tale a Kelpie loves a girl, but is tricked into becoming a beast of burden on her father's farm after she finds out his true nature. After a year of such work the girl and her family consult a fairy doctor who asks the Kelpie if he would choose to be a mortal man so he in turn asks the girl if she still wants to marry him[6]; she says yes and he chooses to become mortal so the two are married (McNeill, 2001). In a less cheerful story from Scotland a Kelpie falls in love with a mortal woman and courts her. They wed and she bears him a son, but one day she realizes his true nature and flees. Heartbroken, the Kelpie remains in their small home, raising their child, and waiting futilely for her to return.

Some Bean Feasa were also known to have Leannán Sí, as in the case of Eibhlin Ni Ghuinniola, about whom it was said: '*A 'fairy lover', a leannán sí, was often seen with [her] as she gathered plants.*' (O Crualaoich, 2003, p. 191) It was believed in such cases that it was through this connection to the Otherworld that these women gained their knowledge of magic and cures, although a Leannán Sí was not always involved with the wise women. Some then could maintain a relationship with a fairy lover and also remain at least for a time in our world and would benefit from the knowledge gained from their fairy associations.

As we can see the threads of myth and folklore provide two distinct, but perhaps intertwined, views of the Leannán Sí. The Leannán Sí as a distinct being seduces and inspires, gives creativity, but drains away life. The related beings like the Geancánach and Baobhan Sith similarly use their beauty and appeal to gain lovers who they destroy in the taking, feeding on either their life force or blood. In contrast the more general fairy lovers may bless or ruin their human lover, may steal them from this world, abandon them to it, or be constant companions. One is a more overtly malevolent, seductive figure, which is a distinct type of being in its own right; the other a more ambiguous term applied to different beings, which in its own way embodies all that Fairy itself is – alluring, sometimes dangerous, sometimes generous.

Land Spirits

Considered to be fairies, Land Spirits are unique because they are not Otherworldly spirits, but spirits that are bound entirely to this world. A Land Spirit may be the embodiment of a river, tree, rock, or other physical object in our world, for example. Unlike a fairy who makes a home in a river, a Land Spirit is the actual soul of that river and it is bound to the health and physical existence of that river. If a fairy who lives in an oak loses the oak it can find another home; if the Land Spirit of an oak loses its oak it loses its existence just as we would if we lose our physical body. The physical item in our world acts as anchor for that spirit. In folklore, Land Spirits are bound to the immediate area around the object they are tied to and unlike Otherworldly fairies they cannot travel. In Ireland Land Spirits are known to appear in the form of birds or animals (O Suilleabhain, 1967).

There is some cross-over in Irish tradition with dangerous spirits-of-place, which may be either Land Spirits or human ghosts bound to locations. These dangerous spirits have names that reflect the places they are tied to or their inherent nature such as Sprid na Charraig an Eidhin (spirit of Carriganine), Sprid na Bearnan (spirit of the gap), and Sprid an Tobac (spirit of the tobacco), each with their own story (O Suilleabhain, 1967). Because these spirits were believed to be malevolent they were protected against using things like an iron chain or black handled knife, or holy water (O Suilleabhain, 1967). Often these spirits were driven out of their locations because of the threat they represented, but it is difficult to know whether they were simply territorial, dangerous by nature, or if their antagonism towards humans was rooted in something else.

This type of fairy is the one that many modern pagans commonly associate with fairies generally; however, they represent only a small amount of actual fairies, and of a very specific type.

Lutins

Lutins are a type of fairy from Brittany described as a shape-shifter somewhat akin to the Kelpie, but whose true form is more similar to a Dwarf, clad in green. Lutins are solitary beings who prefer to live in ponds or lakes and enjoy playing tricks on humans, sometimes assuming the shape of a black horse or goat (Evans-Wentz, 1911). It may be safe to assume these tricks, while terrifying, are generally harmless though as the other main type of fairy in Brittany, the Corrigan, is said to be at war with the Lutins for the Lutins' friendly attitude towards humans (Evans-Wentz, 1911).

Merrows

The Irish version of Mermaids, Merrows are sea-dwelling fairies. The females are much like traditional Mermaids, beautiful and alluring, but the males are said to be hideously ugly. Unlike other kinds of Mermaids, Merrows wear red feather hats in the water and can take the form of hornless cows on land; if their hat is stolen they cannot return to the water (Briggs, 1976). Although sometimes feared as portents of bad weather at sea, generally Merrows are viewed as helpful and friendly beings. Like other types of fairies they will sometimes marry and reproduce with humans and the children of such unions are born looking human, but with some scales (Briggs, 1976).

Pixies

Pixies are one of the most well-known types of fairies; the name is also seen as Pisgies, Piskies, Pisky, Pixy, or Pigseys.

Like most fairies, Pixies can assume different shapes and sizes, from tiny to human-sized. There was an account of two strange fey children found near a village who were described as having a green tint to their skin and dark hair, clothed in pale green, who claimed to have come from a land of perpetual twilight (Briggs, 1976). Although not explicitly identified as Pixies these green children are sometimes thought to have been such[7]. Pixies are usually described as wearing green, red-headed, and bearing the pointed ears we so often associate with all fairies (Briggs, 1976).

One of the most well known of faeries, Pixies are also the most mischievous. They delight in playing tricks on humans and domestic animals, but are generally harmless, although like all fairies if angered they can be deadly. Pixies were known to tangle the manes of horses at night, as well as people's hair while they slept. In Cornwall and western England, Pixies are known to inhabit groves, hills, and river areas, where they are pictured as old men clad in green (MacKillop, 1998).

Another well-known Pixie trick is leading travelers astray in familiar territory. Referred to as being Pixy-led, it is an extremely disconcerting feeling. You could be walking along a section of woodland you've walked a hundred times before, but find yourself totally lost despite being surrounded by well-known landmarks. The effect can last for minutes or hours, and can be broken by turning an item of clothing inside out, pulling some bread from a pocket and leaving it, or showing a wooden cross if you have one on your person. Pixies create fairy rings by riding horses they've stolen in circles; to step fully into such a circle is to be lost to Fairy, while setting only one foot inside grants the ability to see the Pixies (Briggs, 1976).

A lot of our experiences with Pixies revolve around our entertainment value to them, as they like nothing better than to see us running around in annoyed circles. A favorite trick for them in the modern world is to steal car keys – usually when we are already late or in a hurry. They will take the keys, which were left out in plain sight, then watch as we tear our house apart looking for the missing item. Often as soon as we give up looking the keys will reappear sitting out in the open on a table where we would have easily seen them before. They will also borrow or temporarily move other small items, such as jewelry. Like Brownies, Pixies will leave a house if offered clothing.

The Púca

[A]n pucadh da ngairir an spioraid phriobhaideach
Lucerna Fidelium
(The púca he was called the secret spirit)

The Púca – also called by a wide array of variant names including Phooka, Pooka, Pwca (Welsh), Bucca (Cornish) and Puck (English) – is a type of being found in folklore across hundreds of years. Some even connect Shakespeare's character Puck to the folkloric Púca, although Shakespeare naturally took a lot of literary liberties. Puca was used in early Middle English as a name for the Devil (Williams, 1991). The old Irish Púca is given as 'a Goblin, sprite' and similarly the modern Irish is given as Hobgoblin (eDIL, n.d.; O Donaill, 1977). These translations give a clue to the Púca's nature, which may be described as mischievous, but can in folklore be either helpful or harmful. In some sources the Púca was seen as purely evil and dangerous, while others described it as potentially helpful and willing to do work around the home if treated well (McKillop, 1998).

The Púca is known to take on many forms, most often appearing as a dark horse, but also as an eagle, bat, bull, goat, a human man, or a more typical Goblin-like small fairy; in the 1950 movie *'Harvey'* there is a Púca that is said to take the form of giant rabbit (Briggs, 1976; Yeats, 1888; McKillop, 1998). The form I am most personally familiar with is the black goat. In the form of a horse the Púca will lure riders onto its back and then take them on a wild ride only to dump them in a ditch. This is a reasonably harmless trick though given that the Kelpies and Each Uisge when pulling the same trick end it by drowning and eating their riders. The Púca has also been known to work on farms and in mills, both in human form and in horse form (Briggs, 1976). This, perhaps, best encapsulates the Púca's personality, using the horse form to both trick and cause minor harm as well as to work and help. In other stories the Púca will sometimes trick a person, even cruelly, and reward them later. In one case a Púca gave a piper a ride, forcing him to play as they went, only to have the piper find the next day that the gold he thought he'd been paid had turned to leaves and his pipes would play nothing but the noises of geese; but when he tried to tell the priest later and demonstrate, he found that his playing had become the best of any piper in the area (Yeats, 1888). Perhaps that is the best summary of the Púca after all.

The Púca is a mysterious being, if indeed there is only one of him as some claim, or a complicated type if there are more than one. Generally all of the above named beings – the Púca, Pwca, Bucca and Puck – are considered together to be the same. However, while it may be that they are different cultural iterations of one being, it might also be that they are simply similar enough to be classed together. The Welsh Bucca is said to be a single being who was once a God, while the English Puck is thought by some to perhaps be a type of Pixie (Evans-Wentz, 1911). In contrast some older Irish folklore would clearly indicate the Púca was not solitary, but a group of beings. It was said by one person interviewed in Ireland at the turn of the 20th century that the 'Pookas' were men who went invisibly to racecourses mounted on 'good horses' (Evans-Wentz, 1911). In Welsh and British folklore the Pwca and Puck were both said to mislead travelers and the British Puck stole clothes (Briggs, 1976; Purkiss, 2000).

The Púca also had a special association with autumn and with the turning of the year from summer to winter. In some areas it was said that any berries that remained on the bushes after Michealmas (September 29) belonged to the Púca, who would spoil them for human consumption (Briggs, 1976). In other areas it is said that it is after Samhain (October 31) that all the remaining berries belong to the Púca, and that he would urinate or spit on them to claim them. In either case it is clear that he was entitled to a portion of the wild harvest, the food that grew without being cultivated. The Púca was also associated more generally with roaming on and around Samhain and it was said that Samhain was sacred to him (Yeats, 1888).

Although generally helpful the Púca can play pranks that can be malicious and if it's necessary to convince one to leave a home or area, folklore would suggest the same method used (albeit less intentionally) that rids a home of a Brownie – the gift of clothes (Briggs, 1976; Yeats, 1888). In particular the gift of fine quality clothes, as the Púca seems to have high standards. If, however, you feel you have a Púca around that you enjoy you might try offering it the traditional cream or the less common offering of fish, as some say they enjoy that (Evans-Wentz, 1911).

Red Caps

One of the most dangerous types of Goblins. Although there are some stories of the occasional more benevolent Red Cap these seem to be rare exceptions to a general rule of malevolence. These fairies appear as wizened old men, bucktoothed, talon fingered, bearing a pike, and clad in iron boots and a grisly Red Cap that is dyed in human blood (Briggs, 1976). Red Caps are known to haunt ruins where murders have happened, apparently either drawn by that energy or preferring it. They are all-but impervious to injury and iron does not ward them off, but it is said they will flee from a cross or recited scripture (Briggs, 1976). This may perhaps indicate that they were once humans, I might surmise wicked men, brought over to Fairy who still fear their old faith. In at least one case a human lord was known to have a Red Cap as a fairy familiar and it protected him from all harm done by weapons (Briggs, 1976).

The Selkie

The Seal Folk, called Roan, Roane or Rón in Ireland and Selkies or Silkies in Scotland, are shapechangers who can appear as humans or as seals. Stories of these beings appear on the coasts of Ireland, Scotland, the Orkneys, and Shetland and persist today in these areas. They are primarily associated with the sea and beaches, and their stories often originate with fisherman and people whose livelihood is tied to the ocean. Roan are creatures of the Between, existing between land and sea, between human and seal form. Although I will discuss the Roan and Selkies here as a single group it is worth noting that they are not entirely interchangeable and the Roan are noted to be more gentle and forgiving while the Selkies are more vengeful against those who harm them (Briggs, 1976).

Roan can be either male or female, and appear in either seal or human form, as they are true shape-shifters. They appear in the form of seals unless they remove their seal skin, at which point they appear human, but their stories make it clear this is not an innate magic, but a power invested in the seal skin itself (Briggs, 1976). It is a point of interest that the magic does not seem to lie within the Roan themselves, but rather is invested in their seal skin, which is part of them, but which they do not seem to have an awareness of; if the skin is taken or stolen they cannot automatically find it or sense where it is. In Orcadian lore they were said to be limited in when or how often they could transform, either only taking human form on midsummer night, or once every seven or nine days (Towrie, 2016). In Scottish lore it was sometimes said that their true form was human, but they used the magic seal skin to take the form of seals (Briggs, 1976). As seals they are indistinguishable from ordinary seals, but with human intelligence, and they are more prone to follow boats and aid fisherman. Some interpretations of stories cast the male Selkies as more noble while the females seem more animalistic although both are unreliable in their interactions and fidelity with humans (Silver, 1999; Monaghan, 2009).

In folklore Roan will sometimes appear in seal form and aid fisherman during storms and they have been known to help drowning sailors by supporting them and helping them safely to shore. In other tales they will herd fish towards the sailors' nets to help them get a big catch, particularly if the fisher's family is tied to the Roan. Selkies who are angry with humans for harming them are known to raise storms against fisherman, although the Roan are more likely to try to teach the person a lesson and gain a promise from them to stop harming seals (Briggs, 1976). For example, in one story a seal hunter injures a large seal, dropping his knife in the process, and is later taken out into the sea by a male Roan where he is asked if the knife is his and then told that only he can heal the wound he caused. He does this and then is pressed to swear an oath to never hunt another seal (Briggs, 1976). Upon being returned safely to his family he finds that he has been rewarded with gold, despite the fact that he had previously killed many seals and that the entire incident was predicated on his attack of a seal.

Most stories about them involve amorous interactions between Roan and humans. Where human women are involved, the Seal Man will emerge from the sea to court her. Sometimes this is a simple encounter, other times he may convince her to run away with him to his kingdom beneath the waves, where she will be lost to the mortal world. In Orkney it is said that the Selkie men are drawn particularly to unhappy women, both single and married, and there is even a folkloric method for a woman to conjure a Selkie lover if she desires one (Towrie, 2016). The stories involving human men and Seal Women, however, are much different; they generally involve a man who stumbles upon a group of Roan on the beach, and watches them change shape from a hiding place. Once in human form they leave their seal skins to go dance along the shore and the human sneaks down and steals one of the skins. When the Roan return to the ocean the one whose skin was stolen is trapped in her human form, and the man emerges and claims her as his bride. They will live peacefully together, with the Seal Woman as a faithful wife, so long as she never reclaims her seal skin. In most lore the couple will live happily for years, raising a family until one of the children discovers the hidden seal skin and tells the mother. Once she regains her skin she returns to the ocean, and no bonds – not even love of her children – can keep her on land; in some stories she will abandon her children while in others she will take them with her into the ocean (Briggs, 1976; Towrie, 2016). In at least one story, however, the seal-wife simply asked for her sealskin back and was given it, after which she left her husband and three sons to return to the sea; this incident reflecting the normal procedure for divorce at the time (Silver, 1999). Half-Selkie/half-human children were known to have webbed hands or feet, a trait that was passed down family lines, and several families claim such ancestry (Briggs, 1976).

Roan and the closely related Selkies are fascinating beings, perhaps the most human-seeming and acting of all the Other Crowd. Their interactions with humans are usually benign and sometimes even show genuine caring, although they are as prone to be tragic as any human-fey interaction can be. They are also noteworthy because when they have children with humans the children usually remain in the human world rather than becoming part of Fairy, as we see in most stories of human/fairy mixing. Ultimately, perhaps, the great appeal of the Roan is their very humanness, embedded as it is within an inherently non-human being.

Further Resources on Selkies

Black, G., (1903), *County Folklore Volume 3: Orkney and Shetlands*
Williamson, Duncan (1992), *Tales of the Seal People: Scottish Folk Tales*
www.educationscotland.gov.uk/scotlandsstories/aselkiestory/
echoes.devin.com/selkie/selkie.html

Movies

The Secret of Roan Inish
Song of the Sea

Slua Sí

I have already mentioned that some fairies are more naturally kindly inclined towards us than others, and some are generally more malicious. Those that fall under the auspices of the Unseelie Court are generally feared, but one type that is especially feared is the Slua Sí (Fairy Host). In Scottish folklore the most daunting fairies are those of the Sluagh (Briggs, 1976). The Slua travels in whirlwinds, or on the wind more generally and because of this the whirlwind is called the Séideán Sídhe (fairy blast) or Sitheadh Gaoithe (thrust of wind) and sometimes by the similar sounding name of Sí Gaoithe (fairy wind) (O hOgain, 1995; MacKillop, 1998). Usually invisible to mortal eyes while traveling in the form of a wind, in Scotland the Slua is also said to appear in the form of clouds (Carmichael, 1900). The Slua is most likely to be active at midnight and most often appears at night in general, but can show up at any time, sometimes startling farmers working in the fields (Evans Wentz, 1911). Anyone who had reason to be out at night, and more so if they were out alone, needed to be careful to avoid the Fairy Host.

The Slua Sí were known to force humans to go along with them while they engaged in their malicious endeavors, making the unlucky people aid them in their activities (O Suilleabhain, 1967). These endeavors often included kidnapping other people including brides, a common theme in many different types of fairy stories, and doing the new victim mischief. Anyone caught out alone, especially at night, or in a place they shouldn't be in could be swept up by the Slua with little choice but to go along with the Fairy Host until they were released. People taken this way might be said to be 'in the fairies' (O Suilleabhain, 1967). In folklore people taken by the Slua Sí could be taken and left far away, sometimes in foreign countries with no option but to find their way slowly home, or else may be returned to the place where they were taken mostly unharmed. The Slua is utterly capricious in how they treat those they take.

There are also tales of those who were out walking at night and saw another person who had been or was being taken by the Slua, usually as the Slua was passing near the bystander. A folk method to get the host to release anyone they may have taken is to throw the dust from the road, an iron knife, or your left shoe towards them while saying: 'This is yours; that is mine!' (McNeill, 1956). Those known to have been taken and released were gone to for advice relating to the fairies and seen as being quite knowledgeable about them, just as those who had more amicable relationships with the fairies were consulted (O Suilleabhain, 1967).

The Slua may include fairy horses, hounds, and a variety of fairy beings, as well as the human dead. In Scotland some people believe that the Slua Sí, who are also called the Fairy Host of the Air, are spirits of those humans who died with unforgiven sins or filled with sin (McNeill, 1956; Briggs, 1976; Carmichael, 1900). Evans Wentz related stories of the Slua as both the mortal dead and as fallen angels, showing that the belief was not entirely clear-cut (Evans Wentz, 1911). In Irish folktales related by authors including Yeats and Hyde, however, the Fairy Host are distinct from the human dead and act like fairies in other tales, engaging in behavior such as stealing human brides to force them to wed members of their own group. As was discussed in a previous chapter there is no simple division to be found here and it is likely that the Slua represent both fairies who were never human and some who may once have lived as humans, but are now counted among the Fairy Host.

The Fairy Host, like other fairies, are usually invisible to humans, but can be sensed in the appearance of a sudden wind and the sound of voices, armor clinking, or people shouting (O

Suilleabhain, 1967). Hyde describes it in the story *Guleesh Na Guss Dhu* this way: '*He heard a great noise coming like the sound of many people running together, and talking, and laughing, and making sport, and the sound went by him like a whirl of wind...*' (Hyde, 1890, p 76). Some say the Slua appears as a dust devil that moves over roads and hedges as the Good Neighbors travel (JCHAS, 2010). When the whirlwind appeared people would react by averting their eyes, turning their backs, and praying, or else saying: '*Good luck to them, the ladies and gentlemen.*' (O hOgain, 1995; JCHAS, 2010, p. 319) This of course reflects the common practice of appeasing the more dangerous fairies both by speaking of them in polite, positive terms and also of wishing them well, giving a blessing in hopes they respond in kind. This is done to avert any harm caused by the close proximity of the Host and to hopefully avoid drawing their attention in a negative way. The Sí Gaoithe (Fairy Wind), which indicated the Slua was present, could bring illness or cause injury as it passed by, contributing to its fearsome reputation (MacKillop, 1998).

The Slua was known for being mercurial and prone to malicious behavior and unlike more sedentary types of Fair Folk they are not easily appeased, but most often must be warded off, usually with iron, driven away, or out-witted. They are strongly associated with the Unseelie Court and one Queen of the Unseelie, Nicnevin, in particular.

Trows

A type of fairy native to the Shetland and Orkney Isles, Trows can be either the size of giants, human sized, or small wizened man, showing that they are perhaps less a specific kind of fairy but – as with most of the others we have discussed here – a general type. Trows are probably related to the Norse Trolls, but have enough differences to be considered a separate kind of being. The Trows of Shetland are said to prefer night-time and to fear sunlight, which traps them on Earth during the day (Briggs,

1976). They are known to hate a locked door and to often visit homes at night, inviting themselves inside to sit by the fire while the homeowners sleep (Towrie, 2017). Like many other kinds of fairies Trows live in mounds, locally called knowes, and were known to steal people although they usually took brides; they love music and making mischief. They were known most often to wear grey although they may also appear in green, red, black, or white (Briggs, 1976; Bruford, 1991). Folklore around Trows is similar to that of other fairies and features stories of their attempts to steal women being thwarted, their use of magic to turn plants into horses, and occasions where a Trow appeared and demanded a share of a person's food in exchange for a blessing.

Fairy Animals

There are many animals in Fairy, both the fairies who can shape-shift from human-like forms into those of animals as well as beings who are bound in animal form. Generally fairy animals are less intelligent than fairies who can shape-shift into animal form, being closer to a true animal, but they are still Otherworldly and often act in ways we find uncanny. There are a variety of fairy animals in particular that are worth discussing in some depth, although as with the previous sections on types of fairies, some generalities have to be made for brevities sake.

Cu Si

One of the more interesting ones is the fairy hound, or Cu Sí . The Cu Sí are known by many names including Cu Sith (Scottish), Cwn Annwn (Welsh), and when riding with the Wild Hunt may be called the Gabriel Ratchets, Dandy Dogs, or Hell Hounds. They are also sometimes conflated with the ghostly hounds known as the Black Dog, Black Shuck, Hell Hounds, Padfoot, Bogey, Moddey Doo or the Grim. Katherine Briggs divides these supernatural dogs into three categories: supernatural beings, human ghosts in dog form, and ghosts of dogs (Briggs, 1978). For our purposes we will discusses all appearances of Otherworldly dogs, but it is important to understand up front that the subject is complex and that what appears to be a dog may or may not actually be a dog. Which is really just par for the course with anything of Fairy actually. Each unique type of Cu Sí may have its own very specific set of folklore, beliefs, and stories and this section should be understood as a general overview of fairy hounds as a group, rather than a discussion of any specific sub-group or type.

Cu Sí may appear as a huge shaggy black or dark green dog, or as a swift white hound with red eyes and ears, sometimes missing a limb. They are known by their enormous size, often described as being as large as a calf with huge round eyes (Parkinson, 2013). These spectral dogs may be male or female and may appear alone, in pairs, or in packs (Campbell, 2008). A Cu Sí may also appear as a black dog with a white ring around its neck, usually seen on a fairy hill (Evans Wentz, 1911). It is almost impossible to mistake a fairy hound for a mortal dog because of its size and unusual appearance.

The Cu Sí are often associated with the Slua Si, Fairy Rade, and the Wild Hunt. When riding out with the Wild Hunt in particular they usually frighten people, as the Hunt itself is an omen of war, death, and madness, although it can also bring blessings. The Cu Sí as 'spectral black dogs' are seen as omens of death, although it isn't clear whether the dog causes the death or, like the Irish Banshee, the dog shows up to warn of an impending death (Parkinson, 2013). Not all black Cu Sí are bad omens though; in at least some cases the appearance of the black dog was protective. In one story from Swancliffe a man has a black dog appear twice and accompany him through a dark wood only to find out later that the dog had saved him from being robbed and killed by highwaymen (Parkinson, 2013). They may also appear as guardians of treasure, something they are known for in

Scotland as the Cu Sith (Parkinson, 2013). In Ireland Cu Sí are often associated with specific fairy locations where they may be seen over the course of multiple generations and are known to sit and watch people, but they are only considered dangerous if they are disturbed, otherwise they will remain peaceful (Lenihan & Green, 2004). In at least one Irish example a small white fairy dog appeared as an omen of the coming of the Aos Sí to a home, to warn the inhabitants to prepare (Evans Wentz, 1911).

Fairy dogs may appear with the Aos Sí during Fairy Rades, or they may appear wandering on their own, guarding fairy hills, or going ahead of the Gentry to warn of their presence as described above. Black dogs seem to be territorial, favoring churchyards, roadways, and crossroads, especially where gallows have been (Parkinson, 2013). In stories they are often associated with a particular area that is considered haunted (Campbell, 2008). This ties them to the wider idea of fairies and the dead and potentially to being ghosts themselves, as well as being omens of death. Occasionally Cu Sí have been seen standing motionless on fairy hills or even among mortal dogs (Evans Wentz, 1911).

The Cu Sí are often ill-omens, but not every appearance of one presages a death or negative event. Seeing a fairy hound, especially if it is baying or howling, or even hearing one, is usually an omen of death Cu Sí can also appear for other reasons. They may be protecting a person or more often a location, in which case simply leaving the place they are guarding will usually avert any harm. They can also appear inexplicably, without ever directly harming or affecting anyone, and disappear just as mysteriously.

Cat Sí

Another animal we see in folklore is the Cat Sí (fairy cat). Cat Sí are believed to be large, Otherworldly black cats with a single white spot on the chest. The descriptions somewhat resembles the Kellas cats, large wild cats of Scotland, which has led some to theorize that sightings of them may have been the origin of the Cat Sí stories (Matthews, 2005).

Cat Sí are often believed to be shape-changed witches, and are considered to be dangerous. The folk belief was that a witch could assume the form of a Cat Sí eight times, but upon a ninth transformation would become the cat forever (Old Farmer's Almanac, 2012). There are also stories of Cat Sí as true fairies who can take human form and marry into human families. The MacGillivray family claims to have a Cat Sí among its ancestors, and it is said that the clan motto, 'Touch not this cat', comes from this ancestry (MacGillivray, 2000). It may be then that as with so many other types of fairies it is not one or the other that is correct, but that both are possible, with the Cat Sí as a cat-shaped fairy of human-like intelligence or as a previously human witch in the form of a cat.

Fairy cats are usually viewed as malicious spirits and they have a strong association with the dead, but unlike other fairies this isn't because they are believed to be the dead themselves, but rather that they are thought to steal newly dead souls. In Scotland the bodies of the newly dead are carefully watched and special protections are used to ensure that a Cat Sí doesn't sneak in and steal the soul before it has separated from the body (MacGillivray, 2000). Most of these protections depend on doing things to distract the Cat Sí and keep it away from the body, such as sprinkling catnip about the other rooms, or playing games that would draw the Cat Sí's attention (MacGillivray, 2000).

There are particular days associated with the Cat Sí. In some folklore August 17th is the night that a witch might make the ninth transformation into permanent cat form (Old Farmer's Almanac, 2012). Another cites the folk belief that on Samhain a saucer of milk should be left out as an offering to the Cat Sí to gain their blessing, while failing to do so could earn a curse on the household (MacGillivray, 2000).

Fairy Deer

In some stories it is said the deer of the forest are the cattle of the fairies, especially the red deer (McNeill, 1956; Campbell, 1900). Otherworldly deer often appear to lead people into Fairy or to places that fairies wish them to be. For example, it is said that a fairy deer and hare appeared to Thomas the Rhymer to take him back to Fairy when his time on Earth was done (Campbell, 1900). Fairies may assume the form of deer and through magic mortals can be turned into deer (MacKillop, 1998). White deer in particular are associated with the Otherworld.

Fairy Horses

There are two distinct types of fairy horses, that is there are fairies who can assume the form of horses, like the Púca, and there are horses that are native to Fairy. As with other types of fairy animals, the ones who can shape-shift are of a higher intelligence while those who are limited to the horse form are more animalistic. Fairy horses appear as almost ubiquitous with the more noble fairies who are often seen riding them; these horses may be tiny or regular sized and can move swiftly on land, fly through the air, and in some cases run over water or otherwise move through it easily. The fairy horses of the Aos Sí were renowned for their beauty and speed, and Lady Wilde described them as: *'Made of fire and flame and not of dull heavy earth.'*

Fairy Cattle

Fairy cows, especially in Wales where they are called Gwartheg Y Llyn (cattle of the lake), tend to be associated with water particularly as the name implies lakes. In Ireland and Scotland these animals were called Crod Mara (Sea Cattle) and may be brown, red, or black, all usually hornless (Briggs, 1976). The Welsh fairy cows are usually white, a common color for fairy animals.

Generally speaking fairy cows were good natured and positive omens (Briggs, 1976). It was considered fortunate if a farmer had his cows bred by a fairy bull, and several stories feature this theme with either good luck coming to those who appreciated it or ill luck to those who sought to seize the bull or tamper with the cow. Such fairy bulls acted on their own whims, but where described as good natured, sleek, and strong, features, which bred true in their offspring (Briggs, 1976). These fairy cattle may be wild or may belong to the fairies as domestic stock. In some cases though a fairy cow would appear among a mortal herd and lead the entirety of them into a fairy fort or fairy hill (Campbell, 1900).

Swans

Swans are not always what they appear to be and there were old prohibitions against killing a swan, in case it was actually a person or fairy shape-changed. We see a variety of stories where supernatural beings take the form of swans, including Aengus and his dream maiden Caer in the *Aeslinge Oenguso*, and Midir and Etain in the *Tochmarc Etaine*. White is an Otherworldly color that may create a natural association between Fairy and these birds, and they are also animals who by nature are able to travel in all three worlds of land, water, and sky, making them very liminal.

End Notes

1. We may perhaps say that the Fairy Rade is the Seelie version of the Slua Sí, if such a division can be made at all. Certainly the Rade is more orderly and civilized and less overtly malicious, although no less inherently dangerous.

2. Boggarts may also be angered Brownies and there is a somewhat fine semantic line at times between a Hobgoblin and a Brownie.

3. This section originally appeared as an article in *Air n-Aithesc* titled 'Two Views of the Leanann Sidhe'.

4. To be absolute clear here, because English can be annoying,

'fairy lover' meaning a lover who is a member of Fairy, not a human who loves fairies.

5.   I'm not going to address the Selkies as Leannán Sí because that is an entire involved topic of its own, for example, with its own rules and obligations and gets more into abductions and fairy wives/spouses. I will, however, discuss the Selkies in a separate section.

6.   Don't ask me why he still wanted to marry her at that point, I have no idea.

7.   Green is a color associated with death in Celtic lore and it is possible these children were from the land of the dead, i.e. ghosts. However, Pixies themselves were sometimes said to be the spirits of unbaptized children who had died or of the pagan dead, so it is possible these children were Pixies who became lost in our world.

Chapter 6

Fairies in Tradition

Being associated with a ceann féile (chief festival), May Eve and May Day were supposed to be times of greater than usual activity among supernatural beings, Every lios ('fairy fort') in Ireland was said to be opened that night, and their inhabitants moved abroad in great numbers, often changing residence at that time.
Seán Ó Súilleabháin, Nósanna agua Piseoga na nGael

Understanding Fairy and fairies is about more than just knowing what and where Fairy is and how to get there, and who and what the fairies are and what to expect from them. It's also about understanding their place within our world, both how they weave themselves into our reality and how intersectional humans and fairies can be, for good and ill. To that end in this chapter we will look at some ways that fairies and the human world intertwine, and in the next chapter we will discuss direct interactions between the fairies and humans.

Times, Days, and Festivals

When humans go to Fairy time becomes a mercurial and fluid thing that seems out of our control. A day there is too often a year here, or in some cases years there may be only moments here. This may give an impression that our two worlds exist untethered from each other temporally, and yet this impression is deceptive. As little control or even understanding as we may have about the way time works between our two worlds it seems that the beings of Fairy have a great knowledge of the subject that allows them to move easily between our worlds without issue. The fairies are famous for riding out in the Fairy Rade on specific holidays, for preferring or avoiding certain days of our week, and for even preferring certain times of year or times of day. Often specific set amounts of time play a role in how long a human is bound in Fairy or when they may be rescued from it; Thomas the Rhymer was taken for exactly seven years, and Tam Lin could be freed on Samhain night. Lady Wilde relates that the fairies might take a woman for seven years and then return them, and Katherine Briggs says that a changeling could win their freedom after 14 years of captivity. This makes it clear that they are very well aware of the flow of time in our world and are able to choose to interact with our world regularly and at will without missing gaps of years. As Briggs puts it: *'It is possible that the fairies can ignore time, but they are bound to the seasons.'* (Briggs, 1967, p 125)

Times of Day

Fairies are best known for appearing at liminal times, especially dawn and dusk, but also midnight. The turning points of the day, like those of the seasons, are important times of fairy influence and these include dawn, noon, sunset, and midnight (Briggs, 1967). Night in general is a more common time for fairies to be seen, but they are not limited to this of course. We see just as many stories of fairy encounters that happen during the day as during the night, demonstrating that the Fey Folk are in no way bound to the dark hours.

Days of the Week and Tides of the Moon

There are several days of the week that are known be special to the fairies and to be times when they have more influence and are more active than others. Wednesday by some accounts is such a day (Briggs, 1967). According to Lady Wilde, the fairies are most active on Fridays and have the greatest power on this day; it is also on Fridays that they are most likely to abduct people (Wilde, 1888). Briggs refers to Friday as *'the fairies' Sunday'* and agrees that it is the day they have the greatest power over Earthly things (Briggs, 1967). It is uncertain why exactly this day has such great significance to the Fey Folk, but one might surmise that the belief is rooted in a Christian world view that sees Friday as an unlucky day because of its association with Christ's crucifixion. I suspect that the folk beliefs surrounding Friday as unlucky, perhaps shaded with the idea that it was a day with the least divine influence from a monotheistic perspective, lent itself to the view that it was the day when the fairies had the most influence. It is believed that on Friday the fairies approach houses from the west and may enter as they please, going so far as to get into whatever might be cooking for dinner (Campbell, 1900). Because they have special power on this day and are actively abroad, many folk traditions are aimed at either appeasing them or warding against them especially on this day.

Just as there was a day that was seen as almost belonging to the fairies, other days are believed to offer some protection against them. In Scottish lore the fairies were prohibited from being abroad on Thursdays, as that was Saint Columba's Day, and so Thursday was the day a person was safest from fairy interference (McNeill, 1956). In the Highlands it is said that on Thursday the Good People cannot hear anything said about them, and in these areas all the days from Thursday through Sunday are seen as safe from fairy influence (Briggs, 1967). More generally Sunday was viewed as a day that was anathema to the Good People, and they seem to be offended by the mere mention of it (Briggs, 1967).

The fairies are also apparently tied to the cycle of the moon. The full moon and the days immediately before and after it are days of fairy activity (Briggs, 1967).

Holidays Associated with the Fairies

There are several holidays throughout the year associated with the fairies, usually as times when they were known to be more active or more present in our world. Some of these include the quarter days of Bealtaine, Lughnasa, Samhain, and Imbolc[1], as well as June 24th (Saint John's Eve), and New Year's Eve. The importance of Bealtaine and Samhain as turning points of the year, as well as the time around the solar turning points of the solstices, all being significant to the Good People suggests that the fairy beliefs we have today may have once been beliefs from two separate groups, one based on farming and one on herding, which became joined at some point (Briggs, 1967). The fairies are keenly interested in both cows and crops so there is a logic in them being drawn to holidays that focus on such things.

Bealtaine

Bealtaine has many different themes and associations in folklore, but one of the strongest is the idea that fairies are especially active at this time. For example, one belief was that on Bealtaine day it was wise not to lend out any milk, salt, butter, or a coal from the fire, especially to a stranger, lest the person be one of the Good Folk in disguise and take the family's luck for the year (Wilde, 1888; Evans, 1957). A household's luck was intrinsically tied to the items that symbolized it – milk, butter, salt, and fire – and to give any of these to supernatural beings such as the Fair Folk was to voluntarily give them power over you; to do this particularly on Bealtaine or the other fire festivals, when spirits of all kinds were abroad and their powers especially strong, was the height of foolishness.

Every sí was believed to open and the inhabitants to travel out across the land, a process repeated as well at Samhain. Bealtaine was also the time when babies and young brides were most likely to be taken and a person had to take great care when travelling, especially alone. Bealtaine and Samhain were liminal rimes, turning points of the year from one season to another and times traditionally when the rent was due. Because of this shifting there was an association with the time of year and the Good People moving their homes, meaning that they were abroad in greater numbers and more times than usual. At other times of the year a person might still be at risk of running afoul of the Fair Folk – or, if one was lucky and clever, of earning their blessing – but at the turning points like Bealtaine the presence of the Other Crowd was ubiquitous, to the point that it was almost expected to see or experience something Otherworldly. To quote Danaher:

> *Supernatural beings were more than usually active about May Day, and the appearance of a travelling band of fairies, of a mermaid, a púca or a headless coach might, indeed, cause unease or alarm but certainly would occasion no surprise, as such manifestations were only to be expected at this time.*
>
> (Danaher, 1972, p121)

There were two main, possibly interlinked, approaches to dealing with the fairies on Bealtaine. In the old days – and perhaps still in some places – it was traditional to make offerings on Bealtaine morning of milk poured at the base of a fairy thorn or on the threshold of the house, and to take the cows to the sí and bleed them, with some of the blood tasted by the people and the rest given as an offering to the fairies (Evans, 1957). I personally try to avoid making blood offerings during most of the year, but some exceptions may occur on the major holy days, and we see a precedent in both Irish and Norse belief of offering such to the Aos Sí or Elben (Elves) respectively[2]. Any offering of food or drink, left on the doorstep of the house or at any known Fairy place, whether it's a lone fairy tree or fort, was also done and was thought to convey some protection on the person (Danaher, 1972). I would also suggest that offerings of butter, bread, or cakes would be in line with tradition and acceptable. Offerings are an important part of creating a positive reciprocal relationship with the powers of the Otherworld and of averting any potential harm or mischief from them.

Midsummer

Midsummer and the closely related Saint John's Eve on June 24th are days that have a lot of associations with fairies. Generally the encounters with fairies on midsummer in folklore are of a more benevolent or playful nature, although the Amadán na Bruidhne roams in June and is decidedly dangerous. A good theatrical description of fairies around this time of year is seen in Shakespeare's *A Midsummer Night's Dream* where much mischief occurs while the fairies are mingling with mortals in the woods, but ultimately no harm is done. In the story of *Oíche na Féile Eoin* we see the same theme, with a group of boys who are overheard by the fairies claiming not to believe in them being lured away from the bonfires and turned into horses for the night then ridden hard across the country by the Good People only to wake up as boys again under a fairy thorn in the morning (MacLiammóir, 1984). Although the boys endure an unpleasant night they are not truly harmed and afterwards come to believe in the fairies they formerly joked about.

Bonfires are lit at midsummer for luck, blessing, and protection and the ashes of these fires have many uses in protective charms. Similarly bonfires are also lit on Saint John's Eve for the same reasons, with fire-leaping practiced for fertility and good luck. The fairies may appear as a whirlwind and try to extinguish the fires (Wilde, 1888). There were also some older beliefs that several harvest traditions, once associated with Lughnasa, were moved to Saint John's Eve with the advent of Christianity in Ireland, including offering beef into the fires (MacNeill, 1962). People celebrating at the bonfires, such as those held at Cnoc Áine, told stories of seeing the fairies joining in the celebrations.

Lughnasa

Fairies have a vested interest in the harvest although they tend to be more active at the end of it, Samhain, than at the beginning. An anecdotal tale from 1879 said that the 'Sídhfir', the fairy men, used to work the fields during the harvest alongside humans until Saint Patrick declared during a holy mass that the Good People would not achieve Heaven until Judgment Day; from that moment on the fairies would do no work to help take in the harvest (MacNeill, 1962). A similar story recorded in 1942 claimed that the hosts of the air used to help gather the harvest hoping to earn their way back into Heaven, but as in the first story they asked someone to go to the priest with a question. In this case they wanted to know the three groups who would never gain entry to Heaven, and of course their number was included in the answer the priest gave, which caused them to turn from helping people to causing trouble instead (MacNeill, 1962). Although this is clearly given to us through a Christian lens, and with the idea of fairies as fallen angels seeking re-entry to Heaven, it nonetheless ties in with older pagan themes as well, specifically of the strong connection between fairies and the success or failure of the harvest. We can also perhaps see in these stories a reflection of an older idea that fairies once actively aided in the autumn harvest, until they were offended in some way.

There is another very old belief relating to the harvest, that is that the fairies took a tithe of all that was gathered and that the best of what was gathered belonged to them. These two quotes from *The Festival of Lughnasa* illustrate the belief:

The top pickle [best] of all grain belongs to the Gintry [Gentry]; sometimes they claim it, and sometimes not, accordin' as it's required.
County Antrim 1859

The tip-top pickle [best] of all the corn [grain] belonged to them [the Good People]. That was collected from one and all.
County Armagh, 1938

This process is not nearly as peaceful or smooth as it may sound and some of the harvest beliefs hinge on the idea that the Irish fairies, who live in various courts led by an assortment of Queens or Kings, will fight each other for the best harvest of each area. The Good People of County Kerry and County Cork fight each other for the harvest of both counties, for example, and the fairies of Connacht and Ulster fight each other, and whoever wins the crops gathered in that county will be good while the crops of the other county are not (MacNeill, 1962).

Both the Fairy Queen Áine and King Midir have associations with this holiday. It is said that around this time Áine is the consort of the chthonic being Crom Dubh or Crom Cruach, and appears in a very fierce aspect. Midir is known to take children who wander on his sí in the first week of August. The Fairy King Donn is also said to have some connection to Lughnasa, as some folklore recounts offerings of a roosters being made to him at his sí on this date (Logan, 1981).

Samhain

On the night of Samhain the many supernatural beings, including ghosts, roamed freely and the fairy hills were opened, allowing all the creatures of fairy into the mortal world (Estyn Evans, 1957; McNeill, 1961). Just as all the dead were free to return to Earth to visit on Samhain so the realm of Faery was given free rein, reiterating the blurry line between faeries and the dead. As at Bealtaine the denizens of fairy were more likely to be encountered now and it was said that should a person meet a Fairy Rade or the Slua Sí and throw the dust from under his feet at them they would be compelled to release any humans they had taken (Danaher, 1972). This night was one of celebration and merry making, but people preferred to travel in groups, fearing that to walk alone on Samhain risked being taken forever into Fairy (Danaher, 1972). It was thought that dusk and midnight were particularly dangerous times, and that the fairy troops passed to the west side of homes and along waterways, making it best to avoid these times and places (McNeill, 1961). It was also a long time custom to shout out 'seachain' (beware) or 'chughaibh an t-uisce' (water towards you) if one was tossing water out of the home so that any passing fairies would be warned (Danaher, 1972). This was meant to avoid accidently throwing dirty water on the fairies, which would certainly anger them and result in retribution from the offended being.

This is the time that all the fairy sí open up and the inhabitants parade from one hill to the next in grand processions playing music, which some people claim to hear (Danaher, 1972; McNeill, 1961). Anyone who had been kidnapped to Fairy could be freed within the first year and a day from when they were taken, but the spells to do so were strongest on Samhain, as we can see in the ballad of *Tam Lin* (McNeill, 1961). Because the faeries were all abroad it was also the custom in many places to leave them food offerings, but unlike the plates of food left for the dead, the food offerings for fairies might take the form a rich porridge that was made and then placed in a small pit dug in the ground (Sjoestedt, 1949).

All produce left in the fields after this time belonged to the Good People and it was taboo to gather it or eat it. By many accounts the Púca was said to either spit or urinate on anything left out, especially wild berries, while in other accounts it is the fairies more generally that spit on them (MacNeill, 1962; Danaher, 1972). This may be a way to keep people from eating fruit that has gone bad or a way to be certain that the fairies are left their proper due of the wild harvest.

New Year

We don't have any strong midwinter solstice traditions relating to the fairies that have been clearly preserved in folklore, but we do have beliefs from that general time of year. New Year's Eve was another point when the fairies were thought to be more active and more likely to be encountered. In Irish belief it was said that the fairies were likely to be out and about and people should avoid traveling on New Year's Eve to avoid danger (Evans, 1957). The house is decorated with holly on New Year's Eve to ward off the fairies, and the last of the wheat is dressed us a harvest maiden with the belief that this will keep the fairies away until the next harvest (Campbell, 1900).

Fairy Roads

When the Good People travel out, whether in Fairy Rades or otherwise, they do so on established routes. These are known as fairy roads or paths and great care must be taken to avoid them on the festival days and at night, and it is also dangerous to build on them. In Ireland there were several methods for divining if the location of a new house might intersect with such a road, and these were employed before building was begin to ensure the Other Crowd weren't angered. A small shovel might be left in the ground at the site overnight, or a line of stones set up, and if either were disturbed the next morning it indicated that the site should not be used (Evans, 1957). If a person was foolish enough to build on a fairy road anyway than the family who lived in the home would have nothing but bad luck. The milk from the cows would all be spilled, there would be noise at all hours, and in some cases people would even die (Logan, 1981). There was nothing to be done to get the fairies to change their course or reroute their road, it was the humans who had to be aware and be careful not to build on or too near them.

Dependence on Humans

Human and fairy life is intertwined in complex ways, and has been, I believe, possibly forever. There are aspects of this dependence that is obvious and will be discussed in greater depth in the next chapter, including the need by the Good People to take humans for both breeding stock and servants. This dependence is more complex than just what they take from us, however. It has long been a belief, for example, in homes that use fire for heat, that the fire should be kept banked but burning at night for the fairies who come in during the dark hours to warm themselves (Evans, 1957). Why do they do this? No one is certain, but it speaks of a personal level of interaction. They not only expect to be able to enter at will, but to receive a warm welcome (literally) when they are there.

Perhaps one of the most famous areas in which the Other Crowd are known to be dependent on humans relates to childbirth, specifically the skills of the midwife. While we see Queen Mab referred to as the midwife of the fairies, generally speaking it would seem that midwives were a rare commodity and when a woman was ready to deliver a baby the fairies looked to humans for assistance. In some cases this went well, with stories of women called out into the night to deliver such babies being richly rewarded for their efforts, until – after several such deliveries – they finally realized it was a fairy and not a human child they were delivering and they were never called on again. However, in many other versions of these stories, both folkloric and anecdotal, it does not end as well with the human midwife accidentally touching one of her eyes with an ointment she was asked to anoint the newborn's eyes with and gaining true sight into Fairy. Once this occurred and she made it known she could see the Fey Folk for what they were, if she was lucky, only the single eye that possessed the special vision was put out; if she was not lucky she would be blinded entirely. Why do they need to borrow human midwives? We could surmise that the birthrate is so low compared to human birthrates that they have no professional midwives of their own and are forced to borrow from humans to meet this critical need.

In some cases fairies also seem to require human presence or participation in order to engage in specific activities in our world. In *Celtic Twilight*, W. B. Yeats relates a tale of two groups of fairies who want to have a hurling match, but need to find a human willing to play with them in order to be able to touch anything in our world. Similarly, in *The Fairy Faith in Celtic Countries,* W. Y. Evans Wentz gives several anecdotes discussing the fairies' need for human participants in order to have games of hurling or for two factions of the Good People to fight each other. It is possible in this case that the idea of needing a human represents the need for an anchor in world, something of this world to tie them here while they focus on competing. However, I find this somewhat questionable since in many other accounts the Fey Folk can easily go from insubstantial to substantial at will and choose to interact with things in our world, even picking people and animals up and carrying them off. It is also possible, I think, that this need for a human participant has nothing to do with making them more corporeal here and in fact represents the introduction of a neutral third party to witness the competition. A method, if you will, of keeping both sides honest.

Fairies also occasionally borrow from people, reflecting another layer of dependence. In some cases this borrowing may be of grain or produce, which is later paid back, although not always in kind and the Good Neighbors are known to give more than they originally took. In other instances, which may be less easily categorized as borrowing per se, a fairy mother might ask a human mother to nurse her child once or a human might be prevailed on to help fix a broken item (Briggs, 1976). In these cases we may describe this type of borrowing as one of a skill, such as the loan of a midwife mentioned above, rather than of a physical object. Themselves are also known to borrow, or outright steal, handmills as well as borrowing the use of mills at night when humans are not using them. All of these examples show a tendency to borrow things the fairies themselves are in need of, but do not have. However, there is a sense of honor in the borrowing and usually a repayment to the lender not only in kind for the loan in many cases, but also often of good fortune and friendship.

Food and Drink

When a person is in Fairy it is generally unwise to accept any food or drink, because as a rule to eat or drink the offerings of Fairy usually means to be bound to it. There are some exceptions to this, which seem to hinge on the fairies choosing to release a person, but in the bulk of folklore accepting even a bite of food or sip of drink could mean you would never return to mortal Earth. In many stories we see a person saved by the intercession of another, someone who was once mortal and who was themselves taken, who knows the dangers of eating fairy food and warns the new person. For example in a story from Ballard's *Fairies and the Supernatural on Reachrai* from the anthology *The Good People,* a midwife was called to attend a fairy birth and afterwards the fairies asked her to stay with them and she refused, so they offered her something to eat. She was going to accept it, but a young human woman sitting nearby nursing a baby began to sing in Irish: *'Eat nothing, drink nothing, or don't stay the night,'* and the midwife heeded the warning and refused, asking instead be taken back home (Ballard, 1991, p56).

In contrast, however, the fairies have long been known to take food as well as milk from people. It is possible that this does not have the same effect on them when they take it from us because it is owed to them as part of their due for blessing the harvest and prosperity of the herds. This may be part of the wider belief that people long ago entered into an agreement with the Gods and by extension fairies to give them part of the harvest – grain and milk – in exchange for such a blessing, which is still reflected in the idea that the fairies are due a tithe of the harvest each year[3].

There are a variety of folk beliefs based around sharing with the fey to avoid them stealing what they want. One practice was to give any food that was dropped on the ground to them, in the belief that they caused it to be dropped as a way to indicate that they wanted it (Evans-Wentz, 1911). Another was to pour out a small amount of whatever a person was drinking if they were outside, to give some of it to the fairies (Danaher, 1972). In this way we are sharing what we have with them by giving it freely instead of having it taken forcibly or stolen. It is, arguably, better to have a positive reciprocal relationship with them than an antagonistic one.

Fairy Music

The fairies are famous both for their love of musicians and for their own enchanting music. The fairies love good music and dancing and they appreciate true musical talent. As with so many other things Fairy, this is a double-edged blade as the music of Fairy can be both a blessing and a curse, and the gifts that fairies are able to grant to the musicians they favor are often the same.

Musicians have long been one of the groups of people who may be taken by the fairies, but unlike most others, musicians are generally only borrowed, sometimes for as little as a single night, to provide entertainment for the fairies. In at least one case from the Isle of Skye though the man was told when he was returned that he would have to go back to the Fairy Queen when she called him, and so when that day came he left behind his family and rejoined Fairy (Logan, 1981). A musician known to have been taken by the fairies often gained a reputation for his skill and knowledge (Jenkins, 1991). To please the fairies with your talent earned great reward, but to fail to please them or to defy them could be very dangerous. In one story a piper was invited to play for the Gentry and did so, but growing tired he finally said he could play no more; the Fairy Queen asked him for one more song and he refused her so she cursed him, saying that he would never play another song again.

To hear the music of Fairy often means to be enchanted and entrapped by the Otherworld. Many who hear this music never entirely escape the allure of its melody, although some are blessed with great inspiration from it. The renowned Irish musician Turlough O'Carolan was said to have received the gift of his talent and many of his songs by sleeping on a fairy mound (Logan, 1981). However, a group of women who heard fairy music while they were at the shore gathering shellfish danced to the sound until they were physically ill from the exertion (Evans-Wentz, 1911). In other cases people only hear a little bit of the melody and are none the worse for it. Those who have heard the music of Fairy describe it as incomparably beautiful, but also often melancholy or haunting. Once you hear it you never really forget it.

Fairy Rings

One particular bit of folklore that is still especially relevant today is that of fairy rings, also called fairy circles, Elf rings, or Elf circles. In Welsh they may be known as cylch y Tylwyth Teg (literally 'circle of the Fair Family'). The concept of these rings can be found throughout the different Celtic language-speaking countries as well as the various diaspora and some Anglo-Saxon and German lore as well. Fairy rings appear as either a dark circle of grass or as mushrooms growing together in a ring, and less often as a circle of small stones. It is said in folklore and common belief that this ring marks a place where the fairies have danced or where they like to dance. In the 12th century there was an Anglo-Saxon belief that attributed fairy rings to the dancing of female Elves (Hall, 2007). The fairies love of dancing is well known as is their penchant to take people who disturb their revelry, either as a punishment or through a desire to keep the person in Fairy (Evans-Wentz, 1911).

Fairy rings can appear in different sizes, from three feet across to ten times that size (Bennett, 1991; Gwyndaf, 1991). If they were the sort made of darker green within a field of grass then they would be either moss or much darker green grass and were notable because 'no rushes or anything grew on it' (Gwyndaf, 1991). From a scientific perspective fairy rings are created by the fungus mycelium and when they grow above ground can include a variety of mushroom species, both poisonous and edible. Even the dark grass circles are the result of mycelium though, as the fungus naturally grows upwards and outwards in an expanding circle and affects the nutrient content of the soil, resulting in the visible fairy ring effect (Mushroom Appreciation, 2016). Of course, the scientific explanation doesn't necessarily contradict the fairylore explanation, and the two beliefs are compatible with each other. In some folklore it isn't the fairies' dancing that causes the circle, but rather the existence of the circle that draws the fairies to dance there (Bennett, 2001).

A person who comes upon an active fairy ring might see the dancers within it, and even the instruments, but hear nothing from outside, although in other stories hearing the music acts as a lure to draw an unsuspecting mortal in. Most people had a clear aversion to the idea of entering a fairy ring as it was known to do so risked the fairies coming and taking the person away. In one Welsh story preserved in the late 20th century a person was questioned about why they avoided fairy rings and they relayed the tale of a boy named Robin Jones who entered a fairy circle one evening; he saw the fairies dancing and after what seemed to him a few hours in their company he asked to leave only to return home to find that a hundred years had passed (Gwyndaf, 1991). In a similar tale a man stopped outside a fairy ring, just to watch the fairies dance within for a few hours, and lost fifteen years of time for his dallying (Gwyndaf, 1991). Some fairy rings appear to have been used as a sort of trap to intentionally lure mortals, especially children, that the Fey Folk wished to take and these people if they entered the ring would never be returned (Evans-Wentz, 1911). Other times, however, it seems to be only chance that leads a person to find fairies dancing in a ring; in accounts from Brittany some who join them are treated well and released unharmed while those who offend them while they dance are forced to join the circle until they collapse from exhaustion or die (Evans-Wentz, 1911).

Once in a fairy ring, by choice or by compulsion, a person could not leave unless they were freed by the Good Folk or rescued by another human being. Often the person would dance for what seemed like a night to them, or even only a few minutes, and then be allowed to leave only to find that a year or more had passed. In one Scottish take a man fell asleep in the middle of a fairy ring and woke to find himself being carried through the air by the angry fairies who dumped him in a city many miles away (Briggs, 1978). Several options were available for those seeking to rescue a comrade from a fairy ring. One Welsh method of securing a person's release was to place a stick of rowan across the boundary of the ring, breaking it (Gwyndaf, 1991). Some suggest throwing specific herbs, including thyme, into the circle, and of course iron is seen as superlative method of both disrupting a fairy ring and protecting oneself from angry fey (Hartland, 1891). Any iron object would suffice and could be used to break the edge of the ring or could be tossed into the circle to disrupt the dancing. Another method was for someone safely outside the circle to reach in, sometimes by stepping on the perimeter of the ring, and grab the person as they danced past (Briggs, 1978). Even if they were rescued though, many times the person could not truly be saved, and those who had danced with the fairies in a fairy ring were known to pine away afterwards or else, if they had been taken for a length of time and allowed to leave they might rapidly age or turn to dust when the truth of their long absence from mortal Earth was revealed to them in their home place, now occupied by strangers (Brigg, 1978).

There is a strong belief that if one finds a fairy ring it should not be disturbed, not only because of the possible danger, but also because there is a sacredness to the space set aside within them. If one were to damage a mushroom associated with a fairy ring, reparations would be offered to avoid punishment (Bennett, 1991). In Scotland and Wales it was generally unthinkable by those who believed in the Good Folk to consider intentionally damaging the ring or mushrooms, and it was believed that those who did so would be cursed (Bennett, 1991; Gwyndaf, 1991). In one Irish story a farmer who knowingly built a barn on a fairy ring fell unconscious afterwards and had a vision telling him to take down the barn (Wilde, 1888).

Fairy rings are still found today although perhaps fewer people see the footsteps of the fey in them, and more see the science of mycelium. In the spirit of tradition though it doesn't have to be one or the other, but can be both, in truth, and we can still see the enchantment and sacredness of the footsteps of the Good People in fairy rings without denying the knowledge of their natural cause. If you keep your eyes open and your senses sharp you may find a ring of dark grass or newly grown mushrooms in your yard or the area you live in.

Although perhaps you'll think twice about stepping across its boundary.

Scottish Fairies and the Teind to Hell

There's an interesting folkloric belief in Scotland that says the Good Neighbors owe a teind (tithe) to Hell that must be paid regularly. This idea first appears in writing in two poems and spread from there, entering wider belief and becoming popular particularly in the modern period. One thing that makes the teind interesting is that it is not found in Ireland or other Celtic areas with shared fairy beliefs, nor was it a common idea throughout Scotland until a much later period. Originally the concept of the teind was seen only along the southern border. For example in his extensive writing on the Scottish fairies in the 17th century the Rev. Robert Kirk makes no mention of such a teind. It does appear in one 16th century witchcraft trial in Edinburgh, but only one, despite the many times fairies were discussed by accused witches. Despite this, today it is an idea that is familiar to many people who are interested in the Good Folk, and it is often accepted as both factual and ubiquitous to all fairies.

The evidence relating to the teind suggests that this may be a focused regional belief rather than a more widespread one, appearing first in the areas around the river Tweed. The textual evidence for it is tied by place and personal names into the area around Dryburgh Abbey and Melrose along the Tweed as we see in its first appearance in *Thomas of Erceldoune*, later known as *Thomas the Rhymer*, a 15th century poem (Murray, 1918). The second oldest literary source for the teind is the ballad of *Tam Lin* dating to the 16th century, set at Carterhaugh in Selkirk, also near the Tweed, along one of its tributaries (Murray, 1922). The two locations are about eight miles apart. The Rev. Kirk was living and writing in Aberfoyle, about 80 miles to the north, which may explain why he seems to have had no knowledge of this tithe. This geographic difference may have been significant, and part of the explanation for why the teind seems to have been so strongly present in one specific area and almost unknown elsewhere until the story of it spread much later.

The teind is based in the idea that the fairies must pay a tribute to Hell on a regular basis, generally said to be every seven years (Briggs, 1976). The exact agreement and terms vary by source, while agreeing on the general concept. The single witch-craft confession claimed it was a yearly tithe and the two poems clearly state it is paid every seven years. It is also called both a teind in some variations and a kane in others; teind in Scots means tithe, a payment of a tenth part, while kane is a Scots word for a payment by a renter to his landlord (Lyle, 1970). The difference between a teind and a kane is significant, as the first implies the loss of a tenth of the population every seven years, if we assume seven years was the standard, and the second does not. Indeed the various texts of Tam Lin often imply that he expects to be the only one given to Hell as he says, *'I fear 'twill be myself'* (Lyle, 1970). There may be more logic to the idea of a single offering rather than of a tenth of the entire population being given every year or every seven years, but the evidence exists to support either interpretation.

In the 16th century trial of Alison Pearson, the accused witch confessed to learning her craft from the fairies and said that, *'every year the tithe of them [the fairies) were taken away to Hell'* (Scott, 1830). *Thomas of Erceldoune* references the Devil fetching his fee from the fairies and suggests that Thomas will be chosen because he is so strong and pleasant:

To Morne, of helle the foulle fende,
Amange this folke will feche his fee;
And thou arte mekill mane and hende,
I trowe wele he wode chese thee.
(Murray, 1918)
(In the morning, the foul fiend of Hell,
Among this folk will fetch his fee;
And you are very strong and pleasant,
I well believe he would choose you)

Similarly Tam Lin, while pleading with his lover to save him from his fate, says that:

But aye at every seven years,
They pay the teind to Hell;
And I am sae fat and fair of flesh
I fear 'twill be mysell.
(Child, 1802)

This seems to suggest two important things. Firstly the tithe was a regularly anticipated event and secondly those chosen for the teind are picked for physical health and personality. As with tithes of crops it is the best that are chosen and given, so in both poems the ones who would be given for this tithe try to avoid their fate. Although the teind in general has a heavily Christian overtone one might see in this aspect perhaps hints of an older pagan reflection, where a sacrificial animal chosen for a deity would always be of the best quality, unblemished, and usually of good temperament.

The core concept behind this payment seems to be the idea that the fairies are the vassals or subjects of Hell and its ruler and so owe it and him rent on a set basis. This rent is paid, we might say, in the currency of Hell – people. Lyle's article *The Teind to Hell in Tam Lin* argues that the belief in the teind grew out of a need to explain the belief in changelings (Lyle, 1970). From this perspective in seeking to understand why fairies stole human beings, people came to fit them and their motives into a Christian worldview. Fairies were seen as fallen angels who lived as tenants to the Devil, trapped as it were outside of both Heaven and Hell they needed to pay rent to their landlord and did so by stealing humans to spare having to give up their own folk. A key aspect to this argument is the fact that in both poems the teind is due to be paid the next morning and the men in the story can be saved that night if they escape Fairy before the payment is made (Lyle, 1970). In Tam Lin this occurs explicitly on Samhain, a time in Scotland when the bi-annual rents were traditionally paid, supporting the idea that the tithe or kane was a rent payment (Lyle, 1970).

It is entirely possible that Lyle is correct and that the teind is a later folk belief, dating to the mid second millennia, and created to explain why fairies were thought to steal humans away from their own kind. Certainly it has many layers of such belief attached to it, including the taking of humans and danger to those humans should they remain in Fairy and not return to mortal Earth, and it is impossible to ever know the ultimate roots of the beliefs now. However, it is also possible that the ideas behind the teind may reflect older, highly localized beliefs that might tentatively be suggested were originally related to offerings or sacrifices to the spirits of the area or perhaps a deity of the river Tweed. One could guess that these offerings may originally have been of goods or animals, but were later confused with the stories of fairy abductions and changelings to create the folklore in its current form. If the Christian overtones are stripped away and we remove the references to Hell and the Devil, which may safely be said to be much later additions to any potentially earlier beliefs, what is left is a septennial sacrifice of either a single individual or a tenth portion – a tithe – paid as a form of rent by the fairy inhabitants of the area of the river Tweed around Melrose. One might even go further and suggest that during the pagan period this payment was most likely from the human inhabitants to the fey in that area or perhaps to the deity of that river itself. The Celts, et al., were known for worshiping river deities and for making votive sacrifices to rivers, so such an idea is not at all out of place with what is known of native pagan religion (MacCulloch, 1911). Indeed, there are some parallels to Manx tradition where it is said in a 16th century poem to Manannán that every landholder had to pay the God a yearly rent in the form of rushes (MacQuarrie, 1997). Traditional Fairy Faith beliefs as well would support the idea of the importance of specific areas to very specific beings and practices as well as the idea that a belief might be highly localized, especially prior to modern technology and the spread of literacy (Evans-Wentz, 1911). It is possible that after Christianization the beliefs were either changed to reflect the new cosmology, to fit into the new belief system, or else over time the older beliefs were confused and twisted when they stopped being followed and melded with other extant fairy beliefs about changelings.

So, ultimately, we can conclude that the teind is a fascinating and unique belief found in the southern area of Scotland in about the 16th century. At that point it reflected the idea that the fairies paid rent to Hell in the form of lives, preferably stolen human ones, probably once every seven years. A person who had been taken by the fey could avoid being this teind if they could be rescued from Fairy, or flee it, on the eve of the payment, otherwise if they were fair enough and well-mannered enough the Fairy Queen may give them in payment. This fitted into the worldview at the time, which placed fairies as beings that were neither good nor evil and existed between the realms of Heaven and Hell, but owed allegiance to Hell as fallen angels, albeit not demons themselves. The belief itself might be a way to explain why the fairies took humans to begin with and left changelings, or it could perhaps be an echo of an older pagan practice or offering sacrifices to the spirits themselves for the humans to pay rent, as it were, to live in the territory of the Gods or fey. Ultimately we will never know with certainty, but it is an interesting subject to contemplate.

Elfshot

In both Irish and Scottish fairylore 'elfshot' or 'elf-arrows' are a type of small weapon used by the Good Folk, and in Scotland also by witches, against people and livestock. The ubiquitous weapons of the fey, elfshot caused a variety of maladies to those struck by them. The arrows themselves, when found on the ground, are small Neolithic flint arrowheads, but when used by the Gentry are invisible to mortal eyes as are the wounds they cause. Finding such a small piece of flint or primitive arrowhead lying on the ground might lead a person to believe they had found a fairy-dart (O hOgain, 1995) and indeed such arrows are occasionally found and thought to be significant and powerful, for good or ill.

In Scotland they were called 'saighead sith' (fairy arrows) and finding one on the ground was believed to bring a person good luck (McNeill, 1956). Indeed although being struck by one could be calamitous, finding one was auspicious and it would be kept afterwards as a talisman. While some believed a found elf-arrow should be thrown in water or buried lest it draw Otherworldly attentions, to others it was a powerful talisman, although it had to be kept covered from sunlight and not allowed to touch the ground again (Black, 1894; Wilde, 1888; Evans, 1957). It was believed in Scotland that elf-arrows could not be found if a person was searching for one, but were only found by accident and usually in an odd or unexpected way (Black, 1894). This might include appearing in one's possessions or clothing after a walk outdoors or even in one's shoe. Lady Wilde, however, mentions the Irish belief that 'fairy stones' were often found near sí (fairy hills) lying on the ground, and adds no particular prohibition against intentionally looking for them. To possess an elf-arrow was good luck and they had magical uses as well, being used in cures for sick cattle as well as herbal charms (Wilde, 1888; Evans, 1957). There are several examples of found elfshot from Scotland that were set in silver and worn as pendants, because of the belief that they were protective talismans.

When used as weapons by the Other Crowd elfshot was thought to be the direct cause of elf-stroke or fairy-stroke. This fairy-stroke could take the form of a sudden seizure or paralysis, cramping, pain, bruising, wasting sicknesses, and even death (Briggs, 1976). The most distinctive type of elfshot was a sudden, inexplicable shooting pain, usually internal (Hall, 2007). The fairies might use elfshot for anything from punishing someone for a minor offense, in which case the effect might be slight and temporary, to tormenting a person with great pain and suffering if they were truly angry. If they wanted to take a person they might use elfshot to paralyze them then switch the person with a changeling or a glamoured item such as a log (Briggs, 1976). If they wanted to take cattle a similar procedure was used, where the animal was shot and would waste away and die, thus going to the fairies (O hOgain, 1995). The phrase 'fairy stroke' in Old Irish is 'póc aosáin', which literally means 'fairies' kiss'; áesán itself means both fairies and the sickness caused by fairies.

Witches as well as fairies were said to use elfshot, especially in Scotland. In several witch trial people confessed to using elfshot to harm others, and Isobel Gowdie in her confession claimed to have seen the shot being made when she was visiting among the fairies (Briggs, 1976). In her telling she said she had gone with the fairies and saw the Devil himself making the shot and handing it to 'Elf boys' who sharpened them and prepared them. She claimed that they were then given to the mortal witches to be used with a short chant and that the shot was fired by being flicked off the thumb with a fingernail (Black, 1894; Briggs, 1976). In Ireland witches were not known to use elfshot, rather having a reputation for 'blinking' or putting the evil eye on cattle or people instead, but there were other similarities between Irish witches and fairies and it was said that witches learned from the fairies (Jenkins, 1991; Wilde, 1888).

Cures for elfshot varied. For people there are a variety of charms, drinks, and salves to be found in the old Anglo-Saxon Leechbooks. Usually a person would be diagnosed with an Elf-related ailment, often involving sudden internal pain or an illness that was traditionally attributed to Elves, then a cure would be prepared and given in conjunction with a chanted or spoken charm or prayer (Hall, 2007; Jolly;1996). For horses as well the Leechbook offers possible cures that involve a combination of actions, including shedding the animal's blood, and spoken charms (Jolly, 1996). For cattle, animals might be rubbed with salt water and made to drink a portion, given water that had both salt and silver in it, or rubbed with a found elf-arrow, which was believed to have curative powers (Black, 1894). One approach in Ireland was to spill a bit of the cow's blood in a ceremony dedicating the animal to Saint Martin (Evans, 1957). Often a specialist, a fairy doctor or wise woman (Bean Feasa), would be called in first to verify that a person or animal had been elfshot and if necessary to effect the cure (Jenkins, 1991). In some cases the effect of the shot was deemed permanent and could not be cured at all or the cure applied would not be strong enough to be effective. In some cases, tragically especially in relation to suspected changelings, the cure itself would prove fatal.

Elfshot by any of the many names it has gone by – elf-arrows, fairy arrows, fairy darts, fairy stones, saighead sith – are fascinating items. Terribly dangerous if they strike a person or animal they are a fearsome weapon of the Good People. Their effects can be transitory or permanent and may be mitigated with magical charms and herbal cures, and ironically the same exact shot that causes the injury can be used to cure it when wielded by a well-intentioned human hand. As dangerous as elfshot can be if it strikes a person, it is also a wonderful talisman to possess if you happen to find one – but only if you remember to keep it with proper care, away from sunlight and off the ground, lest the Good Folk come back to reclaim it.

End Notes

1. I include Imbolc because all of the quarter days are mentioned in the sources. However, I have not found any explicit references to fairy traditions or superstitions relating to Imbolc.
2. In Grimm's *Teutonic Mythology* he discusses the practice of offering a cow to the Elves as part of an alfablot
3. The idea of this tithe was discussed in more depth in the previous section on Lughnasa and can be researched further in MacNeill's book *The Festival of Lughnasa*. I did previously mention the power of human food to convert a member of Fairy to a mortal, but I suspect that is situation-specific, that is when they are taking food from us as an offering or a tithe, or taking the essence of the food, it negates the power of that food over them. Only when they are bound to Earth and also consuming the produce of the Earth as it is, unaltered, does it affect them the way that fairy food affects mortals taken into Fairy.

Chapter 7

Mortal Interactions

'I have won me a youth,' the Elf Queen said,
'The fairest that earth may see;
This night I have won young Elph Irving
My cupbearer to be.
His service lasts but for seven sweet years,
And his wage is a kiss of me.'
The Faerie Oak of Corriewater

As we've already seen by looking at fairies in tradition there is a great deal of entanglement between the world of Fairy and mortal Earth, and between the beings of Fairy and humans. There is a dependence between the two peoples that is complex and goes back a long way indeed. This almost symbiotic relationship is more than just a matter of our worlds intersecting, or our need to appease them to ensure good crops. For good or ill they can affect us in profound ways and we can, perhaps, affect them as well. In this chapter I want to take a closer and deeper look specifically at mortal interactions with fairies and what we may be able to learn from these stories.

The Goblin Market

There is a long tradition in folklore of various fairy markets, places that humans sometimes stumble across and that can be perilous or provide opportunities for trade, depending on how the human behaves. Many stories of these markets or fairs appear in collections of folklore from the past several hundred years, when writing down such stories became fashionable, and often reflect similar themes. These stories portray the ambiguous nature of the Good Folk, who may reward those with good manners or severely punish those who they feel are violating their privacy, and the markets themselves can be pleasant or dangerous (Briggs, 1976).

One particularly interesting type of fairy market, mentioned in a poem of the same name by Rossetti written in the late 1850s, is the Goblin market. Literary critics, especially those discussing the poem in the latter part of the 20*th* century, tend to ignore the piece's folklore and fairylore themes and discuss it purely as a work of Victorian literature with cultural, sexual, and feminist undertones. However, the work has strong and clear ties to traditional fairy beliefs and deserves consideration on those merits as well.

The poem is the story of two sisters, Laura and Lizzie. Every *'morning and evening'* the girls would get water at the brook and would hear Goblins calling out, selling fruit. Lizzie warns her sister not to even look at the Goblins, but one time Laura can't resist peeking at them and what they are selling. Lizzie runs away, but Laura stays and the Goblins, who are processing past carrying trays and baskets of fruit, offer her their wares. When she explains she has no money they trade her the fruit for a lock of her golden hair and single tear. She then gorges herself on the fruit and on the juice and afterwards, not knowing if it was night or day, she stumbles home. Her sister meets her at the gate, upset and reminding her of their friend Jeanie who also bought the Goblin fruit and afterwards pined to death searching in vain for another taste, but unable to find the Goblins again. Laura dismisses her sister's concern and says that the next night she will get more fruit to share with Lizzie, mentioning that she already wishes she had more of it to eat herself. The next day Laura is already pining for the fruit, but when evening comes although her sister can still hear the Goblins' call at the brook, Laura cannot. Laura then falls into decline, refusing to eat, her hair turning grey, losing the will to do her chores; remembering their dead friend Jeanie, and in desperation to save her sister, Lizzie takes a silver coin and goes to find the Goblins. They come to her, pleased, and she gives them the coin and asks to take the fruit, but they insist she eat with them. She refuses and says if they will not sell her the fruit to take she will take her coin back and go. The Goblins become furious and attack her, clawing and hissing, trying to force the fruit into her mouth. Finally, having pinched her black and blue and covered her in fruit juice, but failing to force her to eat, the Goblins admit defeat and give her back her coin and leave. Lizzie flees home and tells Laura to lick the fruit juice off her, and though she cries and the juice is like *'wormwood on her tongue'* she does. Tasting the fruit a second time puts her into a fit; she tears her clothes and leaps around the room until she collapses. Lizzie tends her throughout the night and in the morning Laura awakens completely cured and restored to her previous self. The poem ends with both sisters grown and married, telling their children the story of how their sisterly love for each other saved Laura from a terrible fate and emphasizing the value of sisterhood.

Looking at the story conveyed in the poem several obvious fairy themes are immediately apparent, including the importance of liminal spaces and the dangers of dealing with malicious fairies. Katherine Briggs suggests three main themes for the poem *Goblin Market* as well: the violation of fairy privacy by looking at them, the breaking of the taboo of eating fairy food, and the rescue of a person from Fairyland (Briggs, 1976). All of these concepts can be found in various forms in other stories of fairy markets and fairs, although few are as overtly dark as *Goblin Market*. Even small things in the poem, like Laura choosing to address the Goblins when she speaks to them as 'Good Folk' and the description of them as each deformed in some way yet alluring in their manner hint at traditional fairylore. In the poem both Jeanie and Laura are described as going grey, and this too may reflect a known effect fairies can have on people; in some anecdotes those who have interacted with fairies display premature aging as a result (Narvaez, 2001). And it is also worth noting that after dealing with the Goblins each person loses track of time entirely, becoming unsure if it is even day or night, with a loss of time or time shifting yet another common occurrence when dealing with fairies (Briggs, 1967).

The Goblins only appear at *'morning and evening'* or in other words the liminal times of dawn and dusk. These times are well known to be likely for fairy encounters and caution is often advised for those travelling at such times (Briggs, 1967). Additionally the girls only hear the Goblins when they are in another liminal place, standing on the banks of the brook, at the very edge of the water filling their pitchers. In this position they are neither on land nor in the water, but between the two. We see a third reference later to another liminal place, when Laura runs home after eating the Goblin fruit, Lizzie meets her at the gate, warning her sister again about the danger as she stands on the threshold between their yard and the outside world, with Laura still on the outside.

Briggs suggests, and I agree, that Rossetti's Goblins – with their cleverly baited trap set to lure mortals to their doom – are certainly Unseelie Court and are strongly reminiscent of the darker tales of fairies to be found in traditional lore (Briggs, 1976). Dealing with such beings, intentionally or accidentally, often proves painful or fatal for the mortal involved. In the poem the reader finds out that the girls were aware of the danger presented by the Goblins, as they had lost a friend previously to the fruit. Lizzie says when talking about Jeanie's death no grass will grow on her grave and the daisies that Lizzie planted there *'never blow'* making it clear that the girls knew her death was unnatural. Briggs relates the maliciousness of Rossetti's Goblins to Bogies, as well as the menacing fairies of Finnbhearra's court, and the malevolent revelers of Lady Wilde's tale of *November Eve*, all of whom cause human suffering (Briggs, 1976). In general it is neither uncommon nor surprising for fairies to be harmful or to seek to either trick people or to steal young women (O Súilleabháin, 1967). However, to exclusively do so is the hallmark of the Unseelie Court, which is said to be inimical to humanity by nature[1].

The first misstep by Laura is to give in to the temptation to look at the Goblins as they pass by with their traveling market. Although they are the ones tempting her to look, and ultimately to taste the fruit, there are old taboos about acknowledging to others that one sees the fairies and especially about watching them when they are going about their business. Although the girls can hear the Goblins they cannot see them unless they intentionally look for them, something Lizzie knows is dangerous as she immediately says: *'We must not look at goblin men'*, and when her sister seems tempted again she says: *'Laura you should not peep at goblin men.'* The fairies are well known to be secretive people who punish those who spy on them and more so those who talk about what they have seen (Briggs, 1976). This perhaps explains Lizzie's panic when Laura looks at the Goblins anyway and tells her sister in detail what she sees, prompting Lizzie to say: *'No, no, no....their evil gifts would harm us'*, stick her fingers in her ears and run away.

The fruit itself seems to be classically taboo fairy food, utterly tempting and dangerous to eat; to eat the food of Fairy as a mortal is to be trapped in that world and lost to the mortal realm. It is a widespread belief in fairy stories, especially Irish ones, that a person should never eat the food or drink anything of Fairy, or they will be trapped there, and often a person who is tempted will be warned by another human among the Fey Folk not to take what is offered (Ballard, 2001). The danger of the fruit is demonstrated by the story within the poem of Jeanie who ate the fruit and pined away. If the food does act as other fairy food on the mortal, one may assume that, like some uses of elfshot, Jeanie may not have died in truth, but rather was taken as a changeling with the fruit binding her to Fairyland. Briggs, however, suggests that the fruit is a deadly part of a trap designed to murder the unwary (Briggs, 1976). In either case those who eat it are doomed in the sense that they are lost to mortal Earth, although it does raise the interesting question of the connection between the dead and the fey, which has always been ambiguous. The fruit may also reflect the idea of fairy glamour, where something is given the illusion of something else, in this case whatever its true nature the Goblin fruit appears to be incomparably perfect and delicious, so wonderful that after tasting it no mortal food is good enough and the person refuses to eat. It is also worth noting that Laura does not pay for the Goblin fruit with money, but with parts of herself, with her hair and with her tear, the two substances echoing the nature of the two materials – earth and water – that she stood between when she first heard the Goblins speaking. Lizzie, however, goes to the Goblins with silver to buy their fruit to take home and ultimately returns with her coin in her pocket.

The final theme mentioned by Briggs is the rescue from Fairyland and this may be the least obvious although it is certainly present in the poem. Although Laura has not fully been taken into Fairy she is clearly under its enchantment from eating the Goblin fruit and is close to death. Usually in examples of rescue from Fairyland a person must either have a way to force the fey to release their captive or, as in the story of *Tam Lin*, must endure trials to earn the captive back. In this case it is through trials that the presumptive captive is freed, as well as a somewhat impossible quest being achieved. Normally once a person tastes the Goblin fruit they are no longer able to hear the Goblins, and thus can never find them to get a second taste; the first taste alone then dooms them. In this case the only way that Laura can be saved is for her sister to follow in her footsteps, to go as she did to find the Goblin Market, but instead of buying the fruit with pieces of herself in trade, Lizzie pays with silver. She resists giving in to temptation and eating the fruit, instead insisting that she must have some to bring away with her. She endures the assault of the Goblins without complaint, without running away, and without fighting back, only focusing on not allowing any of the fruit into her mouth. She retrieves her money and returns from the liminal space, like her sister no longer knowing if it was day or night. Having endured the trial she is able to administer the cure to her sister, a second taste of the Goblin fruit, which is now bitter instead of sweet, but ultimately frees Laura from the fairies' influence.

Goblin Market is a complex story and often overlooked in fairylore, yet it deserves a place alongside other older traditional tales. The market itself with its liminal location and constant movement, and its summer fruit at all times of year, as well as the deeper themes of buying death – or perhaps freedom from it – from the Goblins with pieces of mortality (literally pieces of the person themselves) fit in well with other traditional tales. The Goblins themselves are much like classical depictions of Bogeys or the darker sort of deformed Goblins found in some folklore. The poem can stand as a cautionary tale of dealing foolishly with the dangerous fairies, or of what happens when one gives in to obvious temptations and ignores the hidden costs. The Goblin Market, ultimately is a place where you can only buy the illusion of what you want and only sell what you should not part with.

Fairies, Humans, and Sex

One of the most consistent threads among the folklore, and one that I've touched on previously in the sections on the Leannán Sí, is also one that seems to endlessly fascinate modern people: fairies and humans as lovers. While some today like to scoff at the concept as the fodder of lascivious imaginations and trashy novels it is actually an idea that is found and reiterated in mythology and folklore as well as in anecdotes in the modern period. It was common for the Anglo-Saxon word for Elf to be glossed with Incubus, precisely because of their reputation for sexual interactions with women.

Probably the oldest examples we have of these stories come from mythology, although I admit it gets murky to delve into this in the Irish where the Gods and the Aos Sí are often only thinly divided. We have the story of Niamh and Oisín, where Niamh is usually described as a woman of Fairy although she can equally be called a Goddess as a daughter of Manannan. Although it involves reincarnation and a Goddess reborn as a human, we also have the story of Midhir and Etain, where Etain is born as a human girl and is courted and won by the Fairy King/God Midhir. There is Áine, who we know is a Goddess, but is also a Fairy Queen, and who is the progenitor of the Fitzgeralds; she took the Earl of Desmond as her lover and gave him a son, Geirriod. In a similar vein there is the McCarthy family who are said to be descended from Cliodhna – Goddess and Fairy Queen. In the second two stories there are overtones of the sovereignty Goddess marrying a mortal lord to legitimize his rule, but in all the stories we see an Otherworldly being taking a mortal as a lover and in three of the tales having children with them. We could also add the conception of Cu Chulainn to this, although it is a bit more metaphysical in some versions, as we see Lugh – again a God and one of the Aos Sí at this point – coming to Deichtine either in reality or in a dream and fathering Cu Chulainn on her.

Beyond the mythology we also see many examples in older folklore. There were several types of fairies specifically known for seducing mortals, including the aforementioned Leannán Sí as well as her male counterpart the Gean-cánach; these generally did so to the mortal's ultimate detriment. However, stories of mortals having sexual relationships with fairies, often producing children, are found across fairylore and with a wide array of types of fairies including Kelpies, Selkies, Aos Sí, and Lake Maidens. In the Kelpie lore the Kelpie can be male or female and while Kelpies are more known for tricking and harming people in these cases the Kelpie falls in love with the mortal and seduces them. Sometimes the mortal awakes after a tryst and sees their sleeping lover only to notice the telltale bit of water-weed in their hair, or dripping water, or other give-away sign that reveals their nature and the mortal flees. Other times the two wed and only after a child is born does the mortal realize their spouse's true nature and leave; although there is one iteration of the story where a male Kelpie captures and imprisons a mortal girl as his 'wife' and she escapes after a year, usually leaving behind a son. In the Selkies tales the male Selkie woos the mortal girl to his home under the waves, while the female is only taken as a bride to a mortal – in the stories – if her sealskin coat is taken from her. Again, however, children are the usual result of the marriage. You can see the pattern here. The Aos Sí stories appear under a variety of forms usually with the human being kidnapped or taken into Fairy, sometimes willingly sometimes not. The Lake Maidens of Wales usually are willing wives, but come with geasa, and once those taboos are broken they immediately leave, like the Selkie bride finding her sealskin, returning to the waters they came from.

Some versions of the story of the MacLeod Fairy Flag say it was a gift to the family from a fairy lover who had born a MacLeod child. One of the most widespread stories found in fairylore across different Celtic cultures is that of the borrowed midwife who anoints the baby's eyes and accidently touches her own, only to be granted true sight and realize that she has delivered the half-fairy child of a local girl[2]. This girl has been taken into Fairy as the wife of one of its inhabitants and obviously just proven that humans and fairies are in fact cross-fertile. Which shouldn't be surprising since one of the leading theories about changelings is that fairies steal people to supplement their own population, and that doesn't entirely mean the people become fairies so much as it means the people make more fairies, as the midwife tales illustrate. The gender-flip version of this story might be the ballad of *Tam Lin* although Tam Lin is more properly a changeling as opposed to being a true fairy himself; in the story, however, the mortal girl, Janet, does not know that until after she's taken him for her lover and conceived his child. Only when she goes to the well he guards to gather herbs to abort the pregnancy and Tam Lin appears to stop her does she question whether he was ever human[3]. Many of the Scottish witches who confessed to dealing with the fairies also admitted having sexual relations with them, as opposed to the more usual demonic intercourse other witches admitted to. At least one 19th century Bean Feasa was known to have had a fairy lover as well.

In the book *The Good People*, which is an anthology of collected articles about fairies there are several discussions of more modern anecdotes. These come from interviews with people in Ireland, Wales, and Scotland conducted in the 20th century and looking at modern fairy beliefs. It is, in its own way, the next generation of Evans-Wentz's *Fairy Faith in Celtic Countries* and it includes some discussion of fairy lovers and of the children born of these unions. Generally to have a fairy lover carried prohibitions (geasa), often of silence about their existence, but sometimes it might be something like not striking the spouse three times. With the Selkies, who were unwilling brides, the magical sealskin must be hidden, and in Welsh lore a fairy wife was often secured by learning her True Name, which had power over her. The children of these unions were known to be uncanny and in many stories were taken into Fairy by their Otherworldly parent; those who remained in our world generally stood out as odd or unusual in their mannerisms and preferences; like their fairy parent, they tended to behave in ways that seemed to defy human mores or etiquette as often as not. Children born with Selkie heritage were said to long for the sea and often to have webbed hands or feet, as well as dark hair and eyes.

So, we can see that there's a long established pattern of fairies taking human lovers. Sometimes only as lovers, sometimes as spouses, sometimes producing children, sometimes not. Usually the human half of this equation is someone who has broken social boundaries by seeking the fairies out, such as we see in stories of woman going to do their work in places known to belong to Themselves or going to wells known to be Theirs, or of people who are in a liminal state, for example about to be married. Keep in mind as well this wasn't, for the most part, figurative or imagined – not 'on the astral' as some people might say – but occurred in the physical, tangible world. Other people reported seeing these beings in some cases and the resulting children were real, physical children. Usually when the person was taken into Fairy they were thought to have died, which in the parlance of Fairy means they might have actually died in our world. Give that some thought.

Before you go rushing out to find a fairy lover of your own it is worth considering that as often as not these things end badly. And by badly I mean with the death of the mortal partner, sometimes through mischance and sometimes through violence. In other stories the mortal violates a taboo – a geis – set down by the fairy partner and loses them forever, which generally drives the mortal mad. So this whole concept is a bit more dangerous than your average Tinder hook-up, and shouldn't be treated lightly.

Possession by Fairies

One aspect of fairylore that has become quite obscure today is the idea that fairies are able to possess people. However, this idea was quite common in older belief. We find it in the old Anglo-Saxon medical texts alongside the idea of demonic possession. Elves and fairies more generally were believed to cause a variety of physical maladies, and spiritual possession was included among these. In one example found in the marginalia of an Anglo-Saxon manuscript we see a scribe adding the word 'aelfae'

(Elf) to the usual Latin prayer of exorcism giving us '*Adiuro te satanae diabulus aelfea*' (I adjure you devil of Satan, Elf) (Jolly, 1996). The cures for these Elf-sicknesses and possessions were given along with remedies for demonic possession, seizures, and nightmares, perhaps giving us an idea of the sort of things fairy possession was associated with. Another charm found in an Anglo-Saxon Leechbook specifically calls on the Christian God and Jesus in Latin to expel attacks by Elves, which may be interpreted as an exorcism charm in context, as it is followed by a similar charm for exorcising demons (Hall, 2007).

Evans-Wentz writes about an incident in Kilmessan of a girl who was possessed by fairies, a situation that lasted for years and became so severe that the family had the girl put away; finally she was taken to a witch in Drogheda and apparently a cure was able to be worked (Evans Wentz, 1911). The person relating the tale blamed two factors for this situation: the girl's father '*held communion with evil spirits*' and the family home was built partially into a fairy hill (Evans-Wents, 1911, p.34). This may indicate that one must be both open to such influence and also have violated a fairy taboo – in this case the home cutting into a fairy hill – in order for such possession to occur. Some understandings of changelings take the view that it was the spirit that had been taken, not the physical body, which for all intents and purposes results in a case of possession where the original person's body is now inhabited by a fairy spirit (Silver, 1999).

As with the more familiar demonic possession, fairy possession involves the person's spirit or personality being repressed or pushed aside and the possessing spirit taking over. Often the person appears insane or has fits of madness, acting in inexplicable ways. The only option is to drive out the possessing fairy and then use a variety of protections to keep that spirit out.

Methods to break such possessions varied, but included chants calling on higher powers as well as burning specific herbs near the person, and the Anglo-Saxon Leechbooks also recommended consuming different prepared herbal mixtures. Two herbs that are mentioned for fumigation purposes include mugwort and thyme, which would be burned near the person to drive the spirit out.

Changelings

The basic premise of the changeling is that it is a foreign being or object left behind in exchange for a desired human who is stolen into Fairy. In some cases the changeling was said to be one of the Good People who magically appeared to be the human, but usually acted very differently; if it was a baby who had been taken the replacement would typically be sickly, constantly hungry, and impossible to please, while an adult who was taken might display equally dramatic personality changes. A person who had previously been kind and gentle might become cross and cruel, while a child who had before been pleasant and easy tempered would suddenly be mean-spirited and demanding. In other cases the changeling might not be a living thing or spirit at all, but rather would be an object like a stick or log enchanted to look like the person, left to waste away and die while the real person lived on in Fairy. Generally this was understood as the person having been replaced by a changeling although there were some occultists during the Victorian period who came to believe that changelings actually represented a type of possession where the human would be overtaken by a fairy spirit. In 20th and 21st century anthropology, changelings are often viewed as attempts by folklore to explain medical conditions (Silver, 1999).

The primary targets for fairy abduction were babies and brides, but especially those of great beauty and the best temperament. Physical health was usually an important factor and in at least one story a bride who was in the process of being taken is left when she sneezes, because the Fae want only those in perfect health (Lysaght, 1991). Generally speaking humans in liminal states, which included any transitions such as birth or marriage, were at risk of being taken, with babies and children up to age eight or nine being at high risk and women in child-bearing years being in equal danger (Skelbred, 1991; Jenkins, 1991). Other popular targets for abduction included new mothers who might be taken to wet-nurse fairy babies, and may or may not be kept permanently or later returned; similarly some humans such as midwives and musicians might be borrowed, but usually were returned fairly quickly and usually were not replaced with changelings. Those replaced with changelings were those who the Good Folk intended to keep, and the changeling often died or returned to Fairy at some point, leaving the human family to mourn the person they then believed to be dead.

Why the Other Crowd take people is not entirely known, but there are many theories. Probably the most common belief is that the fairies steal people in order to supplement their own numbers (Gwyndaf, 1991). This idea usually hinges on the related belief that the Good People reproduce rarely and with difficulty and that they must therefore look to outside sources such as humans to strengthen their own population; or to be blunt they take humans to use as breeding stock. This is seen particularly in the variety of stories about stolen brides as well as stories of borrowed midwives where the midwife is taken by a fairy man to the bedside of his wife only to find herself delivering the child of a human girl she recognizes, but who everyone thought had died. Another belief was that fairy babies were unusually ugly and so fairies coveted beautiful human babies and would exchange one for the other (Skelbred, 1991). They seem to prefer people who are in some way deviant or have broken societal rules (Jenkins, 1991). This can be seen in both anecdotal evidence where people taken are usually out alone when or where they should not be or have failed to follow the usual protocol for protection, or in ballads and folktales where people are taken while in or near liminal places. On the one hand this can represent one way in which people open themselves up to being taken, but it could also represent a deeper underlying motivation, in which perhaps the people are being taken because they have some quality that the Fey Folk either admire or need more of themselves. This of course is predicated on the idea that changelings are left in place of people taken for some at least nominally positive use; however, it is worth noting that not all theories of fairy abduction are benevolent, by even the most lenient standard. If one favors the idea of the teind to Hell as an actual tithe that occurs and in which humans can be used as substitutes for fairies, then arguably people may be taken to be offered to darker spirits so that the fairies themselves may be spared (Lyle, 1970).

Means of identifying a suspected changeling often involve tricking it into revealing itself. This may be done through careful observation, such as the story of the mother who noted that when she was with her child the baby would cry ceaselessly, but when alone in her room the baby would fall silent and the mother outside the room could hear music (Lysaght, 1991). A Scottish story along similar lines involved a changeling infant who was seen playing straw like bagpipes, or in a variant was seen playing a reed for other fairies to dance to (Bruford, 1991; Evans-Wentz, 1911). In older folklore a variety of tricks are suggested including boiling water in an eggshell, which in the tales will cause the changeling to sit up and declare that as ancient as it is, it has never seen such a thing before; a regional variant involves disposing of ashes in an eggshell (Bruford, 1991). A family could also seek out the advice of a wise person or fairy doctor to assess the suspected changeling and confirm or deny its fairy-nature. Generally if the presence of a changeling was confirmed every attempt was then made to regain the human child; only in very rare cases was the family advised to treat the changeling well and accept it in their family, with the idea that treating it well would earn good treatment for their own child in Fairy (Briggs, 1976).

Because the fear of changelings, and more generally of losing a person to the Good People, was so pervasive there were many protections against it and methods of getting a person back. Looking at protections first we see an array of options, beginning with prohibitions against verbally complementing an infant, lest the words attract the fairies' attention and increase the chance of the child being taken. Although in some contexts red was seen to be a Fairy color it was also used as a protection against fairies, something we see more generally in the use of red thread (with rowan); there is at least some anecdotal evidence of the use of red flannel pinned to children's clothes as a way to keep them from being taken (Lysaght, 1991). In Wales early baptism was common because of the belief that a Christian baptism would protect an infant from being taken (Gwyndaf; 1991). So widespread that they might be termed ubiquitous were beliefs in the power of iron (or steel) to protect babies and particularly of keeping scissors, a knife, a fire poker, or tongs over or near the cradle. Other commonly found protections include burning leather in the room, keeping bread nearby, fire, silver, giving the woman and child milk from a cow that had eaten the herb mothan, and being carefully and perpetually watched (Skelbred, 1991; Evans-Wentz, 1911). In many stories it was a moment's inattention or an adult falling asleep that allowed the changeling swap to happen, compounded by a lack of any other protections in place.

I will warn the reader before we get into this section that, as Bridget Cleary's story illustrated, often the means of forcing a changeling to leave were brutal and could be fatal to the person on the receiving end. There were just as many methods of forcing a changeling to leave as there were protections against them because the belief was that once the changeling was forced to leave, the human child or bride would return. To force a changeling to leave usually involved threatening or harming them, most commonly with iron or fire. In Bridget Cleary's case she was forced to drink an herbal concoction, doused in urine, and jabbed repeatedly with a hot iron poker, as well as having a priest come in and say mass over her; after several days of this she was set on fire and eventually died of her burns (Gíolláin, 1991). A piece of iron might be thrown at the changeling, or in one of the more benign rituals salt could be placed on a shovel blade, marked with a cross and heated in a fire, with a window left open near the changeling (Gwyndaf, 1991). The changeling might be beaten, pelted with refuse and animal dung, or starved in order to force its own people to take it back, with the idea that only this cruel treatment could motivate the changeling's biological parents to return the human child to spare their own offspring (Skelbred, 1991). Fire often played a significant role in these rituals, with some involving the changeling being thrown into a fire or placed on an object that had been heated in a fire (Briggs, 1976). Another ritual to force a changeling to leave involved taking it to a river and bathing it three times in the water, and related practices involved leaving the infant or child at the edge of a body of water – a liminal space – so that the fairies would take it back and return the mortal child; a less kind version involved throwing the changeling into a river (Silver, 1999; Evans-Wentz, 1911). In cases where the changeling left and the human did not return, or the changeling had already died naturally, attempts could be made to force the return of the human captive by burning grass or trees on the nearest fairy hill (Briggs, 1976).

Changelings are found across Celtic folklore and stories of changelings exist in both folklore and more recent anecdotes. The idea that sometimes the Other Crowd take people and that those people may be saved and returned to the human community with effort or may instead be lost forever to their own kind is a pervasive one. Ultimately the fairies may take people to increase their own numbers or to diversify their own gene pool, to possess the beauty of a particular person or for darker reasons, but the folklore is clear that they take people usually with the intent of keeping them. Those who are rescued or otherwise returned are usually permanently altered by their time among the Good People and most often the hard evidence we have shows that attempts to get people back and force assumed-changelings out results in the death of the changeling.

Fairy Familiars

The familiar spirit, often simply called the familiar, is one of the most well known companions of the classical witch. When most people think of the traditional witch's familiar they automatically imagine a demonic one; However, there is a long history of fairies taking the role of the familiar spirit with some witches in Europe, just as some witches met not with the Devil, but with the Queen of Elfland. In these cases the fairies seem to have been less like servitors, as some classic familiars may appear, and more like advisers who aid the witch by giving them knowledge and acting as a go-between for them with the world of Fairy.

There is a great deal of fluidity in the terms used here and what a clergyman might call a demon or devil, the accused witch in turn would call instead a fairy or even an angel. For example Andro Man, a witch tried in Scotland in the 16th century, said that his familiar was an angel who *'favours the Queen of Elfland'*[4] (Wilby, 2005). In Eastern Europe there was a concept of witches or healing women having either good or evil spirits who aided them (Pocs, 1999). In some views what differentiated the familiar as either a fairy or a demon, as either a 'good' spirit or an 'evil' one, was the actions of the human being and the use they put the knowledge they gained from the spirit. This reflects a deep-seated conflation of Elves, fairies, and demons that existed, particularly in England, and shows a striking similarity in the supernatural afflictions caused by and magical cures used against both groups (Hall, 2007). This gives us not only a blurry line between fairies and demons as familiars, but also shows us that there was truly no hard and fast line nor rigid definition separating the two types of spirits in common understanding.

Fairies as familiars are associated with both witches and cunningfolk, that is with both those who used magic for personal reasons and those who used it in service to the community. How a person was defined, like the term used for the familiar itself, was often fluid and could change or be multifaceted, so that one person's witch was another person's cunningperson or seer, and so on. Robert Kirk mentions such fairy familiars being attached to the Scottish Seers who he describes as predominantly male (Wilby, 2005). In later periods such familiars came to be more associated with women, even perhaps finding echoes in the more modern Leannán Sí who guide and give knowledge to the Bean Feasa, but several older accounts claim the fairy familiar as the province of men (O Crualaoich, 2003; Davies, 2003). It may be best to say that fairy familiars were not segregated by the gender of the practitioner, but that both men and women might have them.

Fairy familiars could take the form of animals, particularly dogs, but just as often appeared as ordinary looking people. They were notable only for how very unremarkable they were, looking little different than the common people around them; although they did sometimes wear the fairy color of green they were also noted to wear all black or all white (Wilby, 2005). In some cases, like the fairy who was seen helping a Bean Feasa in Ireland as she gathered herbs, other people besides the witch themselves saw the fairy (O Crualaoich, 2003). It should also be noted that they were clearly visible to the witch as tangible presences, not as dreams or see-through illusions (Wilby, 2005). While modern people may tend to relegate the familiar to the mental realm of guided meditations or spiritual journeys, historically they were real-world manifestations that were seen, heard, and spoken to in the waking world. The reality of the fairy and encountering of the fairy familiar in daily life and while the witch was awake is noted in multiple sources (Wilby, 2005; Davies, 2003).

These fairy familiars were acquired in one of two ways, either met apparently by chance while the person was engaged in some mundane activity or else given to them intentionally as a kind of gift (Wilby, 2005). In several cases of accused witches in Scotland, the witch claimed the Queen of Fairy herself gave them their fairy familiars, while in others it was passed on to them by a family member or other human being. The ones who were assigned by the Queen of Fairy seemed to act in particular as a go-between connecting the witch to Fairyland, relaying messages, and bringing the witch to Fairy to see the Queen at specific times. Those who found the fairy familiar coming to them spontaneously were in times of crisis, in great need due to illness, poverty, or other desperate situations, and would be offered help by the fairy in exchange for listening to the fairy's advice or agreeing to their terms (Wilby, 2005). Once the witch agreed to what the fairy asked or did as the fairy suggested they might continue to deal with that same familiar spirit for a short time or for years (Wilby, 2005). The relationship between the witch and the fairy familiar varied widely from person to person, based on accounts that survived, mostly in witch trials, and could be either formal or more intimate.

The main help fairy familiars offered to those they were attached to came in the form of giving knowledge, both predicting events and teaching the person cures to treat illness (Wilby, 2005). Cunningfolk in particular made their careers through the knowledge of healing gained this way and the ability to cure any person who came to them with their familiar's help. These spirits acted as givers of healing knowledge and as guardians for the witch, and in some cases granted the witch special powers of foresight or second sight directly (Pocs, 1999; Davies, 2003). They would accompany the witch when they went to meet other witches, traveled to see the Fairy Queen – and indeed would advise the witch there on proper behavior, such as kneeling – and when they went to the infamous witches' sabbath (Wilby, 2005; Davies, 2003). This is a marked difference from the role the demonic familiar played in other, particularly continental, lore, where it might be sent out to do the witch's bidding by directly affecting people. The fairy familiar, in contrast, did not generally work the witch's will that way, but rather improved their life by passing information to them and offering them advice and protection.

Having a fairy familiar was not an entirely positive experience, however. Many of the witches and cunningfolk who spoke of such spirits mentioned times were they were frightened by them, even knowing that the fairy meant them no harm, one witch even going so far as to say that when confronted once unexpectedly by her familiar she fell to the ground in a fit (Wilby, 2005). There were also a variety of taboos that existed around such familiar spirits, often extensions of similar taboos seen throughout fairylore. For example, it was considered unwise to speak of one's fairy familiar or to tell others of the things one's familiar did to help. In the trial records, many witches initially denied having such familiars and only admitted it later under hard questioning, fearing breaking this taboo (Wilby, 2005).

The idea of the witch's familiar is a classic one and one that most people have some awareness of; usually the image people immediately think of is the demonic familiar spirit; however, historically the fairy familiar was just as present. There were some key differences between demonic and fairy familiars, the most important perhaps being who the spirit answered to – Devil or Fairy Queen – and the fact that the demonic familiar usually required a ceremony to call it forth while the fairy familiar was noted to appear at its own will, often to the surprise of the witch. Additionally the manner in which the spirit aided the witch also differed significantly between the two types. In other ways, however, it seemed that the difference between the two types of spirits was a semantic one, depending on the opinion of the person describing it as well as the actions and reputation of the person who it was attached to. In modern understanding it is the demonic familiar spirit that has come to be the main one we remember, but we would do well to consider the significance and folklore of the fairy familiar as well.

End Notes

1. Although it should be remembered from our earlier discussion of the two courts that nothing with Fairy is ever that cut-and-dried and there are always exceptions to every rule.
2. In different versions the girl was either thought to be dead, missing, or known to be taken by fairies. In all versions the midwife later sees the husband at a fair and he puts out her eye when he realizes she can see him.
3. Oh Janet, really? Seems like the sort of question you might have wanted to ask a smidge earlier, if it mattered. Like before you lifted your skirt.
4. The quote in Scots is: *'swyis to the Quene of Elphen.'*

Chapter 8

Fairies in the Modern World

The universe is full of magical things patiently waiting for our wits to grow sharper.
Eden Phillpotts

There are those who believe that the fairies have left this world, perhaps after the fashion of Tolkien's Elves in his books, leaving behind our mortal Earth forever. This idea is reinforced by poems such as Corbet's 16th century *Farewell, Rewards, and Fairies,* which proclaimed the fairies all dead and the land utterly changed by Christianity so that there was no more room for the enchantment of the fey. Knowing that the author was a bishop may perhaps explain his particular view on the subject, but it is certainly a sentiment shared by people down to the modern day. A 19th century Scottish account told of a boy who saw a cavalcade of fairies and boldly asked them where they were going, to which one stopped and replied that they would never again be seen in Scotland (Briggs, 1976). There have been other such accounts in poetry and folklore, and I myself have heard people say that the Good People have been driven out of this world long ago and can be found here no longer. However, as Katherine Briggs says: '*Yet, however often they may be reported as gone, the fairies still linger.*' (Briggs, 1976, p 96)

For others the fairies haven't left this world, but have been driven away into the far wilderness or else shun human habitations. From this viewpoint the fairies have become reclusive and impossible to find. People seeking the spirits of the Otherworld often ask how find them to connect to them, where to go – as if those spirits weren't all around them, everywhere, even in people's homes and in our very modern cities. The idea of house fairies, of fairies' dependence on humans in different ways, of fairies as powerful and frightening beings, has eroded until all that is left is a post-modern understanding of Themselves as ephemeral nature spirits. There is a lack of engagement with the enchantment of the world that hides the presence of the spirits all around us, effectively blinding us to what is still all around. Because I don't think that it's the world that's less enchanted, or the fairies who have gone anywhere, so much as that people have lost the desire or will to be aware of what's around them.

People slowly stopped seeing what's there because many people have stopped allowing themselves to embrace the moments of true joy or to feel the moments of atavistic fear that exist in our world separate from humanity. People seek the middle road and reject what W. B. Yeats called the *'unmixed emotions'* of the Gentry, or of children, and in doing so I think people lose that sense of wonder and enchantment. To reclaim it we have to be willing to experience life, to embrace the moments of enchantment when we find them – and once we know them perhaps we can learn how to make them for ourselves. To believe in fairies in the modern world we have to be willing to believe that magic and enchantment still exist, and can still be engaged with. We have to be open to experiences and possibilities instead of immediately seeking to rationalize and explain away anything and everything that is unusual or uncanny.

This chapter looks at evidence of fairies in the modern world from my own experiences, of fairies in Celtic countries and in places the populations who honor them have moved to. It discusses how and why to offer to them and ways to protect against them. It also takes a frank look at the way that popular culture has and is affecting fairylore and is shaping the beliefs as we move forward in the 21st century. For the bulk of its history the stories and anecdotes of the fairies have been passed by word of mouth, songs, and in collections of stories with a sense of genuineness and authority in their telling. But we live now in a world of social media, mass-produced fiction, and an internet reality that is shaped by anyone and everyone who chooses to add to it. The folklore and fairylore of today are quick to change and reflect new truths and new beliefs, and these too need to be understood and fit into the overall picture of what it is to believe in fairies today.

Fairies Outside Celtic Countries

There is an ongoing debate about the presence of Celtic fairies outside traditionally Celtic countries. Some people feel that the Aos Sí, the fairies, are limited to Ireland and historically Celtic lands, anchored to these places usually through their ties to specific geography. I can only speak here to my own experience and what I have found in studying different folklore, which is that where people from a culture go, their spirits also go.

There are no hard-and-fast answers to this question, but as we discuss fairies in the modern world in a book aimed mostly at Celtic fairies, I think we must first address this issue of where in a wider sense one might find them. Every culture that I have studied has some beings that seem to fit the loose definition of fairies. Different cultures interact with these beings in surprisingly similar ways, including offerings and protections that are the same across continents. One school of thought on this is simply that the Otherworldly folk are the same everywhere, but appear to people in ways that those people can best understand through their own cultural filter; another view is that the spirits are influenced by the belief of the people. Personally, I tend to think that while some types of spirits are indeed sedentary, others are pulled or drawn to where the people who honor and offer to them are, so that the fairies travel as the people do.

When the Norse settled Iceland, for example, they found Alfar and Huldufolk there just as there had been in their old home territories. The Wild Hunt is seen in American skies just as in European, although they are more commonly known as 'Ghost

Riders' here. The areas of America heavily settled by the Irish and Scotch-Irish, like Appalachia, have local folklore that includes traditionally Irish spirits like the Banshee and Will'o'the'Wisp. In a folklore journal from 1894, we find an article about the population of an area of Massachusetts' local belief in fairies and Pixies, the former being lucky and the latter malicious. In all these examples, the people clearly felt it perfectly natural and normal to see and experience the types of Otherworldly spirits from their homelands even in these new places.

Local folklore in my area of southeastern New England is not devoid of fairies, and it's clear that people here both presently and in past centuries believed the Fey Folk were around. I know of one story of a man who saw fairies in Connecticut in the late 19th century;[1] he ran a small store in the west part of the state and had a reputation among the local people for seeing and speaking to the Gentry. One day he disappeared, and no one ever found out where he had gone or why, but there were those who said the fairies had taken him.

There is also the story of the Little People's Village in Middlebury, Connecticut, a village of tiny houses. Built about 100 years ago as part of an amusement park attraction (originally called the Fairy Village) it fell into ruin after shutting down and is now the focal point of local folklore that says the Other Crowd inhabit it and can sometimes be heard by visitors. The place is said to be a center of negative energy and the Fair Folk there are said to cause insanity to those who linger too long or offend them. There is one particular object called the 'fairy's throne' and people say if you sit on it you will go mad.

In Connecticut there is a state park, named 'Devil's Hopyard', which has a certain reputation for being haunted; many of the local pagans I know have come to associate this park with the Other Crowd in particular. Why the park is named Devil's Hopyard is unknown, but some stories say that it's because the Devil would sit at the top of the falls and play his fiddle for the local witches to dance to. Certainly the park has a long history in local folklore of spirit activity. One old story tells of a traveler walking near the falls who saw several dark figures leaping through the trees and across the stones; the man fled and the spirits chased him until he reached the nearest town. I have been Pixy-led there with a friend, wandering for hours on a well-trodden path unable to find our goal – until we gave up and immediately arrived where we'd been trying to go the whole time. I've seen a water fairy there; she lives in a pool near a waterfall and dislikes people. There is also a fairy road that crosses through a section of the park, or perhaps I should say at least one fairy road that I am aware of.

I believe that America is full of a wide variety of spirits from many cultures. I know that my grandfather when he came over from Cork never gave up the practice of pouring out a bit of his beer for the Good Neighbors whenever he drank, and even on American soil never doubted that the Good People would cause trouble if not given their due. This is a belief that has been firmly ingrained in me as well. My own experiences since childhood involved both spirits undoubtedly native to this continent as well as those that seem to have immigrated or otherwise been shaped by the beliefs of the Irish who came to this place, as well as a wide array of other cultures. America is more than just a melting pot of human cultures, but in my experience is also a melting pot of spirits, containing a wide diversity, and this diversity seems to go back hundreds of years, since foreigners first began making permanent settlements on this continent.

Popculture, Modern Fiction, and Fairies

Our modern understanding of fairies is in many ways a unique thing in itself and has been shaped less by traditional culture and folklore then by modern fiction and television. The effects of popculture and fiction on Fairy Faith beliefs have been profound, especially with the advent of social media, and I want to address some aspects of modern belief that are rooted in this rather than older beliefs. I think it is important for people to understand what is genuinely older folk belief and what has grown up in the past few decades as modern belief, although I'll say up front that I doubt I can include all of the ways that modern media is influencing neopagan beliefs on this subject.

I also want to be clear at the beginning that pointing out that something is a more modern belief is not necessarily a judgment on that belief. I happen to personally agree with some new beliefs, but I still think it's important to be clear about what is new and what is older. Not only does paganism do itself no favors by putting new beliefs forward as ancient, but I think it's also disrespectful to the traditional cultures and existing folk beliefs to re-write them and then claim the new version is somehow more genuine or older than the existing ones. My goal here is simply to help differentiate between traditional folklore beliefs and modern beliefs rooted in fiction and popculture. The following then is based on my own knowledge of the subject and personal observations, and should be understood as such.

The Summer and Winter Courts

This is one of the ones that I personally like and use myself. However, as far as I can find, it is a newer term for the two courts. Of course as was previously discussed in the section on the Seelie and Unseelie Courts themselves the entire idea of two courts as such is itself probably comparatively new as well, having come into popular belief in the past several hundred years. Within the past decade or so there have been several young adult fiction series and paranormal romance series that have featured the idea of either a Summer and Winter Court of the Fairies or of courts based on all four seasons, or who use the terms Seelie and Unseelie, but also incorporate Summer and Winter as nicknames for each. This concept has been adopted into fairylore more generally by those who dislike the hard Seelie = good, Unseelie =

bad division and feel that Summer and Winter are more ambiguous and less morally loaded terms.

The Dark and Bright Courts

Similar to the Summer and Winter Courts, this is another way to name the Unseelie and Seelie Courts, which has appeared in modern fiction. It avoids the use of the terms good and bad or good and evil, but still carries the connotations of the original terms. The Dark Court is synonymous with the Unseelie Court and contains those who mean humans harm, while the Bright or Light Court are those who mean humans well. I must admit I'm quite fond of this particular one myself.

The Grey Court

Another idea like the Summer and Winter Courts that cannot be found in older folklore as far as I am aware, but which is gaining in modern popularity. The Grey Court is a term I came across in a paranormal romance series based on the Fae, but has also popped up among pagans who believe in fairies as a term for a third, more neutral, court[2] or used as a term for the court of those fairies who are more wild and less civilized than the other two courts. In traditional fairylore, the more wild fairies would have been termed solitary as opposed to the more civilized fairies or those who prefer to be in groups who were known as trooping fairies. The traditional division into courts has always either bifurcated the fey into Seelie and Unseelie, or else seen them divided into a multitude of different courts based on location and who their monarch was.

Unseelie as the Good Guys

To be clear all fairies are mercurial and can be inclined to either help or hurt; however, those termed Seelie were known to be more inclined to helping while those termed Unseelie were known to be more inclined to hurting. The idea that the Unseelie were all or largely just misunderstood good guys, and more so that the Seelie were the real bad guys[3], is entirely from modern fiction, and so common now that it has become a trope of its own. The idea that the Unseelie are just angst-ridden bad boys trying to prove they can be good is really, truly just from modern fiction. Yes there are stories in folklore of beings generally labeled Unseelie doing helpful things or falling in love with mortals and so on, but those were exceptions rather than the norms and also those stories still tended to end tragically. When it comes to Fairy the only generality we can really make is that we can't easily make any generalities.

Fairies are Nice

Fairies can be nice, but fairies are not nice by nature any more than people are. The idea that they all are all the time is entirely modern and an extreme break from actual folklore. I tend to point to the Victorians as the source on this one, but it's hard to pinpoint exactly when and what started this shift and I think in reality it was probably a combination of the Victorian flower fairy obsession, the New Age movement's emphasis on the positive and a conflation with the idea of spirit guides. This leaves us with modern popculture fairies who don't resemble historic ones; certainly Disney's Tinker Bell is an example of the stereotypical modern fairy, but J. M. Barrie's Tinker Bell, from the 1904 play *Peter Pan* and 1911 novel of the same name, was pretty vicious. Fairies in folklore were not to be messed with. They could – and would – kill, maim, or hurt people for what may seem to us to be trifling slights.

Fairies are our Guides

This appears in both books and pagan culture more generally, the idea that fairies are a kind of spirit guide or are more highly evolved beings seeking to help humanity grow and develop. Some of them may perhaps be beings along these lines, there is after all a lot of diversity, and there is the idea in folklore that some people – especially witches – may have a particular individual fairy who helps them. But they are not all like this and I think it is an error to assume that every single fairy is a helpful spirit guide to all of humanity. For many kinds of fairies, such as the Each Uisge (water horse) or Hags, we are nothing but a food source, and to others we simply don't matter at all.

Fairies are Small, Winged Creatures

This one I do solidly blame the Victorians for and the popularity of children's books during that time that featured little winged flower fairies. This compounded with the early 20th century Cottingley Fairy hoax seemed to have profoundly affected how people visualized fairies, something that has since been perpetuated by everything from Disney to the art of Amy Brown. In folklore, however, and many anecdotal accounts the Good People appear in a wide array of forms from animal to human-like from tiny to giant, from beautiful to monstrous. Wings are actually very uncommon features that seems to have been added within the past couple of hundred years, initially in theater productions and later artwork.

Fairies Protect the Environment

Many modern pagans are firmly convinced that fairies are nature spirits and staunch protectors of the environment, an idea that appears in the works of pagan authors as well as movies (I'm looking at you Fern Gully). This is not something supported in actual folklore though, but an idea that seems to have begun and gained popularity with humanity's own growing awareness of environmental concerns. It is true that many of the Fair Folk are extremely territorial and messing with their places is a profoundly bad idea, but this isn't due to a wider drive for them to protect our world so much as an urge for them to protect what belongs to them. There is, to my knowledge, not one single example in myth or folklore of the Good People appearing and warning anyone about the dangers of clear cutting forests, damning rivers, polluting, etc., prior to the modern era. And, yes, those things did happen historically, which is why Europe isn't covered in forest any more and has lost a variety of native species to extinction due to hunting.

Fairies Rescue Abused Children

Fairies in folklore were known to take a variety of human beings for a variety of purposes, not all of them positive. They would take brides and musicians, as well as midwives and nursing mothers. But they were also known to take infants and children and I think this is ultimately the root of the modern idea that they rescued abused children. However, I will argue that saying they were rescuing these children is a modern recasting of the stories to soothe our sensibilities today. The idea appears in fiction dating back to the 1990s, at least, and gives a much nicer explanation for why the children were taken than folklore, which says they were – effectively – breeding stock to supplement low population numbers among the Fey Folk or servants. As with the other examples so far there is nothing in the actual folklore to indicate that the children taken were abused and in fact usually in the stories they seem to have been wanted and well loved, with many tales revolving around the parents' struggle to get the child back.

Maeve as Queen of the Unseelie

I admit this one baffled me when I ran across it. There are certain beings associated as queens of Fairy in Ireland as was discussed in an earlier chapter and Maeve could be counted among them. However, Ireland doesn't have the Seelie and Unseelie Court structure the way Scotland does, and as far as I know there is no Scottish equivalent to the Irish Maeve; also the Irish Maeve would not necessarily fit the mold of the Unseelie, never mind as a Queen of it. There is the English Mab who appears in Shakespeare is a Fairy Queen, but is never mentioned as being Unseelie and is referred to as a midwife to the fairies and is associated with dreams and mischief making. These two are often conflated with each other which can cause some confusion but Mab/Maeve's appearances in early 20th century literature hold to the view of her as a granter of wishes and giver of dreams. It isn't until very recently with *The Dresden Files* and *The Iron Fey* series, as far as I've been able to suss out, and possibly some television shows such as *Merlin, Lost Girl,* and *True Blood,* that Queen Maeve/Mab has been cast in the role of the Unseelie and given a darker personality and inclination. As far as I can tell this is entirely based in modern fiction.

Oak, Ash, and Thorn

If you've spent any time in either Celtic paganism or around modern pagans with an interest in the Fair Folk you may have run across the phrase 'by oak, ash, and thorn', usually either tied to the idea that these three are signs of fairy presence or that they ward off fairy mischief when branches or twigs of each are tied together. The earliest reference that could be turned up for these three trees was Rudyard Kipling's *A Tree Song* from the 1906 book *Puck of Pook's Hill* (this poem was later turned into a folk song that some may be familiar with as it gets a lot of midsummer play, by the name of *Oak, Ash, and Thorn*). I haven't found anything prior to that or any references to these three trees in traditional folklore. In fact, the ash is mentioned as a protection against fairies in many sources while the oak and both the black-thorn and hawthorn are associated to varying degrees with fairies.

These are only a handful of examples of ways that modern fairylore differs from traditional fairylore and has been influ-enced by popculture. Indeed new fiction and new movies continue to come out and the popular ones seem to inevitably find a way to affect what people believe about the Other Crowd. For example, when a recent movie featuring a Selkie came out (and a great movie it was too), which had the plot twist that the Selkie couldn't speak without her sealskin coat, I started seeing people repeating that tidbit as if it were traditional folklore, even though it is not. In a culture today where many people are disconnected from the traditional folklore and plugged into mass media and popculture it should not be surprising that it is fiction and movies that are shaping people's fairy beliefs rather than actual traditional folklore. Unfortunately, most of this material is based in plot devices or attempts to intentionally go against traditional folklore – to have that surprising twist as it were - , so it's best to take pop-culture fairylore with a grain of salt until you've looked into its validity.

Not all modern beliefs should be tossed out or ignored, by any means, and sometimes things evolve as new ideas, but still work well. I have found using alternate names for the two Courts to be both useful and evocative, for example, and I know many people who have created a deep and meaningful connection to their land spirits and the smaller fey based on following the Victorian garden fairy ideas.

Beliefs are not static things, they grow and they evolve. Some beliefs can be traced back to genuinely old roots; sometimes they have been formed within our own generation. Often there is an assumption that only the old has value, and there is a certain logic to that, as the old has been time-tested and proved. Because of this it is common to justify new beliefs with an older back-story, which can then muddy the waters of the actual history. But the new is not necessarily bad, and sometimes the new represents evolutions in old beliefs – although only time will tell which new beliefs last and which ones fade. I'm obviously a big believer in the value of the older beliefs and traditions myself, but I'm also an innovator and modifier as well, because I try to remember that the old beliefs were new once too.

I don't necessarily agree with all the changes and directions that the new beliefs are taking, and in some cases I outright argue against them, but nonetheless belief is a fluid thing. I may not like it, but I can see that in some way or other it has a purpose. In the same way I'm sure not everyone likes the adaptations and changes made to the old beliefs to make them better fit new places and environments, but that doesn't make them less necessary or important. Everything that is living is growing and adapting to the world around it, and that is a good thing; but as we grow and adapt we should always remember the truth of our roots, whether those roots are old or new. We should also always be cautious not to innovate purely for innovations sake, and to allow the beliefs to evolve naturally not to try to force changes for our own benefit or comfort.

Personal Modern Fairy Encounters

Although everything to do with Themselves is tricky, and often carries specific prohibitions about what can and cannot be shared, there are certain experiences that happened that involved more than just myself or which I know it's okay to talk about. These are an array of things and involve, naturally, a variety of different kinds of spirits, but nonetheless I'd like to share some here. Hopefully this will give people an idea of what these things can be like and show that the Fey Folk are still active in the world today[4].

- I had made a habit of offering milk every Friday to the spirits of my home and immediate area. My finances took a downward turn and I couldn't afford to keep up with it so I switched to other things. One Friday a couple of weeks after I stopped offering the milk I was carrying groceries in from my car after going grocery shopping when a gallon of milk was forcibly pulled out of my hand. The container hit the grass and burst. From then on I made sure to offer at least a small bit of milk each week

- Many years ago I had a loose assortment of friends who were all different types of pagans. One full moon we decided to get together and have a ritual and one woman mentioned a spot out in the woods that she had used many times. We all met up in early afternoon and then drove out to the suburban home where her parents lived, before hiking back into the woods about a mile or so. The ritual location was lovely and we had a casual ceremony followed by a long, pleasant conversation that lasted into the early evening. Finally it was fully dark, and even with the full moon above us the forest was closing in so we packed up and started back. After walking for about five minutes we could clearly see the lights from the houses shining through the trees ahead of us. But after ten more minutes the lights were no closer. We climbed over rocks and around trees, through thorns and fallen branches, yet never seemed able to move forward. One other friend and I began to suspect fairy enchantment, as the rest of the group fought to push forward. After perhaps another 15 minutes of walking, my friend and I acknowledged that we were being Pixy-led; we began to laugh and compliment the fairies on such a fine joke. The energy broke with an almost physical snap and within a few minutes we emerged in a backyard a few houses down from where we'd first gone into the woods.
- My friend has had a large shrine/altar for the fairies in her store for 15 years. One year around the equinox we needed to move the shrine, which was an epic undertaking, and took most of a morning. Several days later I noticed a fluorite ring was missing from a jewelry display. We both assumed it had been stolen, which was upsetting. Then my friend found it, days later on the new fairy shrine – covered

in years of dust as if it had been there for a long time. We left it there – if they want an offering enough to take it, they can keep it.

- I have seen fairy hounds twice in my life. The first time, many years ago, a friend and I were sitting in the doorway of a mutual friend's business in the city, beneath the darkness of the early evening sky. Suddenly we both became aware of the eerie silence – the sounds of the city had fallen away, the traffic had stopped going past on the street, everything seemed deserted. As we watched two huge black dogs came trotting down the sidewalk across the street. No one was with them, but they walked calmly and with a purpose. My friend broke the silence and joked that perhaps they would cross the (empty) street and no sooner had the words left his mouth then both dogs changed directions and moved across the street towards us. We immediately fled into the building and closed the door; peering out of the window we looked out to watch the dogs walk past and saw nothing. Literally no dogs, anywhere. Venturing back out we saw the dogs walking down the sidewalk away from us, although it was impossible for them to have passed where we were without us seeing them. They disappeared when the road curved and moments later the sound and traffic returned.

- The second time I saw a fairy hound happened when I was working as an EMT. My partner and I were on a layover at 5am on a winter morning in a city by the shore of Long Island Sound and we had parked in a lot next to a large field fenced off for construction. My partner was reading a book, but I decided to get out and stretch my legs while we waited, despite the cold weather. I walked over near the chain link fence that surrounded that field and noticed something white moving on the far side. As I watched in the darkness the white shape moved steadily towards me;

it seemed to be moving quickly across the field and eventually I realized it was a dog although its gait seemed odd. I looked past it for any sign of a person out for a morning walk with their pet, but saw no one. The white dog, some sort of hound by its shape, was so white that it almost glowed in the pre-dawn darkness and I stood there watching it come straight towards me, trying to puzzle out why it was alone in a fenced in field and why its movement seemed jerky and off even though it moved quickly. When it had crossed about two-thirds of the space between us I finally realized that it had only one front leg – not that it was missing one, but that its front leg was placed in the center of its chest. A wave of fear went over me and before I could think I had turned, run, and jumped back into the ambulance. My partner looked up, startled, and asked me what was wrong, and I told him there was a dog. Looking out he asked me what dog. Sure enough when I looked there was no dog to be seen anywhere, despite the fact that there was nowhere for it to go in the empty field and no time for it to have gone anywhere.

- As I was helping out in my friend's store one day I looked down and realized my wedding ring was gone. I panicked and my friend and I searched everywhere, but there was no trace of it. I made several offerings hoping the ring would turn up, because I knew of the fairies tendency to take jewelry, but it didn't. Months went by and I felt pressed to write my *Fairy Witchcraft* book, which I did, although that's another story. Shortly after I finished the book and submitted it to my publisher my friend found the ring sitting in front of her altar.

- About a decade ago I was at a local state park that has a strong Other Crowd presence. While I was there I left a small pendant, a moonstone with an iolite set above it, as an offering. At my house I have a small room dedicated for ritual use; it is where all my altars are. About a year ago I walked into my ritual room and sitting on the floor in front of my main altar was the pendant I had left as an offering all those years before.

- I had been given a small bracelet as a gift by a friend. I took it off one night and when I went to put it back on it was gone. The lesser fey are fond of taking my jewelry, although so far they've always given it back, eventually, so I was annoyed, but not too worried about it. Several months went by and the bracelet still hadn't reappeared; at this point my family was getting ready to move to another town and I was getting worried. I tried everything I could think of, but no bracelet. Finally I decided that maybe it wasn't Themselves who took it after all, but I'd just lost it. We moved to the new house and a few days after moving in I walked into the bathroom and the bracelet was lying in the middle of the floor.

- About 15 years ago I was hiking in a local state park known by some to have a strong presence of the Good People to it. In this same place I'd been Pixy-led while I was with a friend, and I know of at least one other person who had also been Pixy-led there. This particular day I decided to go off trail at the bottom of the waterfall and hike around the rocky area near the water's edge. I came around a place where the rock face had jutted out and into a small secluded area with a little pool. I stopped; in the pool was a pale, dark haired woman; I knew immediately she wasn't human. She was so pale her skin was literally white and there was an aura of Otherworldliness around her. She was about waist deep in the water and had been running her fingers through her hair when I walked around the cliff. There was a strong feeling of menace in the air that made my hair stand on end. She looked at me. I looked at her. She told me to get out. I backed up and left the way I'd come as fast as I could.

- I have seen the Slua Sí several times in my life. One particular time that I will share I was going out with my children and as I stepped out of my door I felt the wind pick up and looked up towards the road. It was a gaoithe sí, a fairy wind, and the fallen leaves spun around in a rising circle as the whirlwind took them. My children were in the yard in front of me, and there on the road I saw a rider where the whirlwind was, a man on a dark horse, and I heard the sounds of dogs growling and horses moving restlessly, although I only saw the one rider. I looked at him and he looked at me, with my children between us and me frankly terrified, then he was gone. I went immediately and made an offering of cream, and it was honestly one of the most frightening experiences of my life. A little while later I found out that about 10 minutes after I saw this, seven miles across town on another back road six telephone poles were all broken about six feet off the ground and fell together in a row, without explanation. I firmly believe it was the passage of the Slua that caused it.

- Twice at least I believe the Good People have saved my home or my life one way or another. The first time I was in my living room, getting ready to go run some errands when I caught sight of something moving on the wall behind the television, by the outlet where the electronics are plugged in. I walked part way across the room, but there wasn't anything there. I stood for a minute or so, nothing happened, so I went and sat back down. Glancing over the same thing happened again, but I ignored it. The third time it was the more distinctive form of a small person moving back and forth in front of the outlet, so I got up again and walked over this time right up to the outlet. The figure disappeared but a few seconds later the largest cord plugged into the outlet sparked and then started burning. Because I was standing right next to it I had time to pull it out of the wall before anything else caught fire, and the only damage was the cord itself, melted and burned (also probably added some white to my hair).

- I have had many strange experiences with the Other Crowd relating to butterflies and moths, also I mentioned that I believe they have saved my life. Several years ago, just before going to bed, I started to have a severe allergic reaction to something (for which I now have an EpiPen by the way). I was going into anaphylactic shock, which as a former EMT I recognized, but at the time I was scared and made the very irrational decision not to disturb my husband. I went to bed, with my tongue swelling and each breath a struggle. Suddenly my husband jumped up yelling and turned on the light. He swore that a huge moth had just flown, forcefully, into his face, although he could find no evidence of any moth anywhere. A sense of calm came over me and I told him to call 911 and explained that I needed help. And obviously I lived, although I'll admit things got a bit dicey on the ambulance ride. I truly believe that it was the fairy folk who saved me by waking him up.
- At one point we had a relative staying with us for an extended period of time who the house fairies did not like. The day the person moved in, the back door of the house, through which their furniture was being moved, jammed and had to be broken in order to be opened. Once they moved in, their room that had always been the warmest in the house became the coldest and they complained of constantly hearing strange noises when they were in the room. Their phone line and Wi-Fi repeatedly went out, although technicians could find no reason why. Their electronics repeatedly broke, and items went missing from their room and reappeared at odd times. As soon as the person moved out all of these problems stopped. When a

house fairy doesn't like a person they make their feelings known.

- We have a fairy thorn in my yard – which is its own story, actually. Anyway, one day while doing yard work my husband damaged the tree accidentally. He came in and told me and I was very upset (read; freaked out) and told him to go make an offering right away. I went out myself and offered honey and milk, and asked him if he had done that too, but he was still in the middle of mowing the lawn. I emphasized he needed to do it as soon as possible. So a week or so went by and it was about 7am one morning. I was up with my son, who was an infant at the time, while everyone else was still sleeping, when we heard the most Gods-awful loud crashing noise. I rushed to the window with the baby and looking down at the driveway saw that a roughly 20 foot long branch from an oak tree had impaled my husband's car. I went to wake him up, and the first thing I said was something like: 'Did you make that offering to the fairies like I told you to?' He said: 'No I thought you'd done it for me.' So I said: 'Oh no. You should have done your own. You'd better go see what's happened to your car.' The car was totaled and my husband is a lot more careful around that tree now.

- When I was visiting Tulsk, in County Roscommon, I spent time in Uaimh na gCat (the cave of cats) with the group I was traveling with. While we were in the cave I saw the back wall open up and inside was a shining hall, the sí of Cruachan. There were many people, finely dressed, and a long table set with food. I could hear music playing, a flute and fiddle, and the whole place glowed as if it was filled with a golden light.

- On that same trip we also visited Sliabh na Caillighe in County Meath. It's a pretty steep hike up the hill to get there, then it flattens out at the top. While there I felt a very strong presence of Themselves and at one point as dusk was falling I couldn't find the way out; I said as much out loud and immediately my eye was drawn to the gate. I left a small offering of butter in thanks then headed down, walking with a friend. As we walked down we chatted and I found myself, against all wisdom, joking about how I wouldn't be surprised if I fell on my bum[5] because that was the kind of thing that would amuse the Fey Folk. I of course immediately fell on my backside, much to my friend's consternation, as I felt one of my ankle's being grabbed and pulled. No harm was done and I laughed as I stood back up.

These are some of my own personal experiences, but I am far from the only modern person to still experience the Fair Folk today. There is a very good book called *The Fairy Faith – In Search of Fairies* by Simon Young that documents modern fairy anecdotal experiences, and there was a documentary film made by Wellspring Media in 2001 called *The Fairy Faith* that did the same. Both of these are resources for other people's modern experiences and I encourage you to consider them as well.

End Notes
1. The story of Mr. Perry is included, briefly, in the 1938 book *Connecticut: A Guide to its Roads, Lore, and People*, page 460.
2. I can only point out here that the use of Grey Court for a third neutral court sitting between the so-called Light and Dark Courts is exactly how it was used in the paranormal romance series.
3. None of the Fair Folk are 'good guys' by modern human standards. All of them are equally capable of harming or helping, and are mercurial to different degrees as to which they are more inclined towards.
4. For those who have read my previous books on Fairy

Witchcraft some of these anecdotes may be familiar.

5. It's never a good idea to say something like that aloud especially if you already know or suspect there are fairies around. They are pretty good at coming up with their own mischief, but they are also often open to suggestions if you are foolish enough to make them.

Chapter 9

Dealing With Fairies

Meddle and mell
Wi' the fiends o' hell,
And a weirdless wicht ye'll be;
But tak' and len'
Wi' the fairy men,
And ye'll thrive until ye dee.
McNeill, *The Silver Bough*
(Meddle and mingle
With the fiends of Hell
And a luckless creature you'll be;
But take and lend
With the fairy men
And you'll thrive until you die)

We live in a world today that often seems very foreign from the one of historic folklore. To many people the idea that fairies and other spirits are still with us and still active in our world is a difficult concept to process, when our lives so often revolve around social media, commute times, and deadlines. Yet people do still encounter fairies today, we still find anecdotal evidence and stories of these encounters throughout the world. The only thing that has really changed is our own openness and ability to believe what we hear. We have not lost our connection to Fairy; we have lost our sense of enchantment, which is the lens through which we have always viewed the unseen world.

The idea of enchantment resonates strongly with people, especially those who still find themselves drawn to the magic and mystery of the Otherworld, yet enchantment is a concept that seems far removed from our everyday existence. There is a layer of cynicism that resists the idea of enchantment, of the possibility of childlike wonder that we might associate with enchantment. This isn't so much a matter of belief, because the belief is often there, but of a willingness to be open to engagement and experience. We have lost our childlike ability to experience something without trying to dissect it immediately and explain it rationally. Children have us beat when it comes to experiencing the numinous – they don't just believe it, they expect it. They don't need validation or proof, but see the enchantment of the world like gravity or oxygen as a simple given aspect of reality. In contrast, adults believe but only so far, only to a certain degree, and usually hinged on an expectation of the possibility of it being proven or shown to them. In order to deal with fairies today, you must believe in their reality without question.

Enchantment isn't something that we simply wait to find like waders in a stream waiting for the water to carry something to us, but rather it is something actively participated in. We are aware of the enchantment present in the world because our eyes are open to the possibility of it and we are looking for it. Like trying to see a particular type of bird, it isn't enough to know it lives in your area, you also have to keep your eyes open and your perception sharp to spot it. Enchantment is something to actively engage in, not passively experience. Finding Fairy in the modern world means finding enchantment again and regaining our ability to engage with the Unseen world. For those who seek to actively engage with Fairy and its inhabitants today, that means not only believing in them, not only being educated in what they are, but also having an understanding of how to deal with them, both how to make allies among them and how to protect yourself against them.

Approaching Fairy – Balance Between Light and Dark

One of the most difficult challenges that may face people seeking to connect to Fairy in the modern world is probably not one you expect: a need for a balanced view of Fairy and those who inhabit it. As you may have gathered from the section on pop-culture and fairy beliefs there is a split between the older lore, which tends to be much grimmer in nature, and the modern, which tends to romanticize all things fairy. To deal with the Good People in the modern world means finding a middle road between a view that is too fear-ridden and one that is not respectful enough. We cannot deal successfully with these beings if we are either too terrified of them to do anything except ward them off, or if we are so enamored of the idea of them that we refuse to see any danger from them even when we are being led off a cliff.

I cannot deny that I have a lot of frustration about the amount of twee[1] in modern Fairy beliefs and the way that view is changing and shaping many modern witches' views of the Other Crowd into something different and foreign from the older beliefs. It can be easy to want to reject the entire concept of the extremely safe end of the spectrum, which tells us that fairies are nothing but gentle, kind guides. As modern paganism embraces the twee fairy as the norm there can be an urge to go to the other extreme and speak only about the most dangerous and dark of the Good People, to try to drive home the message that they should be respected and even sometimes feared. But ultimately neither extreme is a solution and only creates more problems.

Just as there is balance in nature there is balance in Fairy. The fiercest wolf can be a good mother and even the most timid stag will turn and fight when his life is danger. There is, ultimately, no light without darkness, and no darkness without light, and all things need their opposite for balance. There are fairies who will never see humans as anything except a food source, but there are others who want nothing more than to help us. Even if twee isn't for me – and honestly I may never like it – I can still acknowledge that it is important, because I can see that all aspects of Fairy have value in different ways. In the same way people who tend to favor the light and airy view of fairies would do well to try to see the value in the dark and serious side as well. Both need each other to be whole.

If there's a place for the macabre and the hard then there must also be a place, a need, for the overly sweet and soft. And I can't argue for the need for the grim and bloody if I'm not willing to also acknowledge a place for the safe and delicate. After all, nature needs both wolves and deer, and Fairy needs both sainly and unsainly – blessed and unblessed – because each serves an important purpose. A world with only gentle kind fairies is a world out of balance, just as one with only dangerous, predatory fairies would be.

Just like the twee-loving people and I balance out in some way, I think we each within ourselves have a bit of the other energy as well. I certainly see the value in joy and fun for their own sakes, and I'd like to think that even the most light-hearted, happy, fairies-are-all-goodness sort of person sees the value in solemnity and the necessity of endings as well. And both ends of the spectrum value enchantment – the enchantment of pure joy and the enchantment of shadowy dreams. Enchantment, after all, is the backbone of Fairy whether you like light or dark.

Wholeness is about balance, if not in practice at least in under-standing, and in respecting the need for the entire spectrum. It is so easy to fall into thinking that only our own viewpoint has value, only our own belief is worthwhile, but we can't vilify an entire end of the spectrum and not create repercussions. You can love light-hearted and joyous things – but don't deny the impor-tance and power of the dark and dangerous. You can love the dark and dangerous – but don't deny the importance and power of light-hearted and joyous things. Finding Fairy is a tricky thing, but it's impossible without a sense of enchantment, and perhaps just as impossible without an appreciation of both the sweet and the bitter, the dark and the light.

This is a lesson that must always be kept in mind when seeking to truck with uncanny things.

Seven Basic Guidelines for Dealing with Fairies

The ultimate point of this book is to give people the tools to understand fairies and Fairy from a traditional folklore standpoint. However, I realize that many people are also looking to not just learn about who and what fairies are, but also to connect to them in a more active way. I have my own personal approach to doing this, something I choose to call Fairy Witchcraft, but I want to offer some basic suggestions and guidelines here for those seeking to reach out to Fairy who may not want an entire spiritual structure along with it or who don't consider themselves witches in the practicing-magic sense. These guidelines are suggestions for a beginner just starting out, but should be useful for anyone of any experience level.

Why work with fairies? There are advantages to trucking with uncanny things of course or no one would do it, but it can be and often is a dangerous business and that must be understood at the start. If you have any hesitancy with this or are not sure it's worth the risk, then perhaps give it more thought first. It's not something you need to or should jump into anyway, and it something that once you begin you may find you cannot easily walk away from. Some people may not have as much choice, as the Fey Folk have been known to take an interest in people, whether or not that interest is reciprocated, in which case the following guidelines can be more of a survival guide. Those who successfully navigate dealing with the Fair Folk are usually rewarded with knowledge, luck and health, and by some accounts wealth as well. There are benefits to establishing a good relationship with Otherworldly beings, and those benefits can be very valuable and even tangible. Silence is a vital aspect to successfully dealing with the Good People though, so please keep in mind that if you do find yourself receiving any fairy gifts of the sort that don't turn into leaves at dawn, you should not rush out to tell anyone. Keep your experiences and anything you may receive a secret and you will avoid angering Them. Which is very important because the flipside to the good aspects of dealing with fairies is that when angered their response tends to be extreme and harsh. Also, never forget that nothing is free and anything you get will have a cost. Make sure it's one you are willing to pay.

Nearly every culture has fairies, by one name or another, and so no matter where you are you'll be able to find Otherworldly spirits. I recommend researching and looking into local folklore and stories, because you are likely to encounter not only the fey you expect, but others as well, no matter where you live. If your primary interest is in Celtic fairies then you may find the odds are higher of encountering those kinds, or of course if you live in areas known to have them, but spirits show up in strange places and it's impossible to predict what you may find yourself dealing with. It is best to take a well-rounded approach as much as possible. If you live in an area that has a diverse population or was previously occupied by other cultures, it's a good idea to have at least some idea of what other fairies or fairy-like spirits you may run across.

So, that said, let's get to the list.

1. Start Small

No pun intended on this one, as the name 'wee people' is mostly hyperbole, but if you want to deal with the fey going right to the ones most likely to eat you for dinner or to turn you into something unnatural probably isn't the best idea. So start with the ones most inclined to be favorable to you and that, in the grand scheme, are the least powerful. It's true that in stories ambition and daring are often rewarded. People like the Brahan Seer or Turlough O'Carolan who slept on a fairy mound were rewarded with amazing abilities, but don't ever forget there's also all the others who tried the same thing, failed to please the Fey Folk, and went mad for the effort. The thing about fairies is that some can and will help you and bless you in awesome ways, and some can and will torment you and laugh while they do it. If you begin with something like your house spirit who is already inclined to like you and build a relationship there, you can get the practice in before you move on to bigger things. Although keep in mind you really don't want to anger your house spirit either, so don't slack off just because I said it was a good place to start. Also keep in mind I'm saying 'start' not end – the idea is to slowly build up a network of friends and allies in the Otherworld. Just don't aim too high right out of the gate. Set reasonable goals and be honest about your own abilities and limitations

2. Be Prepared to Pay Them

Some people are really against the whole concept of paying spirits. I suspect these people don't deal with many spirits. But the truth is everything has a cost and the Fair Folk are often quite tit-for-tat in their approach to things. If you do them a favor they will pay you back, because they abhor being in anyone's debt; by the same token if they do something for you, especially at your request, they will fully expect to be paid back for it. And the tricky thing there is if you don't offer something in payment up front sometimes they'll decide to set the price themselves later on. This is not a good thing, because it means you have no control over what they may decide they want from you. Being in unspecified debt to a member of Fairy is a dangerous situation so you are much better off to go into any dealings with Them paying upfront. I recommend butter or cream, but I'm a bit of a traditionalist. I'd avoid offering blood – your own anyway – or anything else with heavy metaphysical implications for you, because offering a piece of yourself can also mean creating a tie to that being or giving it some degree of power over you[2].

3. Negotiate

Speaking of payments you may find yourself in a situation where you are being offered something that you desperately need or want in exchange for something else. Like your firstborn. And no, I'm not kidding. Fairies taking babies is an old practice and it's a lot easier if one of the parents gives them up willingly. Not all changelings were stolen, some were bargained away, and if you think I'm kidding then please, please, don't try to deal with fairies. No, really. Don't. Once it's said aloud, once an offer is made, it's almost impossible to negotiate down from there to give them something less, and it's for them to decide when and how to take the payment. And before anyone thinks I'm being hyperbolic, I have heard of at least one instance of someone in a large public pagan ritual offering their child to the fey, so this does happen, and the fact that it was said in jest doesn't matter at all. The words matter, not the intent. Which is another detail you need to keep in mind when negotiating with anyone of Fairy. Semantics is an art form to them and you must be sure you mean exactly what you say exactly how you say it.

They may ask for something else, but whatever it is you should be asking yourself why they want it and whether you really want to give it up. I mean a soul seems pretty inconsequential until you don't have yours anymore. You may think in that moment that you are willing to agree to give something up, or even agree to serve them, but give that some real serious thought before you bargain your life away. Don't be afraid to negotiate or even to say no. Sometimes it's just not worth it. You can always offer things that have traditionally been given, which I've mentioned already, such as butter, cream, milk, bread, even silver. Just make sure anything you agree to give is something you can give and are willing to give up.

4. Manners are Important

If you want to deal safely with the Good People then you better say 'please' and 'may I?' and generally be on your best behavior. Although there is a prohibition against saying 'thank you'[3], which many people I know agree is best to follow; say something else instead, which isn't 'thanks' such as 'I appreciate this' or 'this was exactly what was needed'. Why no thank you? Some people say it shouldn't be said because it is dismissive and so insults the Good People by implying they are less than we are. Others say that it is an admission of a debt, something that is reinforced in English at least by the etymology of the word thank, which is rooted in the idea of repayment or recompense (see point #2). I believe the idea of admitting a debt is a valid one, given the fairies' obsession with semantics and the root meaning of 'thank you'; by saying 'thanks' you are in effect saying 'I owe you one' and of course they take that literally. The key here is be on your best behavior, be polite, and remember that you aren't the one with the actual power. Which is why you are dealing with them in the first place right?

5. *Keep it Clean*

I don't know if cleanliness really is next to godliness or not but I do know that the Fair Folk detest filth. You want to know a really good way to ensure that the Good People will be against you? Urinate on land that is theirs or throw dirty water on something that belongs to them. A traditional method to keep them out of your home involved dirty water, and it was an old practice to always yell: 'Beware!' before tossing dirty water out a door or window after cleaning, because you did not want to hit a fairy with that water, should one be passing by. There is a story about a woman who would always pour her dirty wash water on a certain rock outside her home until one day a man appeared and told her to stop because that was his home and the home of many other fairies. Terrified the woman never did so again and made sure no one else in her family did either. Fairies are generally beings who embrace proper order and prefer homes that are well kept and tidy (Briggs, 1967). So if you want to work with fairies keep it clean.

6. Don't Overestimate Yourself

This is something of an extension of point #4, but it is separate enough to merit its own point. I don't know why people labor under this delusion that getting a huge attitude and treating the Good Neighbors like you are a deity and they never had been is a thing, but it does seem to be a thing so here we are. I have seen popular pagan authors suggesting people make their own fairy[4] or command fairies to certain tasks and that is just a jerk thing to do, even ignoring the debate about whether or not they may have once been Gods. There is an approach to fairies that involves commanding them, but that is rooted in ceremonial magic and also is a risky road to go down unless you have a good amount of experience. Or desperation. So unless you know exactly what you are doing when it comes to commanding spirits that are more powerful than yourself – you know how to summon them, bind them, and what to do if they break free and come after you – don't go there. Fairies are independent, sentient beings and they can and will act to protect themselves. A good rule of thumb is to treat them more or less the way you would treat another corporeal human being. Unless the fairy starts it first and you are being a jerk in defense of yourself or similar, just don't go there. You go there and so will they and that is not a contest you want to get into unless you are 100 per cent confident you will win – and they have a lot more experience at it. Also, they are much more vicious. So for the love of all that's green and growing don't be a jerk unless and until you have to.

7. Always Cover your Butt

The best laid plans still go sideways so always have a worst-case scenario plan in mind. Know what protections work against which fairies because there is no one-size-fits-all and know when to bluff and when to run. Have an escape plan behind your back-up plan. And know exactly how far you are willing to go and what you are willing to do. I mean when it comes down to it would you kill something? Would you maim something? Remember tip #6? Well I mentioned don't be a jerk unless you have to, but understand if you have to go there you have to go all the way there. You can't half-ass your jerk attitude with the fairies when that attitude is required by a situation. Which, by the way, is exactly why you don't want to lead off with it, because firstly it doesn't leave you a way to up the ante and it also means if your bad attitude backfires then you'll be wearing iron jewelry and lighting up St. John's wort and sulfur every day for a very long time. You don't want to end up in that situation unless there is no alternative, and certainly not because of your own poor choices.

This is also why tip #1 is to start small and build up relationships, because if things do go badly you'll need those allies.

Offerings

Making offerings is a key aspect to building a good relationship with the fairies. There are different modern viewpoints on why we give to the Fey Folk, usually based in how exactly a person related to them. Some people see giving to them as a requirement, fulfilling an agreement that was made long ago when the Tuatha De Danann went into the sí. Some people see it as a form of appeasement, giving to ensure that they are pleased and don't cause any mischief or damage. Some people see it as a gesture of welcome or kindness. To others offerings might be done in gratitude or as a gesture of friendship. And, of course, any or all of these reasons could apply in different situations for the same person. I suppose ultimately in this case it doesn't really matter why you believe it is done, just that you do it.

There are some key things about offerings that I think are important to understand, and that are not often discussed. Firstly, why do we make offerings from a traditional perspective? The main reason historically was twofold: to propitiate the spirits for blessing or to prevent harm, or to maintain an agreed upon exchange. In the first case, when applied to the Good Neighbors, the idea was that if we offered to them willingly they would not take from us forcibly so we see practices like milk being offered at fairy trees or cows being bled in fairy forts on holy days such as Bealtaine. This ties in to some degree with the second idea, which is that there was once an agreement between the Tuatha De Danann and/or Aos Sí and humans that a portion of our milk and grain would be given to them so that they would allow the land to prosper. Basically we give back some of our harvest in acknowledgement that it ultimately comes through their good will. There are also those who traditionally would offer, especially milk or cream, once a week to the fey in their home or immediate area in appreciation for their effort around the area and to ensure no ill luck about the place. Another aspect of this is that if we are taking something from one of their places, visiting where we don't usually go, or feel we have been given a gift by them or – in my opinion – feel we owe them in some way, we should be sure we give something back. As I mentioned in the quick guide to dealing with the fey, you do not want to be in their debt so it is always better to err on the side of caution and offer something if you think you might be in a situation where you possibly owe them anything. Giving is also foundational to creating a relationship with any spirit. Reciprocity is built piece by piece on giving when things are received and offerings are important to that.

Any offering should always be the best of something that you have to give, even if it's a daily offering you are making. The idea here isn't to do something as a throw away action, but to do it with intention and even if it is small and casual it should be meaningful. It should have value, both intrinsically and to you as something that actually costs to give. The cost doesn't necessarily have to be monetary, but it should be something that really matters to you, something that you have an investment in. I burn incense every day to the Gods and it is always either something I've made myself or the best quality one I could find to buy.

Offering to spirits is not a matter of giving second-rate things or whatever you have on hand[5], although I will say that in some situations I have literally given the jewelry I was wearing. In my house we often share our own food with the various spirits we offer to, both in the belief that we are giving what is good enough for us, and because the practice of sharing food with spirits is a long one in many cultures, seen in things like the Dumb Supper and in ancient ritual sites where evidence shows feasting and faunal deposits (people sacrificing animals, eating them and giving them to the Gods and Aos Sí).

When choosing what to give I do look at what would have been a traditional offering, which for the Good Neighbors includes: milk, cream, butter, water, bread, cakes, fresh fruit, vegetables, portions of meals shared by the family, alcohol, and honey. I also trust my intuition though, so there have been occasions where I have given non-traditional things because I strongly felt it was desired. Sometimes I give things like poetry or songs, or my own effort or energy with something, if it seems like that is an appropriate thing to give. And I find that sometimes when something needs to be given I'll just get an idea for what it needs to be – and understand it isn't always something I want to give. For whatever reason I end up offering a lot of silver in the form of jewelry, usually jewelry I have a sentimental attachment to. These aren't things I necessarily want to get rid of, in the sense of I'm not seeking to give them away or eager to give them up. I'd rather keep them, but I've found that when I get that feeling that I need to give something the more I resist it the stronger the feeling gets and the more little omens and indications I'll get that I need to make the offering. Recently, for example, I had a feeling before going somewhere that I was going to need to give one of my favorite necklaces, a larger stone that was a cabochon of an amethyst naturally growing within clear quartz set in silver (my friend had called it a fairy stone when she'd seen it). I did not want to give up this necklace, but nonetheless I wore it when I went where I was going, and while I was there I kept getting that nagging feeling as well an assortment of different things going on indicating that an offering was needed. I tried other things first of course, because I'm stubborn, but finally I gave the fairies what they wanted and after that things shifted in a more positive sense. I've had the same thing happen before over the years, and I try to be philosophical about it. You may sometimes feel called to offer something with metaphysical significance such as your own blood or an oath and in that case you need to really seriously think about all the implications before you do it, especially if you have no familiarity with blood magic or with the power of oaths. When in doubt don't do it is always a good way to go, and try to find a substitute. If you really feel you must, try to talk to someone more experienced first if you can.

So, we've looked at why we offer and what, and in this context we know to whom means the fairies primarily. When we offer is another question we might want to discuss. I mentioned daily offerings, and those are an option for something like a house fairy, although I wouldn't personally recommend it. I sometimes make daily offerings along with divination about the day to come in the morning as part of my morning routine, but these are more random than consistent. These offerings are also fairly small and basic – usually incense and lighting a candle – and are a way to both ask for success and guidance in the divination and offer gratitude for their presence. I also make a weekly offering to the Good People, of cream, because it is traditional and to maintain a right relationship with them. And on the holy days, the holidays I celebrate, I make offerings as well, which I see as part of a long tradition of offering to the fairies on sacred days. If I am traveling I will make offerings when I come to a new place, sort of a peace or friendship offering to the spirits of that place. I don't think there's really any right or wrong for when to make offerings, but I do think if you are pagan/polytheist seeking to establish a relationship with the Fair Folk that making offerings at least on the holy days is a good idea.

I will add this though on the subject of regular offerings to the Other Crowd: it's a commitment that you shouldn't start unless you're willing to follow through with it. There are weeks were I am literally spending the last of my grocery money – or dipping into my gas money – to get the cream to give the Good Neighbors, but they always get theirs, sure enough. I learned my lesson on that one years ago when finances made me decide to stop giving them milk and I had an entire gallon pulled from my hand; as my grandfather would say, if you don't give them their due they'll take it. And in my experience they really will. There is also a story from Irish folklore of a young Catholic woman in the 19th century who always made sure to pour out a little milk for the fairies when she milked her cow, but after converting to Protestantism quit the practice, which was frowned on by her new religion. She then found that every time she milked her cow the milk would be spilled or the pail knocked over, so after a short time returned to pouring a bit out herself; the accidental spilling then stopped. If you have any hesitation about starting a committed schedule of offering then simply don't offer regularly.

Where you leave offerings is really going to depend on your own circumstances and preferences. I follow the school of thought that the fairies consume the essence of the item, the toradh as Campbell would have it, if it's food or drink within the first 24 hours of it being offered and after that the physical item itself can be disposed of. Therefore I leave offerings on my altar for a day then throw them out, or put them outside. In some cases I put them directly outside, but if you choose to do this consider whether the item is safe for any animal that might eat it. Milk, cream, honey, or alcohol are either kept on the altar for a day or poured directly outside. Flammable items like paper, butter, ghee, or herbs, I burn, because of the old Celtic belief (recorded by the Romans) that what is burned with intent in our world appears in the Otherworld. Solid items like silver, jewelry, or weapons, I give to earth or water, again because of archaeological evidence that this is how historic offerings were made in the pagan period.

This should be common sense, but we all know the saying about that... Most of this has been discussing offerings in the context of home or private ritual sites. If you are visiting a historical, archaeological, famous, or natural site please do not leave a tangible, lasting offering there unless there is a policy in place allowing it. It's bad form to leave items, even what you might consider small things like crystals or coins, at sites that might be excavated for study at some point, and it's extremely bad form to leave any sort of trash or litter anywhere. Candle wax, food wrappers, bottles and such are trash and they shouldn't be left at public sacred sites for other people to clean up. If you feel you want to participate in the tradition of the rag trees in Ireland, which involves tying a piece of cloth to a tree by a healing well, then please be aware that the cloth should be natural and one that will decay quickly or it can and will harm the tree. Also understand that the practice was applied specifically to certain trees for a very specific reason and if you aren't 100 per cent sure you understand the reason and which trees, then just don't do it. And never, ever – please! – tie anything except organic cloth to a sacred tree (or any other for that matter). Plastic, synthetic material, and such damages the tree and may kill it over time. When in doubt about what to offer at a sacred/famous/public location pouring out a bit of water is usually a respectful and safe option. You can save the bigger offerings for other private settings later, or ask someone local (if you are traveling) how best to handle what you need to do.

So, I think we've covered every aspect of offerings I can think of, excluding how, which is really a personal detail that I think is up to the individual to decide and also probably depends on your specific path – although it's been touched on throughout in bits and pieces. Offerings should never be taken lightly, and even when they are part of the daily round of our spirituality should never become routine, but should be done mindfully. Whatever we offer should always be understood as important and valuable, or quite frankly it's not worth doing, because if it's being done without the proper intent or without any meaning – offering something with no real value to the person – then it will have no meaning or value to the spirits receiving it either, and in the case of the fairies may even anger them.

Protections

A key aspect to dealing with Otherworldly beings is an awareness that while the goal may be to create positive relationships and build allies, there is always risk involved. Because of this it is important to know how to protect yourself, those you are about and your property if necessary. I know many people prefer to believe that protections against fairies are not generally needed, and ideally they wouldn't be, but it should say something about the potential need for them that folk tradition offers us so very many options in this area.

This section is going to look at a variety of options for protecting against the Good People, should they decide they have a problem with you. I would normally add a bit here about how to tell if that's an issue, but it is usually fairly obvious as the fairies are rarely subtle with their anger. Generally speaking I will say that if you find that all of your luck has turned bad, your health has suddenly and inexplicably taken a turn for the worse, your possessions are being lost or broken, you are losing things that are precious to you, and you are being physically injured then you may very well have an enemy among the Folk. It is also possible that you might find yourself needing to use some of these things to help someone else who is either in trouble with the fairies or who has drawn their attention in a way that could endanger that person.

You may also need to resort to some of these protections for less extreme reasons. Sometimes you may not have angered one of the fairies, but may simply find that you have drawn the attention of one that is too mischievous or troublesome and you'd rather not be stuck dealing with it. You might be in a situation at particular location where you cross paths with something hostile and you need to protect yourself. Or you may be someone who generally works well with the Fey Folk, but you have children in your home and you want to have protections around them to be sure they are safe, given the fairies' interest in taking human children. Sometimes you just need to have particular areas that are protected against their presence. I ran into an issue with my second child who is able to see spirits where she, at the age of three or four, was frightened seeing things in her room that she felt were dangerous. Putting protections on her room with her help made her feel safe and established a 'fairy-free zone' that she could go to when she needed.

Whatever the reason, it is important to be aware of what you can do to protect yourself and others. Always keep in mind though that there is no one thing that works on all fairies, which is perhaps part of why we see such a wide array of protection options.

Iron is the most common thing recommended as protection against faeries, and can take the form of a horseshoe hung up over the door, a knife or pair of scissors under the mattress, or an iron nail in the pocket. In my experience the majority of fairies can't bear the touch of iron, probably in the range of two-thirds of them. The others though have no problem with it, and those would include any being that naturally exists in proximity to iron ore or by its nature deals with iron. For example mine faeries, forge spirits, and most house spirits, as well as some of the Aos Sí who are connected to smithing.

Why iron? No one agrees and there is certainly no definitive answer, but many people have theories. One common one is that the Tuatha De used bronze and part of why the Gaels drove them out was the Gaels' use of iron, and that this in turn developed into the fairies' aversion to iron, either as a genuine aversion or as a psychological abhorrence. It does seem unlikely that smith Gods would be averse to any metal, but iron is a newer material to be worked by humans. Some also argue in the same vein that as humans developed iron we drove the fairy beings out of our world because they could not handle the refined metal. Some also argue that it was the process of forging itself that endowed iron with a magical quality and granted it the ability to protect from fairy enchantments; it is true that blacksmiths have a reputation in folk tradition and mythology as magic workers. In the end of course no one really knows why, but it is a ubiquitously recommended protection in Celtic folklore and elsewhere.

My own theory is that it is because of the strong grounding nature of iron versus the inherently magical nature of fairies. Iron draws and grounds magical energy. Fairies by their nature not only use this same energy, but also often seem to be made up of it, particularly if you go by how Robert Kirk describes them in *The Secret Commonwealth of Elves, Fauns, and Fairies*: '...*said to be of a middle Nature betwixt Man and Angel, as were Daemons thought to be of old; intelligent fluidious Spirits, and light changable Bodies, (lyke those called Astral) somewhat of the Nature of a condensed Cloud.*' I don't believe all fairies are '*astral*' as he describes them because some are clearly capable of physical interaction with us and our world, but certainly they all rely heavily on magic, which iron interferes with and dispels, and that may be enough reason for them to avoid it.

True forged iron is hard to come by these days and, although it is the best protection, steel will also work. Generally the type of item isn't as important as the material in this case so anything made of iron or steel that you can procure can be used for protective purposes although in folklore the most common items recommended are black handled knives, knives more generally, scissors, nails, horse shoes, and fire tongs (Campbell, 1900,

Briggs, 1976; Danaher, 1972).

There seems to be a lot of confusion about the apotropaic qualities of iron. So, I want to quickly clear some points up. Iron is said in folklore to protect against a wide range of spirits and negative magics including (most of) the Good Neighbors as well as, ghosts, demons, and witches. Iron objects deter the majority of the Other Crowd who are averse to its presence and things like knives, scissors, nails, and horseshoes were recommended as protective objects because even the presence of such an item is enough to keep the fairies away from a person or area. It is said that cemeteries had iron fences to contain any ghosts inside. Similarly older folklore said that demons were also repelled by iron, and it was believed to break the magic of witches. A horseshoe hung up above a doorway kept out a wide range of spirits as well as protecting from baneful magic.

Many people are familiar with the term 'cold iron' and associate it today with pure or simply worked forged iron – what is technically called 'pig iron' or 'crude iron'. Historically the term cold iron was a poetic term for any iron weapon and is synonymous today with the term 'cold steel'. When you see a reference to cold iron it is talking about an iron weapon, usually a sword or knife. This may explain in part why most of the recommendation for iron objects refer to bladed or sharp items, which have not only the quality of the item as a protective force, but also the inherent threat of the items nature.

As to iron and steel; they are effectively the same substance and have been treated that way in folklore and for apotropaic purposes historically. Steel is between 90 percent and 98 per cent iron depending on the alloy, so a steel object is obviously mostly an iron object.

Those who are seeking to encourage the presence of the Gentry should remember their dislike of iron and limit its presence. On the other hand those seeking protection from Otherworldly influence would do well to keep iron or steel objects around. Remember though that I said earlier it is a protection against most of the Good Neighbors. In folklore there are some fey it is known to have no effect on, including Etins, Redcaps, and spirits associated with mines or forges. Other protections are required for those, such as salt or silver.

In my experience iron ore and stones with high iron content work the same as iron, but to a weaker degree, i.e. hematite, which is about 70-ish per cent iron and magnetite (72 per cent iron). Both work to deflect negative magic and to deter ghosts, negative spirits, and the fey who are sensitive to iron, but not as intensely as worked iron, even so-called 'pig iron'.

Iron ore is most often hematite or magnetite along with a few others with a slightly lower iron content so it makes sense that they work in a similar fashion to iron. A variety of crystals also have iron as a component, which is what give them their color, such as peridot, but usually not in an amount that would act as an effective deterrent. Although I think it's unlikely any fey would wear them or desire to be around them and if you offer crystals to the Other Crowd I might suggest looking for ones without iron content, but that's not exactly here nor there.

There are several ways to use iron to protect your home from fairies, if it's needed. In Celtic tradition you could hang a horseshoe, points up, over your doorway, which would also act to bless the home and draw luck to you. For protection against fairies you can also place an iron knife or scissors in a strategic place. Another method found in Germanic and Norse traditions is to hammer an iron nail into a post near the doorway or alternatively part of the door frame. Additionally, it is said to be as effective to draw a circle using an iron nail or knife around what you want to protect (Gundarsson, 2007).

A more modern, but still useful method, is the use of iron water. Fill a small spray bottle with water and add iron filings, iron dust, or a piece of iron, and allow to sit for a few days. The water can be sprayed into a room or around the home as needed.

As always keep in mind that the use of iron will not affect all fairies, as some, including house fairies, are not bothered by it. For those that are sensitive to it, though, it is a superlative protection. For this reason those who seek to work with fairies must be very cautious about using this metal, as it will drive away most fairies as well as interfering with some types of magic and other spirits. One should never, for example, cut a plant to be harvested for magical purposes with an iron knife as this will drive away the plant's spirit.

Besides iron there are a variety of other options for protection against the Good People including salt, fire, four leaf clovers, bells, several different kinds of herbs, hag stones, and turning clothes inside out. These are all things that are established as effective in folklore and have been tried and tested, as it were. Keep in mind though that what is being discussed here is ultimately only a sample of the protections against fairies and there are many others out there. The herbs I mention for example are only a small number of the ones that are known to protect against fairy influence, so you should research this on your own if the subject really interests you.

Although not as widely recommended as iron, salt also has protective qualities. In some cases salt works better than iron at driving out dangerous fairies. Salt was sprinkled on cows who had just calved to protect them from fairy influence, salt was used with fire and water to bless pastures, and salt was used to protect butter from the influence of fairies and witches (McNeill, 1962). Salt is said to symbolize eternity and carrying it is a strong protection (Briggs, 1976). The idea of using salt by sprinkling it around yourself, often in a circle, is one that has entered pop culture thanks to movies such as *Hocus Pocus* and television shows like *Supernatural*, but the core idea behind this is rooted in older folklore; salt is used in purification and so it is believed that impure – or as the Scottish might say unsainly – beings cannot be around it. One method to force fairies to release people from a fairy hill is to dig into the mound and throw salt and ashes into the open earth, as fire and salt are powerful forces against fairy magic (Logan, 1981).

Although often seen today as being cliché, the four leaf clover has a long use in folk tradition. The main power of the four leaf clover against the Good People is its ability to dispel their glamour and allow a human to see truly (Briggs, 1976). This is because glamour and enchantment are some of the main powers that are used to mislead people; by making them think a handful of leaves are a fistful of gold coins, perhaps, or that a dreary cave is a palace, the Fair Folk can control people to their own benefit and the person's misfortune. The four leaf clover gives some power back to the human by taking away this advantage. If you have such a talisman it should be carried on you or kept in something that you keep on you in order to be effective. Often in folk charms such an herb would be sown into a person's clothing.

Bells and the sound of bells ringing are also said to frighten away any malicious spirits. Most references to this specify church bells; however, folklore makes it clear that any kind of bell, including those worn by Morris Men, and those attached to livestock, will have the same effect (Briggs, 1976). I was always told, although I could not say where I learned this, that the ringing of bells will have no effect on most spirits, but only certain types that are most inclined towards causing us harm. For those spirits the sound of bells is piercing and very painful. This may well be true as it should be kept in mind that the Fairy Rade and the Fairy Queen when she rides out is often described as accompanied by the sound of bells ringing, and descriptions say that the horses would have bells woven into their manes, making it clear that the more Seelie types of fairies neither fear bells nor flee from their sounds.

Certain herbs are protection against fairies as well, and these include St. John's wort, broom, yarrow, and rowan berries, although it is also said that some of the Aos Sí live on rowan berries (Briggs, 1976; McNeill, 1962). Tying a red ribbon on cattle or horses was thought to keep fairies away, as was tying a rowan twig on to a cow's tail, or lightly striking the animals with rowan or hazel switches (O hOgain, 1995; O hOgain, 2006). The color red itself seems to have a warding effect against some fairies, which can be seen in its use not only with certain herbs and berries, but also in the combination of rowan twigs and red thread, or rowan, amber, and red thread, to protect against fairies and negative magic. Ash may be substituted for rowan if necessary (Briggs, 1976). Although mugwort may be best known among witches today as an herb for psychic empowerment, in the old Leechcraft texts it was burned and otherwise used to drive off spirits, especially Elves, and can still be used as a protection against Elven enchantment and to break their magic on a person. Protections against harm from the Other Crowd included primrose and gorse scattered on the doorstep, and rowan branches hung over the doorway (Evans, 1957). Yarrow was hung in the home to ward off illness, and a loop of ash might be used to protect a person against Themselves; it was also said looking through the loop would allow someone to see them even through glamour (Evans, 1957; Danaher, 1972). St John's wort is said to protect against fairy enchantments, and grant luck, prosperity, and blessing. In Irish tradition St John's wort is one of the seven herbs that cannot be affected by anything supernatural (Wilde, 1991). Verbena is another herb recommended for protection, as are daisies and it is said a child wearing daisies cannot be taken by the fey (Briggs, 1976). All of these can be used in various ways that include carrying on your person, sowing into clothes, burning, hanging up in the home, or scattering near doorways. I have broom hanging in my children's rooms for example, as a protection, and I have rowan bound with red thread over the entrance to my house.

Hagstones are stones that naturally have a hole in them, usually from the action of water wearing through. To be clear, by the way, they do not work if the hole is artificially created; the stone must be found with the hole in it as a natural artifact. Hagstones are usually found in water, either salt or fresh water, and are protection against not only fairies, but also various types of negative magic and influences. Traditionally they might be hung up in a stable to keep fairies from either putting Elf-knots in the manes of horses or taking the animals out at night and riding them into exhaustion. They can also be used hung over the bed to ward off nightmares and similar fairy interference with sleeping humans.

Turning clothes is a method of protection recommended particularly for breaking enchantments that cause confusion, such as being Pixy-led. This can be as simple as turning socks inside out although the usual preference is to turn your coat inside out. Briggs suggests that this works because it represents a change of identity that effectively dispels the existing magic.

There are also an assortment of other protections to consider. Amber works as a protection against the fey, and is often used to protect babies and children. Sulfur is a protection against fairies, particularly those of the Norse tradition (Gundarsson, 2007). Bread, which can be used as an offering, is also a protection against fairies being as Briggs says 'a symbol of life' (Briggs, 1976). The Rev. Robert Kirk mentioned the use of bread as a protection against fairies as well, when he discussed ways to keep them from taking women in childbed. Many sources in folklore mention the use of Christian holy symbols, particularly the cross, as a way to drive off fairies or protect against them, although the poem *Alice Brand* makes it clear that this method is not effective against all fairies, especially those who were once human. Given that in that poem the Fairy King sends a fairy who is exempt from the influence of holy symbols to attack the protagonists knowing that they may resort to prayer or a cross, I would not personally trust my safety to this method unless there was no other option.

When outdoors if you find yourself in danger from anything

fey, one method to protect yourself is to cross running water. It is best if the water you cross is south-running, as anything moving southwards, like anything moving sunwise, has positive and blessing qualities. This method of protection is also said to work against ghosts and malignant spirits (Wilde, 1887). Although leaping running water is a good method if caught outdoors, don't forget that some beings like the Kelpie make their homes in water and will not be stopped by it (Briggs, 1976). Iron should be carried any time you think you may be going somewhere with potential danger, ideally a black handled iron knife[6], or else ashes from the hearth fire, and if one is being misled or tormented by the Good People one could turn their jacket inside out to confuse them, as previously mentioned, or in more dire circumstances you could splash urine on your hands and face[7] (Danaher, 1972). Of course the most commonly used protection may simply be staying away from places known to be Theirs and avoiding any chance encounters.

A variety of protections focus specifically on laboring and nursing mothers as well as newborns. To keep a new mother and infant safe they would be given milk from a cow who had eaten the herb mothan (McNeill, 1956). Rev. The Kirk suggested putting bread, a Bible, or cold iron with a woman in labor to protect her from being taken.

If you believe a group of passing fairies, particularly the Slua, has taken a human with them and want to get them to release the person you should throw the dust from the road, an iron knife, or your left shoe and say: 'This is yours; that is mine!' (McNeill, 1956). Throwing iron seems to be an effective method for getting the fey to release a person if the person is in sight, and I might suggest in cases of fairy possession or suspected influence that it would be worth trying iron on or near the person as well.

In some extreme cases a person might show indications of being on the receiving end of negative fairy magic, which will have very specific symptoms. At any point that a situation, especially one involving a person being affected or harmed by fairy magic, is beyond your ability to handle you should not hesitate to look for someone more knowledgeable or experienced. For example, traditionally if a person was suffering from the ill-willing attention of one of the fairy people, a fairy doctor must be found. That is a person with special knowledge of the fairies, who can diagnose the exact issue, be it elfshot or fairy blast, and come up with the appropriate charm, chant, or herb to cure the person (Wilde, 1887). There will always be some times and situations that call for an expert, and it's wise to know your own limitations and abilities so you are confident of what you can and cannot handle.

Getting Started

I think the first step to dealing with fairies is to read as much folklore about them as possible. Not the watered-down fairytales, but the real folklore, the gathered stories collected from people who actually believed and still believe in these beings. Suspend your own disbelief if you haven't quite gotten to a point yet yourself to see them as real and take what you read at face value – don't try to rationalize it away or explain what might have caused it. Just take it in for what it is. Believe that the person telling the experience believed it.

Next reach out to your house fairy[8]. Set aside a small area for them, ideally in the kitchen or wherever people most often gather. Maybe leave some milk there on occasion. Try to be as welcoming as you can be, knowing this spirit is there and has always been there. A house fairy, by the way, is not the same as a Brownie, or at least not necessarily, but rather is a generic term for the sort of domestic fairy that is found in any home. House fairies are seen in many different cultures, in many different forms, and usually like to live in or around the hearth, which in modern parlance is the kitchen. They can and do influence the overall mood of a home and can affect the luck and health of people living in a place. I should also mention that you may have one or many as some are solitary and some are social (aka trooping), but since there is so much variety its really impossible for me to speak in anything except generalities about them here. My house has one solitary house fairy as well as a collection of social ones; the two groups – if you will – exist apart from each other but all within the house, so such a situation is also a possibility. The point here isn't so much to worry about exactly what kind of house fairy you have, but to try to make friends with it.

When you feel that you have a solid connection with your house fairy, based on your own intuition and personal measure, then start slowly expanding out. How you do this is up to you, based on your own comfort zone. If you like the idea of safe fairies maybe look at connecting to garden or smaller plant fairies. If you are aware of locations around you with fairy activity perhaps spend some time there and feel out the energy. Try visiting Fairy in dreams or with spiritual journeywork.

Know how to protect yourself, and know what to do to make friends (hint – give them gifts and be nice). Follow the seven guidelines I mentioned at the beginning of this chapter. And know that you will make mistakes, and those mistakes will sometimes have lasting consequences. You will get in over your head sometimes, you will meet things that scare you and things that try to hurt you – and you will get hurt sometimes. But if you persevere you'll also learn a lot and slowly build connections and allies. It's got a steep learning curve, but it also has its rewards.

Fortune favors the bold. Just remember to be canny as well as courageous.

End Notes

1. Twee – excessively cute, sweet, delicate; often used of an affectation of daintiness or quaintness. Think the new Disney Tinker Bell (not the original from the 1904 play – she was properly vicious).

2. There are – no surprises here – some exceptions to this, but please use common sense. If you are asking for healing then yes you may be required to offer or pay with something like hair or blood. That's fine. I wouldn't suggest giving something like blood up front, but if it's being requested, don't hesitate to ask why and really consider the answer. Ultimately you are an adult and can make your own decisions about what you feel is safe to do or give.

3. This is discussed by both Katherine Briggs and in anecdotal evidence, although the reasoning is obscure. I do not personally remember where I first heard of this prohibition, but I have known it for a very long time.

4. In fairness while they called it a fairy they were actually talking about making a thoughtform or golem. But still the principle of creating your own fairy servant is pretty offensive so here we are.

5. I'll add one exception to that, in emergency situations obviously, you may end up offering what you have on hand, but it should still be the best you can muster.

6. Danaher also discusses the power of a black handled iron knife against the fey in *The Year in Ireland*; although no one seems able to offer a clear reason why it must be black handled such an item is referenced often enough in folklore that I would be confident relying on it for protection.

7. The Good People detest filth and things like dirty wash water and urine are known to disgust them, and so act as protections against them.

8. It doesn't matter what your living situation is, provided only that you live in a building that usually has people sleeping in it. Even hotels and motels have what could be loosely termed house fairies in them. You don't have to own the building, you don't have to be the primary resident, you don't even have to be a permanent resident. If you are sleeping there for any length of time you can reach out to the spirit of that house.

Conclusion

Find what you love and let it kill you.

*Let it drain you of your all. Let it cling onto your back and weigh
you down into eventual nothingness.*

Let it kill you and let it devour your remains.

*For all things will kill you, both slowly and fastly, but it's much
better to be killed by a lover.*

Charles Bukowski

People have always had a certain fascination with the world of
Fairy, and there have always been those who found a special
connection to it and the beings within it. Folklore is full of stories
of people who earned favor among the fairies with their
boldness, cleverness, and good manners, as well as people who
suffered for offending them. Looking at the array of fairylore is
like looking at a colorful quilt spread out in front of us, and
knowing that the surface we see, as dazzling and artful as it may
be, conceals another side that we aren't seeing.

The more you seek to study Fairy the more you begin to
understand that every answer is a contradiction and every truth
has its equally true opposite. It is a maddening maze to work
through trying to find your way to solid answers, and at some
point you will realize that in this case at least it really is the
journey that has value, not the destination. I like to think that
Thomas the Rhymer realized that as well, as he rode for forty
days and nights, in darkness, in deserts, wading through blood;
that it wasn't where he was going that was the goal, but the
process of getting there.

If you have read through this entire text than you have read a
great deal about fairies and Fairy. Hopefully you have gained
some small insight into the traditional beliefs and some of the
aspects of fairylore that are increasingly being lost in modern

paganism. Perhaps you already knew some of these things, or perhaps this was all new to you. Either way I hope that this journey has had some value for you.

It pains me to think of centuries or more of belief and practice, which were vital and central to people's lives, just fading away and being lost. The old fairy beliefs have a lot of power and wisdom to them, if we take the time to learn them. And it really does bother me to see people not making any effort to learn the old ways – which are there to be found and learned with a little bit of effort – and instead relying just on their own imaginations, intuition, and modern pulp fiction coming out with things that directly contradict the old beliefs. Basically doing things that would never have been done previously for specific reasons, usually relating to safety. And sometimes that doesn't end well for them.

Preserving the old beliefs matters, and we should care about it – and bringing those beliefs into modern times doesn't mean erasing the past and making it all up anew, but realizing that those beings and beliefs never went anywhere and have been and are still with us – all we have to do is understand how they evolved with us into this century. Because they did.

We live in a world today where the old fairy beliefs are quickly being lost. This isn't anything new, more than a hundred years ago people were already aware that this was happening, that the cynicism, skepticism, and desire by people not to seem backwards or superstitious was eroding away the old fairy beliefs. Douglas Hyde, a collector of Irish folklore, said in 1911: *'My own experience is that beliefs in the Sidhe folk, and in other denizen of the invisible world is, in many places, rapidly dying.'* (Evans-Wentz, 1911, p26) He then goes on to relate how even in his time people had largely forgotten that a certain hill was named Mullach na Sidhe (hilltop of the fairies), and that another place, Cluain Siabhra (meadow of the fairies) had been mistakenly associated with 'shiver' because people didn't remember the correct name or the stories about the place. His experience as someone who was actively gathering these stories illustrated an important point that is still valid today: what we do not continue to value and actively pass on will die with us.

This book has been my attempt to draw attention back to the older traditional beliefs. In our world today where belief is shaped less by tradition and lore that has been passed down through generations and more by personal opinions and imagination the old ways and beliefs are still there to be found, but it requires effort. We must be willing to look beyond the bulk of what is offered to readers today by pagan publishers and look instead to the older sources and to the living cultures, to the storytellers; to the wisdom of tradition and to the modern experiences that still happen and reflect the older lore. The fairy beliefs, like the fairies themselves, still exist if we are willing to look for them and willing to embrace knowledge that had, until recently, been passed down through generations. This book then, is the summary of much of what I know and what tradition tells us about the fairies, as well as some of my own modern experiences. It is a distillation of the information and beliefs that are available, gathered here into a single resource.

People seeking to deal with fairies in the modern world have just as many opportunities as people a hundred or a thousand years ago did. The question is whether you will choose to do so or not. Ideally now you have the knowledge and tools to begin.

As I finished this book I found myself thinking of the quote by Bukowski that started this chapter and how very much his words can be applied to the fey and the Otherworld. What we love consumes us in the end, whether it is fair or fierce, and because of our love we fling ourselves willingly into our own destruction. That is probably why it was always better to fear the fairies than to be enchanted by them – fear brings a healthy caution and a measure of safety, but enchantment brings a desire for that which will destroy us in the end, one way or another.

And yet...all things die and all lives end. So maybe Bukowski's right, better to be killed by what we love.

Resources

Books

This is a list of some of the books that I find more essential to begin with when starting a study of fairies:

A Dictionary of Fairies by Katherine Briggs – an essential look at a wide array of different fairies and folklore including some stories.

A Practical Guide to Irish Spirituality: Sli Aon Dhraoi by Lora O'Brien – a great overall introduction to modern Irish paganism and ways to relate to the native powers of Ireland. I'd also recommend the author's older book, *Irish Witchcraft from an Irish Witch*.

Fairy and Folktales of the Irish Peasantry by W. B. Yeats – a look at folklore and belief, especially fairylore.

The Gaelic Otherworld by John Campbell – an overview of Scottish folk beliefs and folklore.

The Fairy Faith in Celtic Countries by W. Y. Evans Wentz – the classic text on the Fairy Faith. It's a bit dated at this point having come out in 1911, but it includes fairy beliefs from a wide array of Celtic cultures.

Scottish Herbs and Fairy Lore – by Ellen Evert Hopman – a great book on traditional Scottish fairy beliefs and related practices.

Faeries by Brian Froud and Alan Lee – excellent artwork and some great tidbits of folklore sprinkled in.

Elves, Wights and Trolls by Kveldulfr Gundarson – a look at Norse and German fairy beliefs and some comparison with the Celtic beliefs. Very useful for looking at how different closely related cultures viewed their fairies.

The Secret Commonwealth of Elves, Fauns and Fairies by The Reverend Robert Kirk – written in the 17th century, it's a short, but fascinating look at traditional Scottish fairy beliefs.

The Secret Commonwealth and the Fairy Belief Complex by Brian Walsh – a review and analysis of the Rev Kirk's book, but extremely insightful and should be read in addition to Kirk's book for its commentary on beliefs about fairies.

Meeting the Other Crowd by Eddie Lenihan and Carolyn Green – an excellent book on Irish fairylore.

The Good People: New Fairylore Essays, edited by Peter Narvez – a collection of scholarly essays discussing a variety of aspects of fairylore and including a wide array of anecdotal evidence.

Elves in Anglo-Saxon England by Alaric Hall – a very thorough discussion of how Elves were viewed and understood historically in England. Although not explicitly Celtic there is cultural overlap and influence that merits study here.

Movies

Besides books there are some movies that I've found helpful in conveying the general feel of the beliefs themselves, and these include:*The Secret of Roan Inish* (1995) Sony Pictures – the story of a family that used to live on a remote Irish island, but has moved to the mainland and their connection to the seal people, called roan.

Into the West (2011) Echo Bridge Home Entertainment – two boys try to free a horse they believe to be a Pooka.

Legend (1986) Universal Studios – a complex story of good and evil, full of unicorns and fairies.

The Secret of Kells (2010) New Video Group – an animated film about a boy apprenticed to a monk who befriends a forest spirit.

Labyrinth (1986) Sony Pictures – the story of a girl's quest to regain her little brother from the Goblin King after she accidently gives him away.

Song of the Sea (2014) Universal Studios – an amazing animated film that tells the tale of Ben and his sister Saoirse who is the last Selkie left and the only one who can save all the Irish Aos Sí with her song – except she's mute. (This one is my younger daughter's favorite movie.)

The Last Unicorn (1982) Shout! Factory – an animated film about the last unicorns attempt to find out where all of the other unicorns have gone, and eventually to free them.

Fairy Faith (2001) Wellspring Media – a documentary by a Canadian film maker who traveled around North America, Ireland, and the United Kingdom interviewing people about their beliefs relating to the Fair Folk. Unfortunately out of production and hard to find on DVD now, but you can watch it on YouTube.

Kin (2013) Five Knights Production – part of a series, hard to easily describe in words, but this short film is visceral and very fey. It can be watched on Vimeo: vimeo.com/73747093

A Note on Anecdotal Evidence

Often when you start to look for books on paganism one of the first pieces of advice you might get from more experienced people is to avoid things published prior to and during the Victorian era (with the exception of much older manuscripts, particularly myths) or books that rely too much on these as sources. Generally speaking this is good advice as this period was a time when scholarship was heavy on unsupported supposition and opinion and short on factual evidence. There is, however, one large exception to this general rule that I'd like to address today because it's an important one, especially for those who have an interest in fairylore.

There was a movement during this same time period for folklorists and anthropologists to begin collecting the stories of the people, both the old folk tales that had been passed on for generations and also stories of personal experiences and family lore. The motives for doing so were likely less than ideal in some cases, but the result is a multitude of books that are full of stories that relate people's first or second hand experiences with the Good Neighbors and the complex beliefs surrounding them over the past several hundred years. For modern people, especially those interested in the Fairy Faith as a viable system, these stories are vital. While the usual rule of thumb may be to avoid books dated prior to the mid-1900s or so when we are looking at books of folklore, the rules are different. Although I still advocate being careful with anything sold as 'retellings' because those usually involve a lot of fictitious additions, and translations, because they often alter material in the translating, there are many important folklore collections to be found from the 1800s.

Of course when we read these stories we must still be cautious to watch for the editor's influence on them. It is usually easy to tell where the person writing them down has inserted their own opinions into the narrative or where they have simply written down exactly what they were told as it was told to them. In many cases we get a mixed result where there may be a great deal of wonderful anecdotal information preserved, but we must pick through secondary opinions to get to it. We see this with the *Fairy Faith in Celtic Countries*, which espouses some popular theories of its time that should not be trusted now – like the fairies as native British pygmies – while also giving us some valuable folklore. We shouldn't throw out the baby with the bathwater, but rather learn the discernment to judge what is valuable and what is just some Victorian academic's personal opinion.

We also need to keep in mind something else. Anecdotal evidence is not limited to a hundred years ago – it still exists today. We have the strangest habit as a culture (speaking especially of Americans here) of giving some credit to people a hundred years ago for actually possibly having had some genuine experience of the Otherworld while simultaneously doing everything possible to rationalize away people in our time saying the same things. We can believe that a hundred years ago someone saw or experienced Fairy, but simultaneously believe that no one can really have those same experiences today except intangibly in dreams or meditations. And yet people do still see and experience Fairy as they always have; we are just more reluctant to talk about it today because of the strength of the disbelief. Not to say we should immediately believe every claim by every person, because discernment is always valuable, under any circumstances, but I'd caution against deciding that our own cynicism should be the measure for everyone. What we personally see or understand is not the limit or ability of everyone else. It may be best to find a balance between a healthy skepticism and an attitude that espouses, as Shakespeare's character Hamlet said: *'There are more things on heaven and Earth than are dreamt of in your philosophy.'* There have been some efforts to collect modern anecdotes, such as *Seeing Fairies* by Marjorie Johnson and Simon Young as well as an excellent documentary *The Fairy Faith – In Search of Fairies*. These modern collections are just as important as the older ones because they show that the beliefs are still vital and alive, if less visible.

Ultimately anecdotal evidence is important because it gives us a snapshot of the beliefs of the people at different points of time. It shows us not only what they believed, but also in practical terms how they felt the different worlds interacted and affected each other. Reading a range of anecdotal evidence across different periods of time is important, and for those interested in fairylore it is essential to see the beliefs in different areas and the changes to beliefs over time. We can learn a great deal from this material, if we are willing to embrace the older as well as the new.

Appendix A

Fairies, Witches, and Dangerous Magic

When many people think of the classical image of the witch it comes with the implicit shadow of the Devil looming over it and an inherent sense of danger. When the folklore is studied in Scotland and Ireland, however, it is not cloven hooves and hellfire that mark many witches, but the touch of Fairy and inter-action with the Otherworld that made them what they were, and for some of us what we are still. But people are right nonetheless to associate this kind of fairy-touched witchcraft with dangerous magic, the sort that up-ends social orders and defies the status quo, the sort that runs wild under the night sky singing to itself of madness and mystery, the sort that seeks to give power to those who society sees as powerless. And that sort of magic is without a doubt dangerous, because it is boundless and unrestricted by what Yeats called (in another context entirely) *'the nets of wrong and right'*.

From a traditional point of view the cunningfolk and wise women[1] worked with the right order and helped the community, but the witch worked against that order – and so did the fairies. Witches might steal a cow's milk, or stop butter from churning, or take a person's health, or a family's luck – and so might the fairies. Elfshot was wielded by the Good People, but it was also used by witches. Witches might take the form of hares to travel the countryside – and so might fairies. A witch's purpose was often personal, instead of communal, and might seem inexplicable to their neighbors, in the same way that the Other Crowd seemed to operate with their own concerns in mind, regardless of the human community. The witch defied the social order, retaliating against offenses and taking actions to ensure their own success and prosperity instead of that of the greater communal good, a good that often enough was at odds with the witch's own interests, exactly as people might view the Good Folk acting for their own good over human interests.

Isobel Gowdie said that it was from the Fair Folk that she and the other witches got elfshot and by some accounts it was from the fairies that Biddy Early obtained her famous blue bottle. Alison Pearson, a confessed witch from Scotland, said that she learned her knowledge of herbs and herbal cures from the fairies, and I have previously discussed the claims by some historic witches that they were given familiar spirits from Fairy. The idea of witches gaining knowledge from Otherworldly sources is an old one, and in itself an idea that threatened the proper order, because things taught to people by the Gentry were inherently out-of-bounds and in defiance of a system that sought to regulate and control information and education. The Other Crowd give people weapons to fight against other humans – elfshot, Otherworldly arrows that humans cannot generally even see to defend against; they give herbal knowledge that provides magical cures in defiance of established medicine; they give visions of what is and what may be to help a witch find lost items and predict the future[2].

Along these lines when questioned a variety of witches in Scotland claimed to serve not the Devil, but the Queen of Elphen or Elfhame, saying that it was this Queen who they would be brought to visit and who they served in some capacity. We can perhaps see echoes of this concept in ballads such as *Tam Lin* or *Thomas the Rhymer*; in the first Tam Lin is a mortal who is taken to serve the Queen of Fairies, apparently by guarding a well at Carterhaugh, and in the latter Thomas is taken by the Queen of Elfland to serve her for seven years in an unspecified manner before being returned to the mortal world. In the case of witches it was a very literal defiance of social order, where the witch's ultimate allegiance was to no Earthly person or Heavenly power (by Christian standards) but to the monarch of the Otherworld itself, usually bound by formal pledges or oaths and by a renunciation of mortal order in the form of the Church.

In the examples we have of historic witches associated with fairies, whether we look at those brought to trial or those renowned in more positive ways, we most often see people who were otherwise socially powerless or limited by the society of their times. People who were poor, marginalized, struggling, even victimized by the social order. Scottish witch Bessie Dunlop claimed that she made her pact with the fairies when her husband and child were desperately ill, for example. Sometimes, as in the cases of Biddy Early or Alison Pearson, the practice of magic and of dealing with the fairies seemed to be directly related to a major life change; the death of her husband in Biddy Early's case, and an illness in Pearson's. Both arguably directly impacted the person's social status and ability to fend for themselves within their society, and both arguably gained status from their fairy-related practices, although Pearson was eventually caught up in Scotland's witchcraft persecutions. Witchcraft, ultimately, was and still should be a way for people to gain or regain control of their own lives.

The Other Crowd are dangerous and unpredictable in many ways, and so can witches be, which is what we see when we look at history; because anyone who worked outside of what was deemed the proper social order was a wild card as far as that social order was concerned. In Old Irish the Good Folk are called 'Túathgeinte', literally leftwards or northwards people, with túath having connotations of evil, wicked, and of motion to the north instead of the luckier and more beneficent rightward/southward motions. In exactly the same context we have the words túathaid – person with magical powers – and túaithech – witch, or magic worker. In both cases the concepts are directly linked with the idea that dessel, with the sun, righthandwise, was lucky and fortuitous while túathal or túathbel, against the sun, lefthandwise, was unlucky and related to ill-luck and confusion. Both fairies and some witches[3] then went against the right order, turning against the sun instead of with it.

The magic of the Good Neighbors that was taught to these witches – what I in modern practice call Fairy Witchcraft – was about empowering the powerless and giving the witch a way to meet their own needs and to ensure their own safety. It was knowledge and magic that removed the person, to some degree, from human society and this removal made them dangerous because it realigned their allegiance in unpredictable ways. This is magic that is meant to effect real change for the benefit of the witch, not necessarily for some nebulous greater good. There was – is – a cost, of course, because there is always a cost in dealing with Themselves, and sometimes that cost was heavy. But it gave and gives hope to people who were suffering and hopeless, and offers control to those who otherwise are at the mercy of others.

Walking with the sun, righthandwise, is trusting the system, whether that system is religion or something else, to bless you and take care of you because you are walking the expected way, the well-worn way. Walking against the sun, lefthandwise, is taking your fate in your own hands and disrupting that system, going against that order; it is walking with the Other Crowd into danger and uncertainty because you believe ultimately the knowledge you gain there is the greater blessing. Fairies and witches have a long history together, and it is all dangerous magic.

Which is exactly as it should be, because dangerous magic gets things done in the end.

Come, heart, where hill is heaped upon hill,
For there the mystical brotherhood
Of hollow wood and the hilly wood
And the changing moon work out their will.
W. B. Yeats, *Into the Twilight*

End Notes

1. Understand, however, that these terms are fluid and one person's cunningman was another person's witch, perspective being everything in these cases.

2. Not that the Brahan Seer was a witch, necessarily, but some stories do say that it was from the fairies he got his famous seeing stone, and certainly some say that Biddy Early could look into her blue bottle and see things.

3. There are multiple words in Old Irish that mean witch, and it should be understood that túaithech is only one and has particular connotations not seen in the others. I have discussed this in a previous blog post 'Nuances of the word 'Witchcraft' and 'Witch' in Old Irish'.

Appendix B

Some Humor and Suggestions for Using Popculture

You May Have Fairy Blood If...

So there's a post on a major blogsite about eight ways to tell if you may have fairy blood. The list is heavily prejudiced towards a modern (post-Victorian) view of fairies and specifically of winged flower fairies as far as I can tell. It also includes an array of characteristics that could apply to many people for many reasons, like feeling the need to lighten the mood in serious situations with humor.

Now in the traditional lore there are stories of people who have fairy ancestry of various sorts, from the children of Selkies and fisherman to those who have a human mother and Aos Sí or Alfar father. But I would tend to use a very different measure, myself, when discussing whether someone might have 'fairy blood'. You'll quickly see a theme for my criteria, but I'll say that I'm not just getting this from folklore, and that I do believe there are more things on Heaven and Earth as Shakespeare's Hamlet said.

The following is just my own list, feel free to disregard if it doesn't appeal to you. And I know it won't to many people.

You may have fairy blood if....

1. An aversion or reaction to iron and iron alloys – it's pretty traditional in most stories for the Good Neighbors to have issues with iron, which is why it's such a powerful protection against them. This same thing can also apply to other traditional fairy protections.
2. A flamingly inappropriate sense of humor – laughing when other people are crying, or laughing when other people are

very angry. In many stories fairies are described crying at happy occasions or laughing at funerals. The jokes they play on people are also often extreme and lean towards the macabre.

3. An unusual charisma or ability to charm people – if we look at stories that mention people with mixed ancestry they are usually described this way.

4. A reputation for magical skill or healing – same as above.

5. An unusual physical appearance – in stories this can be exceedingly pale, fair, dark, tall, beautiful, Otherworldly or so on.

6. Intense emotions that may be described as inflexible – again based on looking at how folklore portrays fairies, they are often described as quick to anger, quick to love, and difficult to sway.

7. A love of both the beautiful and the broken – in folklore the fey love luxury and fine things. They also have a penchant for the grotesque.

Using Popculture as a Tool, or Teaching My Kids about Fairies

We've looked at the ways that popculture is affecting fairy beliefs, and the impression that may have left is that popculture is a bad thing, but it isn't really. The issue is making sure that we are controlling the way it influences our beliefs instead of passively absorbing it and allowing our beliefs to be shifted without realizing it. To illustrate what I mean I want to share my own approach in handling how I am using modern fairy beliefs and mass media to help teach my children about the Other Crowd.

The main focus of my actual day to day, rubber-hits-the-road spirituality is the Otherworldly spirits and land spirits. I also have three children currently aged three, eight, and twelve, which is an interesting spread to deal with. I have always held to the belief that we should raise our children with our beliefs and let them decide what they want to do from there, so from birth my kids have been raised pagan. Teaching them about the Gods has been fairly easy – they see what I do on holy days, they hear the stories, they see the altar, the offerings. I read them the mythology, much of which can be found in child-friendly versions. My husband is a very casual sort of Egyptian pagan, but they see his version of spirituality too and it offers a nice counter-point, I think to my own.

Teaching them about the Other Crowd is a whole other kettle of fish, almost literally.

You see, I realized very early with my oldest that I was swimming against the popculture tide, for the most part, on this one. Because the pagan Gods generally are untouched by modern younger kids' shows and movies, with few exceptions, but while I'm over here railing against twee little fairies and the dangers of assuming too much safety with the fey, Disney, Nickelodeon, Hollywood in general and a glut of children's fiction is teaching kids – mine included – the exact opposite of everything I'm saying to them.

And here is the real crux of the problem – I can't tell them that the happy nice fairies don't exist, nor that there aren't any winged little ones either. Because as much as I might emphasize the darker dangerous sort for the sake of caution I don't deny that Fairy is a dizzying array and variety of beings in nearly every imaginable form and temperament. There are nice little garden fey, and winged sprites, and gentle fairies who are shy and unassuming; there are all the kind and harmless things that can be imagined and probably many beyond our imagining. And there are also things that eat us for dinner, and dye their hats in our blood, and drown kids for sport. And none of it is really that cut and dried at all because really it's not black and white, but infinite shades of grey that constantly shift and change, and just when you think you've sorted out who's on which side of the divide of good and bad or safe and dangerous all the lines have moved and everything's topsy turvy. The cute little winged fairy is biting a chunk out of your hand and the giant monstrous fey is helping you in exchange for nothing but a good word. Because that's the only constant in Fairy, that it's never constant by our measure.

But little children don't think well in nuances and degrees, they like concretes – good and bad, dark and light, either/or. Basically things I'm not good at. I can talk plenty about the dangers of Fairy and the need for caution to adults with decades of fairies-are-watered-down-angels-meant-to-serve-us ingrained in them, but that's born of my soul-weariness from constant over-exposure to the saccharine-sweet bubblegum approach that denies everything traditional fairylore ever was or still is. When it comes to my own children, I was baffled as to how to reach them without either scaring them so badly they iron plated themselves, or failing to get through to them at all and watching them merrily trip into danger face first.

Paracelsus once said: 'Poison is in everything, and no thing is without poison. The dosage makes it either a poison or a remedy.' I decided this was good advice in this situation as well, if I made it work for me. Popculture was the problem, but popculture could also be the solution. There are, after all, some decent movies out there with fairies in them, or fairy themes: The Secret of Kells, Song of the Sea, Labyrinth (especially for my older daughter), Spiderwick Chronicles, The Secret of Roan Innish, Into the West, even Lord of the Rings and The Hobbit when they get older. None of these are perfect, but if I watch them with my kids I can gently bring up the disconnects from the older folklore and redirect them in a better direction. I can make a fun movie into a subtle teaching experience. If I'm clever (and I certainly try) I can work in the actual methods of dealing with them safely. I can read them, and tell them, the old stories too of course, and teach them what I do and the folklore, but they are less interested in that than in the captivation of a good movie. Because as much as it pains me, child of books that I am, while my kids like to read and like stories well enough their imaginations are captured by movies in a way that reaches the places I need to speak to right now. And unlike boring old mom talking, a fun movie will get all three of them, diverse ages or no, sitting down together and paying attention. So I have to make popculture my weapon instead of letting it be used against me.

So one weekend we tried two new animated movies, *Epic* and *Strange Magic*, borrowed from the local library. Very different movies, but both were good in their own ways.

Epic is the story of a teenage girl who goes to live with her estranged father after her mother dies. He is obsessed with proving that in the woods by his house live an advanced civilization of tiny people – read: fairies. Meanwhile the fairies are divided into two opposing factions, the Boggans who are bad fey intent on spreading rot and decay, and the Leafmen who are good fey who fight the Boggans and whose Queen is the only power that can reverse the damage the Boggans cause. The girl decides to run away and stumbles across the Fairy Queen as she's being attacked; the girl ends up being shrunk down to fairy sized (about two inches) and entrusted with a magic pod that will choose the new Queen. And adventure ensues.

Pros: sticks to the rigid ideas of good and bad with the fey; likable characters; teaches kids to be aware of what's around them; time runs differently

Cons: balance is mentioned as necessary, but is portrayed as endless war. The only true wisdom is held by the good side and the evil side is just mindlessly bad and destructive. This movie also reinforces the 'fairies are tiny' idea.

Lessons I was able to teach my kids after watching: things aren't what they appear to be. Things that appear harmless can be dangerous. Things that appear unpleasant can be helpful. Time runs differently in Fairy.

Strange Magic: a story of two Fairy Kingdoms, one of Elves and winged fairies (all tiny) and one of Goblin-like creatures (also tiny) led by a winged King who looks a lot like a cross between a cricket and a fairy. The Bog King hates love and has imprisoned the only fairy who can make a love potion. The Fairy Princess Marianne has her heart broken by an unfaithful fiancé, who then tries to get her back so he can be King. When her younger sister's best friend, an Elf who is in love with the sister, gets tricked into sneaking into the dark kingdom to free the fairy to make the love potion (by the fiancé who wants it to use on Marianne) adventure ensues.

Pros: great message about not judging by appearance; good isn't always good and bad isn't always bad; nice trickster fairy in the mix. Strong female lead.

Cons: singing. Lots of singing; painfully campy at times. Another tiny fairies movie.

Lessons I was able to teach my kids; don't judge good or bad on looks, what seems fair can be treacherous, and what seems ugly can be trustworthy. Also don't judge beauty by our own standards, what we think is beautiful may be ugly to other beings, and what other beings find beautiful may seem ugly to us.

I'm still not a fan of popculture fairies, but I'm adapting. And my children and I are finding common ground to pass on the old ways in a new day and age.

Author's Note

Many people are curious about the Fey Folk, and yet also find themselves wondering how to learn about them and if it's safe to connect to them. For some people it's not an option – they will be around whether you want them to be or not – so its self-defense to learn how to be safe. For other people, well, there's an advantage to respecting them and being on their good side, that's worth the effort. And there's also that saying about 'no risk no reward'.

I should add that being successful at any dangerous real-world pursuit means never forgetting your place in things or thinking you have more power than you do. Arrogance and overconfidence kills. The same applies exactly to dealing with the Other Crowd. Know exactly what you can do and how far you can push, and never forget where you fit into the food chain (and it isn't at the top).

Sometimes people ask me why I don't talk much about personal practice and experience with the Other Crowd, beyond a handful of anecdotes that I repeat and some fairly generic for-public-consumption stories that I have shared here. I'm pretty free with talking about experiences that occurred with other people, about being Pixy-led, or seeing fairy hounds, or items being taken and returned. And I will talk about the numinous, about the Gods even the liminal Gods, pretty easily. So why not share more of the deeper personal things?

It's a hard thing to talk about for many reasons. Certainly one is that I worry about people questioning my sanity as I talk about these experiences. It's funny how we, as Pagans or Polytheists, can talk about things with Gods and people are, if not supportive, at least more willing to consider possibilities; even ghosts are met with a basic assumption of the person's sanity. But when it comes to the Other Crowd, at least in my experience, people are far quicker to jump to 'crazy' to explain away something. And of course I worry that in speaking about it I'll say too much and lose their favor, which is a concern supported by folklore – the quote may go that the 'first rule of fight club is don't talk about fight club', but in my experience that is far more applicable to fairies. There's also always the worry that people simply won't believe me because it's so difficult to convey these experiences in words without making them sound trite and contrived. Even I don't think some of them sound believable when I tell them, and I was there when they happened. So there's the fear that people just won't believe what I'm saying is true.

And there's the worry that they will.

I feel often like I am talking out of both sides of my mouth, saying on one side to seek Themselves out for their blessings and friendship and on the other to avoid them because of their mercurial nature and danger. And the Heaven and Hell of it, if you'll pardon the expression, is that both are equally true. Because I do think there's value in keeping the old ways and the reciprocal relationship with the Good Folk that has existed for many hundreds, if not thousands, of years – and indeed part of my service to Them as a priestess is to do what I can to keep those old beliefs and traditions viable – and I think that people should be encouraged to do that. But I also think that modern pop-culture has done the Fairy Faith no favors and that people do need to be reminded of the respect and fear that They are due and why they are due it. So it's seek Them out and encourage Their interest in you, but at the same time be cautious of Them and don't get Them too interested. And if that's a contradiction, then consider it your first lesson in fairywork.

I talk a lot about the darker side of Fairy and the dangers of the beings who dwell within it, and I do that on purpose. The Otherworld and its inhabitants are not the stuff of young adult novels or *Lord of the Rings* fan fiction. I see too many people who plunge head first into seeking the Gentry out, heedless of any potential danger, and my instinct is to warn people. I'll use the analogy of hiking here, that hiking on a summer day seems really appealing because it's so beautiful and looks so easy – you just start walking in the woods, isn't that nice? And you know most of the time it will just be nice and pleasant and nothing bad will happen. Nothing at all will happen except for you getting some exercise. But – oh, there's always a but isn't there? – anyone who is an experienced hiker knows that there's always a chance of getting lost, or falling and getting hurt, or being attacked by an animal, or eating something that looks familiar, but isn't what you thought it was, or... or. You see? And that's what I might say that Fairy is like. And if you get lost or hurt or attacked you had really better know what to do about it.

And there's a part of me that doesn't like to talk about some things I've seen or experienced because I worry that it may give people the wrong idea, may make things seem more alluring or good than they actually are. It may make people forget the danger. It may create that urge in people where they want to have that same experience because they are hearing the beautiful experience and not grasping the fuller context.

I am not yet forty years old and I have seen things that I will never stop seeing – not horrible, terrifying things either, but things so beautiful it breaks the heart and so enchanting it makes everything in mortal life seem a pale shadow in comparison. Beauty is a poison in its own way, and it sinks into the bone beyond removing. The stories talk about that too, but we don't want to see it most of the time because we like the idea that people can be saved from Fairy in the end and return to their lives and be happy here. But once you've heard that music and once you've seen those shining halls you lose a part of yourself to the sound and sight of it and there is no real coming back from that. The old stories talk about that too you know. And ultimately I don't want the responsibility of leading someone else where I am, aching for a world that isn't here and that nothing here compares to.

Fairywork is worth doing and it has benefits that make it worth the risk, like any other dangerous thing. But it is dangerous both in Fairy's ability to actually harm a person and the way its enchantment changes a person. It is something that must be done with care and with constant vigilance to be done well, or something that must be done lightly to be done safely, or something that can and will consume a person. I suppose I talk about the things I do because I'd rather be a horrible warning than a great example, to paraphrase Aird.

And so when I talk about it I try to talk enough to encourage people to want to do it, but not enough about my personal deep experiences to give the impression that losing your soul to it should be a life goal. And I try to emphasize the danger so that if things go sideways people can't say they didn't know the pitfalls and bears were there along the trail the whole time.

More and more I think some of us are being pushed to talk and teach about this, and we each offer different – and important – pieces of the puzzle. Some of those pieces are heavily filtered through specific concepts, like environmentalism and New Age spirituality. Some of those pieces are filtered through traditional cultures and folklore. Some are shiny and colorful; some are sharp and dark. All call people, one way or another, back to a place very foreign from here.

One thing I am certain of though is that the spirits of the Otherworld are not done with us or our world, not yet. If anything they seem to be working to reconnect and re-establish their footing here – and not just the kindly ones.

Morgan Daimler, Dark Moon, January 2017

Bibliography

Acland, A., (1997) *Tam Lin Balladry*

Aislinge Oenguso

Ashliman, D., (2004) *Folk and Fairy Tales*

Ballard, L., (1991) *Fairies and the Supernatural on Reachrai*

Bedell, J., (2007) *Hildur, Queen of the Elves, and Other Icelandic Legends*

Bennett, M., (1991) *Balquhidder Revisited: Fairylore in the Scottish Highlands, 1690-1990*

Bitel, L., (1991) In Visu Noctis: Dreams in European Hagiography and Histories, 450-900, *History of Religions vol. 31*

Black, G., (1894) *Scottish Charms and Amulets*

Blain, J., (2000) *Wights and Ancestors: Heathenism in a Living Landscape*

Briggs, K., (1967) *The Fairies in Tradition and Literature*

—- (1976) *A Dictionary of Fairies*

—- (1978) *The Vanishing People*

Bruford, A., (1991) *Trolls, Hillfolk, Finns, and Picts: The Identity of the Good Neighbors in Orkney and Shetland*

Campbell, G., (1900) *Superstitions of the Highlands and Islands of Scotland*

Campbell, J., (1900) *The Gaelic Otherworld*

Chambers, R., (1842) *Popular Rhymes, Fireside Stories, and Amusements of Scotland*

Child, F., (1802) *Tam Lin*

-— (1882) The *English and Scottish Popular Ballads*

Cox, M., (1904) *Introduction to Folklore*

Croker, T., (1825) *Fairy Legends and Traditions of Southern Ireland*

Curtin, J., (1895) *Tales of the Fairies and of the Ghost World*

Daimler., M (2014). The Witch, the Bean Feasa, and the Fairy Doctor in Irish Culture. *Air n-Aithesc*, vol 1 issue 2, Aug. 2014

Dalyell, J., (1801) *Scottish Poems of the Sixteenth Century*

Danaher, K., (1972) *The Year in Ireland*

—- (1967) *Folktales of the Irish Countryside*

Davies, O., (2003) *Popular Magic: Cunningfolk in English History*

De Chopur in Da Muccida

De Gabail an t-Sida

DSL (2016) *Dictionary of the Scots Language*

eDIL (n.d.) Electronic Dictionary of the Irish Language http://edil.qub.ac.uk/browse

Evans, E., (1957) *Irish folk Ways*

Evans-Wentz, W., (1911) *The Fairy Faith in Celtic Countries*

Firth Green, R., (2016) *Elf Queens and Holy Friars: Fairy Beliefs and the Medieval Church*

Froud, B., and Lee, A., (2002) *Faeries*

Froud, B., (1998) *Good Faeries, Bad Faeries*

Goblin (2016) *Online Etymology Dictionary*

Gregory, A., (1920) *Visions and Beliefs in the West of Ireland*

Grimm, J., (1883) *Teutonic Mythology volume 2*

Gruber, B., (2007) *Iceland: Searching for Elves and Hidden People*

Gundarsson, K., (2007) *Elves, Wights, and Trolls*

Gwyndaf, R., (1991) *Fairylore: Memorates and Legends from Welsh Oral Tradition*

Hall, A., (2005) Getting Shot of Elves: Healing, Witchcraft and Fairies in the Scottish Witchcraft Trials. Folklore Vol. 116, No. 1 (Apr., 2005)

—- (2007) *Elves in Anglo-Saxon England*

—- (2004) The Meaning of Elf and Elves in Medieval England, Retrieved from http://www.alarichall.org.uk/ahphdful.pdf

—- (2011) The Contemporary Evidence for Early Medieval Witchcraft-Beliefs. Retrieved from https://www.academia.edu/1528964/The_Contemporary_Evidence_for_Early_Medieval_Witchcraft-Beliefs

Harms, D., Clark, J., and Peterson, J., (2015) *The Book of Oberon*

Harper, D., (2017) 'Elf'; Online Etymology Dictionary

Hartland, E., (1891) *The Science of Fairy Tales*

Harvard Classics (1914) *Volume 40: English Poetry I: from Chaucer to Gray*

Helrune, S., (2016) *Essays from the Crossroads*

Hyde, D., (1910) *Beside the Fire: A Collection of Irish Gaelic Folk Stories*

JCHAS (2010) Journal of the Cork Historical and Archaeological Society

Jamieson, J., (1808) *An Etymological Dictionary of the Scottish Language*

Jenkins, R., (1991) *Witches and Fairies: Supernatural Aggression and Deviance Among the Irish Peasantry*

Johnson, M., (2014) *Seeing Fairies*

Jolly, K., (1996) *Popular Religion in Late Saxon England; Elf Charms in Context*

Jones, M (2003) *The Wild Hunt*. Retrieved from http://www.maryjones.us/jce/wildhunt.html

Kirk, R., (1691) *The Secret Commonwealth of Elves, Fauns, and Fairies*

Lecouteux, C., (1995) *Demons and Spirits of the Land: Ancestral Lore and Practices*

—- (1992) *Witches, Werewolves and Fairies: Shapeshifters and Astral Doubles in the Middle Ages*

—- (2000) *The Tradition of Household Spirits*

—- (1999) *Phantom Armies of the Night: The Wild Hunt and the Ghostly Processions of the Undead*

Lenihan, E., and Green, C., (2003) *Meeting the Other Crowd: The Fairy Stories of Hidden Ireland*

Linton, E., (1861) *Witch Stories*

Locke, T., (2013) *The Fairy Doctor*. Retrieved from http://www.irishabroad.com/blogs/PostView.aspx?pid=4404

Lockey, N., (1882) *Nature, vol. 26*

Logan, P., (1981) *The Old Gods: The Facts about Irish Fairies*

Lyle, E., (1970). The Teind to Hell in Tam Lin

Lysaght, P., (1991) *Fairylore from the Midlands of Ireland*

—- (1986) *The Banshee: The Irish Death Messenger*

MacCulloch, J., (1911) *Religion of the Ancient Celts*

MacDonald, L., (1993) People of the Mounds. Dalriada Magazine

MacGillivray, Deborah. (2000). *The Cait Sí*

MacLiammóir, M., (1984) *Faery Nights Oícheanta Sí: Stories on Ancient Irish Festivals*

MacManus, D., (1959) *The Middle Kingdom: The Faerie World of Ireland*

MacQuarrie, C., (1997) The Waves of Manannan

Magic and Religious Cures (2014). Ask About Ireland. Retrieved from http://www.askaboutireland.ie/reading-room/history-heritage/folklore-of-ireland/folklore-in-ireland/healers-and-healing/magic-and-religious-cures/

McKillop, J., (1998) *Dictionary of Celtic Mythology*

McNeill, F., (1956) *Silver Bough*

McNeil, H., (2001) *The Celtic Breeze*

Merriman, B., (1780) *Cúirt an Mheán Oíche*

Monaghan, P., (2009) *The Encyclopedia of Celtic Mythology and Folklore*

Murray, J., (1918) *The Romance and Prophecies of Thomas of Erceldoune*

—- (1922) *The Complaynt of Scotland*

Mushroom Appreciation (2016) Fanciful Fairy Rings

Narvaez, P., (2001) *The Good People*

O Crualaoich, G., (2003) *The Book of the Cailleach*

—- (2005) Reading the Bean Feasa. Folklore Vol. 116, No. 1 (Apr., 2005)

O Donaill, (1977) *Foclóir Gaeilge-Béarla*

O Giolláin, D., (1991) *The Fairy Belief and Official Religion in Ireland*

O hOgain, D., (1995) *Irish Superstitions*

O Súilleabháin, S., (1967) *Nósanna agus Piseoga na nGael*

Parkinson, D., (2013) *Phantom Black Dogs* http://www.mysterious-britain.co.uk/folklore/phantom-black-dogs.html

Pitcairn, R., (1843) *Ancient Criminal Trials in Scotland, vol 1, part 3*

Pocs, E., (1999) *Between the Living and the Dead*

Purkiss, D., (2000) *At the Bottom of the Garden*

Rieti, B., (1991). 'The Blast' in *Newfoundland Fairy Tradition*

—- (1991) *Strange Terrain: The Fairy World in Newfoundland*

Rossetti, C., (1862) *Goblin Market*

Sands, Brymer, Murray, and Cochran, (1819) The Edinburgh Magazine and Literary Miscellany, vol. 83

Scott, W., (1830) *Letters on Demonology and Witchcraft*

Shakespeare, W., (1974) *The Complete Works of William Shakespeare*

Sikes, W., (1881) *British Goblins: Welsh Folklore, Fairy Mythology, Legends, and Traditions*

Silver, C., (1999) *Strange and Secret People: Fairies and Victorian Consciousness*

Skelbred, A., (1991) *Rites of Passage as Meeting Place: Christianity and Fairylore in Connection with the Unclean Woman and the Unchristened Child*

Spenser, E., (1590) *The Faerie Queene*

Táin Bó Cuailigne

Táin Bó Regamna

Tam Lin (1997) Child Ballad 39A http://tam-lin.org/versions/39A.html

Tochmarc Etaine

Towrie, S., (2016) The Selkie Folk http://www.orkneyjar.com/folklore/selkiefolk/index.html

—- (2016) *Orkney's Standing Stones*

—- (2017) *Trows*

Walsh, B., (2002) *The Secret Commonwealth and the Fairy Belief Complex*

Wedin, W., (1998) *The Sí, the Tuatha De Danann, and the Fairies in Yeats's Early Works*

Wilby, E., (2010) *The Visions of Isobel Gowdie*

Wilde, E., (1888) *Ancient Legends, Mystic Charms & Superstitions of Ireland*

—- (1920) *Visions and Beliefs in the West of Ireland*

Williams, M., (2016) *Ireland's Immortals: A History of the Gods of*

Irish Myth

Williams, N., (1991) *Semantics of the Word Fairy: Making Meaning out of Thin Air*

Wooding, J., (2000). The Otherworld Voyage in Early Irish Literature

Yeats, W., (1888) *Fairy and Folktales of the Irish Peasantry*

—- (1892) *Irish Fairy Tales*

—- (1893) *Celtic Twilight*

You might also enjoy…

978 1 78535 051 1 (Paperback)
978 1 78535 052 8 (ebook)

Following the call of the Old Gods along the path of the
Fair Folk

An in depth manual for practicing Fairy Witchcraft including
theology, fairy lore, rituals, holidays, and magical practices.

Moon Books

PAGANISM & SHAMANISM

What is Paganism? A religion, a spirituality, an alternative
belief system, nature worship? You can find support for all
these definitions (and many more) in dictionaries,
encyclopaedias, and text books of religion, but subscribe to
any one and the truth will evade you. Above all Paganism is a
creative pursuit, an encounter with reality, an exploration of
meaning and an expression of the soul. Druids, Heathens,
Wiccans and others, all contribute their insights and literary
riches to the Pagan tradition. Moon Books invites you to begin
or to deepen your own encounter, right here, right now.
If you have enjoyed this book, why not tell other readers by
posting a review on your preferred book site.

Recent bestsellers from Moon Books are:

Journey to the Dark Goddess
How to Return to Your Soul
Jane Meredith
Discover the powerful secrets of the Dark Goddess and
transform your depression, grief and pain into healing
and integration.
Paperback: 978-1-84694-677-6 ebook: 978-1-78099-223-5

Shamanic Reiki
Expanded Ways of Working with Universal Life Force Energy
Llyn Roberts, Robert Levy
Shamanism and Reiki are each powerful ways of healing;
together, their power multiplies. *Shamanic Reiki* introduces
techniques to help healers and Reiki practitioners tap ancient
healing wisdom.
Paperback: 978-1-84694-037-8 ebook: 978-1-84694-650-9

Pagan Portals – The Awen Alone
Walking the Path of the Solitary Druid
Joanna van der Hoeven
An introductory guide for the solitary Druid, *The Awen Alone*
will accompany you as you explore, and seek out your own
place within the natural world.
Paperback: 978-1-78279-547-6 ebook: 978-1-78279-546-9

A Kitchen Witch's World of Magical Herbs & Plants
Rachel Patterson
A journey into the magical world of herbs and plants, filled with
magical uses, folklore, history and practical magic. By popular
writer, blogger and kitchen witch, Tansy Firedragon.
Paperback: 978-1-78279-621-3 ebook: 978-1-78279-620-6

Medicine for the Soul
The Complete Book of Shamanic Healing
Ross Heaven
All you will ever need to know about shamanic healing and
how to become your own shaman...
Paperback: 978-1-78099-419-2 ebook: 978-1-78099-420-8

Shaman Pathways – The Druid Shaman
Exploring the Celtic Otherworld
Danu Forest
A practical guide to Celtic shamanism with exercises and
techniques as well as traditional lore for exploring the Celtic
Otherworld.
Paperback: 978-1-78099-615-8 ebook: 978-1-78099-616-5

Traditional Witchcraft for the Woods and Forests
A Witch's Guide to the Woodland with Guided Meditations and
Pathworking
Melusine Draco
A Witch's guide to walking alone in the woods, with guided
meditations and pathworking.
Paperback: 978-1-84694-803-9 ebook: 978-1-84694-804-6

Wild Earth, Wild Soul
A Manual for an Ecstatic Culture
Bill Pfeiffer
Imagine a nature-based culture so alive and so connected,
spreading like wildfire. This book is the first flame...
Paperback: 978-1-78099-187-0 ebook: 978-1-78099-188-7

Naming the Goddess
Trevor Greenfield
Naming the Goddess is written by over eighty adherents and scholars of Goddess and Goddess Spirituality.
Paperback: 978-1-78279-476-9 ebook: 978-1-78279-475-2

Shapeshifting into Higher Consciousness
Heal and Transform Yourself and Our World with Ancient Shamanic and Modern Methods
Llyn Roberts
Ancient and modern methods that you can use every day to transform yourself and make a positive difference in the world.
Paperback: 978-1-84694-843-5 ebook: 978-1-84694-844-2

Readers of ebooks can buy or view any of these bestsellers by clicking on the live link in the title. Most titles are published in paperback and as an ebook. Paperbacks are available in traditional bookshops. Both print and ebook formats are available online.

Find more titles and sign up to our readers' newsletter at
http://www.johnhuntpublishing.com/paganism
Follow us on Facebook at
https://www.facebook.com/MoonBooks
and Twitter at https://twitter.com/MoonBooksJHP